A Handbook of
Data
Envelopment
Analysis
@ Stata

Choonjoo Lee

The suggested citation for the content and code in this
book is

Choonjoo Lee. (2022). *A Handbook of Data Envelopment
Analysis @ Stata*. Middletown, DE, USA: Amazon KDP.

To

Misun Park, Jinwoo and Chaeyoon

PREFACE

I presented "Data Envelopment Analysis in Stata" at the 2009 Stata Conference DC held in Washington DC, USA on July 30-31, 2009, showing that a DEA program is needed and possible in Stata. https://www.stata.com/meeting/dcconf09/
During the presentation, I received less of a response from the traditional Stata enthusiasts than I had expected. Perhaps they were hesitant to ask questions because I seemed unfamiliar with English communication, or perhaps the subject of the presentation, which dealt with non-statistical and mathematical methods, was unfamiliar to them.
After the conference paper was posted online, I received messages through email thanking me for sharing how to install the program, even asking for more general Stata usage tips. Some students in doctoral programs who wanted to implement DEA analysis using big data in Stata for their thesis reached out to me, and professors who teach economics at universities also contacted me expressing interest in using the DEA program in their lectures.
The problem was that the program we released at the time was just a rough draft that myself and a student had worked on together without any background in software engineering, and it only showed that DEA was possible in Stata. Therefore, it took several hours to calculate the efficiency of five DMUs. To make it practical, it was necessary to program the linear programming, which is the core engine of DEA, efficiently.
I fell in love with Stata's concise and compact appeal when I first encountered it in a quantitative economics class in 2001, and I learned about DEA thanks to Professor Lee, Jeong-Dong of Seoul National University in 2003. I was disappointed that DEA was not implemented in Stata and tried to do it without a clear plan, but it wasn't until 2009 that I was able to accomplish what I had wanted to try.
In any case, the 2009 Stata Conference made me realize that there were Stata users interested in DEA, and I wanted to let them know about the program, so in 2010 I published a paper in the Stata Journal on how to use the upgraded user-written Stata program "dea.ado," which had been optimized for calculation efficiency. (Ji, Y. B., & Lee, C. Data envelopment analysis, The Stata Journal (2010) 10, Number 2. , 267-280.)

In 2010, at the 2010 Stata Conference Boston, I presented "An Efficient Data Envelopment Analysis with Large Data Set in Stata", which addressed the issue of tolerance in the Stata program when using large data sets for DEA calculations. In 2011, at the 2011 Stata Conference Boston, I presented "Malmquist productivity index using DEA frontier in Stata" and discussed the application of panel data analysis.

In 2012, at the Stata Conference San Diego 2012, I presented "Allocative Efficiency Analysis using DEA in Stata" and discussed the application of production economics. In 2013, at the 2013 Stata Conference, I presented "Mathematical Optimization in Stata: LP and MILP" and expanded the topic to include MILP as well as LP. In 2019, at the Oceania Stata conference, I presented "Technology forecasting using data envelopment analysis in Stata" and discussed the application of technology forecasting methods. In July of the same year, at the Stata Chicago Conference, I presented "The matching problem using Stata" and discussed the strategic application of mathematical methods.

These results would not have been possible without the help of Yong-bae Ji, Kyung-Rok Lee, Byung-Ihn Lim, and Byung-ki Jung, who were with me on weekends and evenings. I also want to thank the anonymous persons who generously commented on and encouraged the released program. I am also grateful to the Stata Corp. officials who made it possible for me to present the program at the conference. And when I was in College Station, Texas, I sincerely thank Chris & Gretchen Farrar, who invited to Stata Corp. with my family and have been constant friends.

Looking back over the past 20 years since I learned about Stata, the two things that stand out to me are: first, the "DEA program using Stata" that I released on the internet as open source software in 2013 is being used globally by users as shown in the following figures; second, in 2019, Stata officially began offering Linear Programming and is currently offering it as a default program for running some DEA.

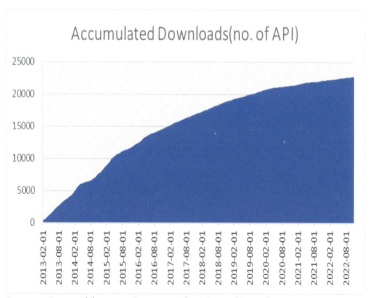

Source: https://sourceforge.net/projects/deas/

The two things I mentioned earlier are both significant accomplishments and meaningful reasons for me, but I also feel that I need to share the shortcomings and think about how to further develop them for those who are interested in the program.

Now is a timely opportunity for me to share my experiences and for those interested in the program professionally to take on a role, as the user-written DEA program provided in this book has both advantages and disadvantages. The DEA-related programs provided generally utilize the two-phase revised Simplex method to solve linear programming problems, so they have the advantages and limitations of the original Simplex. The LP raw source code can be checked by users, which helps in understanding the results, but understanding the inside of the black box requires a basic understanding of data science, unlike programs that provide results as a black box. In addition, the linear programming provided as the default in the new Stata program uses the Interior point method. Therefore, it is necessary to select the appropriate program according to the type of problem the user has.

In addition, the code was written by someone who is not a professional programmer, so it is only recommended for use for academic purposes.

Choonjoo Lee
Korea National Defense University
Republic of Korea
December 28, 2022

CONTENTS

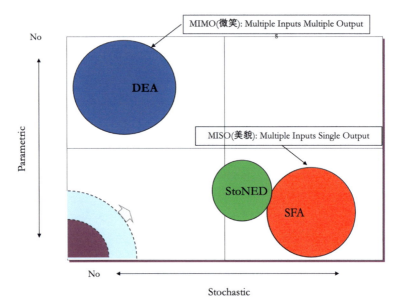

ACKNOWLEDGMENTS

The publication of this book would not have been possible without the guidance and stimulation of Professor Jeong-Dong Lee of Seoul National University. I would like to express my deepest gratitude to Yong-bae Ji, Kyung-Rok Lee, Byung-Ihn Lim, and Byung-ki Jung who have been with us for a long time to develop the DEA program in Stata. I would also like to thank Stata staffs, anonymous reviewers, and friends Chris & Gretchen Farrar for helping to bring the DEA program to the public at the Stata conference. Since the program was made public, your anonymous questions and advice have stimulated and encouraged me to publish this book.

DATA Integer, real, cardinal, ordinal, context, negative, cross sectional, panel, physical, value, input, output, variable, …

 ENVELOPMENT returns to scale, convex combination, piece-wise linear combination, disposability, …

 ANALYSIS orientation, distance measurement, efficiency, time series, frontier change, efficiency change, (non)radial, technical, allocative, stage, optimization, cost, revenue, profit, value, benchmarking, managerial control, interpretation, approach,(non)parametric, (non)stochastic,…

1 INTRODUCTION

1.1 The Objectives of the Book

This book was written for users who want to implement Data Envelopment Analysis in Stata. It is particularly useful for those who are curious about the various programs available that offer linear programming in a black box form and want to understand and implement linear programming themselves. It will also be helpful for those who want to program data envelopment analysis in linear programming and mixed integer linear programming.

DEA (Data Envelopment Analysis) is being used in a variety of fields such as production economics, management, public policy, military studies, etc. Recently, there have been efforts to model new programs that incorporate artificial intelligence techniques to efficiently analyze big data. There is also an international journal dedicated to DEA. As the range of applications of DEA expands, it is important to consider the possibility of opening the "inside black box" of linear programming to search for methods that are suitable for the characteristics of the analysis target.

Therefore, this book's important goal is not to provide readers with a fully completed program, but rather to serve as a test bed for considering your problems.

1

1.2 Installing the necessary software

The DEA code dealt with in this book is not automatically installed as a package even if you purchase and install the Stata program. This is because it is a program written by the user. Fortunately, Stata can execute not only officially provided commands but also various types of commands written by users - user-written commands, the Stata Journal, Stata Technical Bulletin, and the SSC archive.

To use the Stata user-written command used in this book, you need to connect to the internet and type the following in the Stata command window:

. net install *dea*

    This will download and install the DEA package from the internet. You can then use the DEA commands in your Stata program.

    Note: You may need to specify the path to your Stata program if it is not in the default location. For example, you can do this by adding the path to the command:

. net install *dea*, from("C:\Program Files\Stata15\ado\plus")

    This will install the DEA package to the "ado/plus" folder in your Stata installation directory.

. net get st0193.pkg

    The Stata command will save the required packages to the user-specified working directory. You can also get the same result by typing the following:

. use http://www.stata-journal.com/software/sj10-2/, clear

    Note that the program installed in the above command is the initial version presented by the authors in the 2010 Stata Journal. To use the latest version of the code, you can download it from the Source: https://sourceforge.net/projects/deas/ site or copy the code provided in the appendix of this book to a Stata execution file. To use the user-written ado file in Stata, simply follow the general instructions for using Stata.

2 THE FDH MODEL

This chapter discusses Free Disposal Hull (FDH) model for efficiency measurement. The FDH model was introduced and developed from the discussions of Deprins, Simar, and Tulkens (1984), Thrall (1999), and Cherchye and Post (2000) in the field of production economics. Free Disposal Hull model only assumes the free disposability in defining the production possibility set from the observations. Free disposability means if a specific pair of input and output is producible, any pairs of more input and less output for the specific one is also producible. FDH model allows the free disposability to construct the production possibility set. Accordingly, the frontier line for FDH model is developed from the observed inputs and outputs allowing the free disposability.

One version of FDH model aims to minimize inputs while satisfying at least the given output levels. This is called the input-oriented model. The other one is called the output-oriented model that attempts to maximize outputs without requiring more inputs. The scores of efficiencies in FDH model are between 0 and 1.

The FDH model is a non-parametric method to measure the efficiency of production units (i.e., Decision Making Units). It is known for its ability to provide users with more realistic point of view, by taking each numeric unit into account instead of using a convex combination of them. Therefore, due to its non-convexity nature, FDH model relaxes the convexity assumption of basic DEA models-CCR, BCC- and it requires mixed integer programming method to be solved since it's not linearly drawn.

3

2.1 Data

Table 2.1 data was taken from Cooper, Seiford, and Tone (2006, p.75, Table 3.7) for the FDH analysis. The data consist of five stores that use two inputs (employee, area) to produce two outputs (sales, profits).

<Table 2.1> Data of 5 Stores

Store	Employee	Area	Sales	Profits
A	10	20	70	6
B	15	15	100	3
C	20	30	80	5
D	25	15	100	2
E	12	9	90	8

2.2 Model Description

There are two versions of FDH model: input-oriented and output-oriented FDH models. The input-oriented model focuses on minimizing input value while satisfying the output value. The output-oriented model attempts to maximize the output value without requiring more input values (Jeong-dong Lee & Dong-hyun Oh, 2012).

The input-oriented FDH model can be mathematically expressed as follows:

$$\min_{\theta,\lambda} \theta^k \qquad (2.1)$$

subject to
$$\theta^k x_m^k \geq \sum_{j=1}^{J} x_m^j \lambda^j \quad (m = 1,2,\ldots,M);$$

$$y_n^k \leq \sum_{j=1}^{J} y_n^j \lambda^j \quad (n = 1,2,\ldots,N);$$

$$\sum_{j=1}^{J} \lambda^j = 1;$$
$$\lambda^j \in \{0,1\}$$

The output-oriented FDH model can be mathematically expressed as follows:

$$\max_{\theta,\lambda} \theta^k \tag{2.2}$$

subject to $\quad x_m^k \geq \sum_{j=1}^{J} x_m^j \lambda^j \quad (m = 1,2,\dots,M);$

$$\theta^k y_n^k \leq \sum_{j=1}^{J} y_n^j \lambda^j \quad (n = 1,2,\dots,N);$$

$$\sum_{j=1}^{J} \lambda^j = 1;$$

$$\lambda^j \in \{0,1\}$$

In the FDH model, if specific inputs produce specific outputs, these specific values are reproducible and can be used as a reference. These valid inputs/outputs are collectively referred to as the production possibility set (P or PPS). <Figure 2.1> is a graphical representation of the production possibility sets when seven DMUs (A, B, C, D, E, F, G) are observed to engage in activities in which they input one element of x and produce one element of y, assuming free disposability. (a) shows the set of DMUs included in the production possibility set when free disposability is assumed (see appendix for do file). (b) shows the production possibility sets under the assumptions of constant returns to scale (CRS) and variable returns to scale (VRS) for comparison with the FDH production possibility set. It can be seen that the size of the production possibility set is in the order of CRS, VRS, and FDH.

If we look at the case of DMU F in <Figure 2.1> (b), we can see that the distance from F to the frontier is greater in the order of CRS>VRS>FDH. Therefore, if we use the distance from the frontier to measure efficiency, we can define DMUs located above the frontier as efficient DMUs, so we can estimate that the efficiency value is in the order of FDH>VRS>CRS. The method of measuring efficiency using the distance from the frontier to the point where the dotted line drawn horizontally from F meets the frontier in <Figure 2.1> (b) is called input-oriented, and the method of measuring efficiency using the distance from the frontier to the point where the dotted line drawn vertically from F meets the frontier, which is not

5

shown in the figure, is called output-oriented.

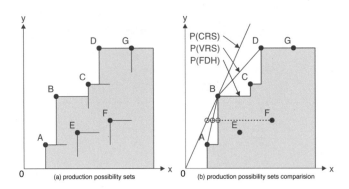

<Figure 2.1> (a) FDH production possibility sets, (b) production possibility sets comparison for RTS

    <Figure 2.2> shows a graph of PPS for two input elements, x1 and x2. It can be seen that DMUs A, B, C, and F are located on the frontier of the PPS, while DMUs D and E are located inside the PPS. If we want to assign efficiency values less than 1 to DMUs located inside the PPS, how can this be done? The orientation FDH model draws a line connecting the corresponding DMU from the origin O and indicates the point at which the line passes through the frontier, as shown in the figure, and then uses a distance function. That is, in the case of DMU D, the line connecting O and D passes through $\overline{OA}$ and $\overline{OD}$, and the relative ratio $m(\overline{OA})/m(\overline{OD})$ of the distances between these two lines can be used as the efficiency value. This model for measuring efficiency is based on radial-relative to frontier-orientation.

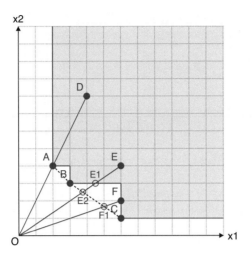

<Figure 2.2> FDH production possibility sets and convexity assumption for two inputs (x1, x2)

FDH model constructs all producible inputs/outputs, including values of lesser output values (below specific values and onwards); however, it excludes values that are in between specific points, producing stair-like graph. Therefore, the term "free disposability" means to include input values that produce results that are desirable but keep inputs in bare minimum. More details can be found in Cooper et al. (2007, pp.117-119).

2.3 FDH Analysis @ Stata

The following command loads into memory the data set of 'cooper_table3.7.dta', a Stata-format dataset previously saved by *save* command from your working directory.

. use "D:\data\cooper_table3.7.dta"

And you can use the command *list* to Result Window the values of variables (see Result Window 2.1).

. list

	dmu	i_empl~e	i_area	o_sales	o_prof~s
1.	store A	10	20	70	6
2.	store B	15	15	100	3
3.	store C	20	30	80	5
4.	store D	25	15	100	2
5.	store E	12	9	90	8

Result Window 2.1

The syntax of the *dea* command for FDH analysis is:

dea inputvars(min=1) = outputvars(min=1) [if] [in] [using/ *filename*], fdh [ort(i|in|input|o|out|output) stage (integer 2) tol1(real 1e-14) tol2(real 1e-8) trace saving(*filename*) replace]

Where *inputvars* and *outputvars* mean input and output variable lists, respectively. *dea* for FDH analysis requires the user to select the input and output variables from the user designated data file and solves FDH models by options specified.

The *dea* program requires initial data set that contains the input and output variables for observed production units. Variable names must be identified by *inputvars* for input variable and by *outputvars* for output variables to allow that *dea* program can identify and handle the multiple input-output data set. And the variable name of DMUs must be specified by "dmu" and the option must be specified by "fdh" to solve FDH model using *dea* command.

The program can accommodate unlimited number of inputs/outputs with unlimited number of DMUs. The only limitation is the memory of computer used to run *dea* and the number of observations (DMUs) than the combined number of inputs and outputs to solve the MILP (Mixed Integer Linear Programming) problem. The result file reports the information including reference points and slacks in FDH models. This information can be used to analyze the inefficient production units, for examples, where the source of inefficiency comes from and how could improve an inefficient unit to the desired level.

saving(*filename*) option creates a *filename*.dta file that contains the results of FDH including the information of the DMUs, inputs and outputs data used, ranks of Decision Making Units (DMUs), efficiency scores, reference sets, and slacks. The log file "fdh.log" will be created in the working directory. The *dea* program requires the input and output variables and data sets and the options to be defined for the FDH model selection. Based on the data and options specified in the *dea* program, the *dea* program conducts the matrix operations and linear programming to produce the results data sets that are available for print or can be used for further analysis.

You can estimate the FDH model with input-oriented two stage using the following command to get the results shown in Result Window 2.2:

. dea i_employee i_area= o_sales o_profits, fdh ort(in) stage(2)

```
options: ORT(IN) STAGE(2)
FDH-INPUT Oriented DEA Efficiency Results:
                                    ref:        ref:        ref:
                    rank     theta  store_A     store_B     store_C
dmu:store_A          1        1       1           0           0
dmu:store_B          1        1       0           1           0
dmu:store_C          5       .6       0           0           0
dmu:store_D          4        1       0           1           0
dmu:store_E          1        1       0           0           0

                    ref:      ref:     islack:     islack:     oslack:
                    store_D   store_E  i_employee  i_area      o_sales
dmu:store_A          0         0         0           0           0
dmu:store_B          0         0         0           0           0
dmu:store_C          0         1         0           9          10
dmu:store_D          0         0        10           0           0
dmu:store_E          0         1         0           0           0

                    oslack:
                    o_profits
dmu:store_A          0
dmu:store_B          0
dmu:store_C          3
dmu:store_D          1
dmu:store_E          0
```

Result Window 2.2

In Result Window 2.2, the options for the model are input-oriented and the model was solved using two stage revised simplex to apply two-stage optimization. It can be seen that the applied model is FDH. DMU store_C has an efficiency (theta) of 0.6, ranking 5th, and it is possible to interpret that in order to improve the inputs efficiently, it is necessary to refer to DMU store_E (ref:

9

store_E) by 100%. Also, when DMU store_C is connected to the origin, if the point where it meets the frontier is designated as C', it can be known from the information on slack that the DMU located at C' has a technical efficiency value of 1, but it is not pareto-optimum, but weak-efficient. In other words, in Result Window 2.2, it can be seen that DMU store_C's slack is islack: i_area 9, oslack: o_sales 10, oslack: o_profits 3, all of which are larger than 0.

Also, you can estimate the FDH model with output-oriented single stage using the following command to get the results shown in Result Window 2.3:

. dea i_employee i_area= o_sales o_profits, fdh ort(out) stage(1)

```
options: ORT(OUT) STAGE(1)
FDH-OUTPUT Oriented DEA Efficiency Results:
                                  ref:      ref:      ref:
                rank      theta   store_A   store_B   store_C
dmu:store_A     1         1       1         0         0
dmu:store_B     1         1       0         1         0
dmu:store_C     5         1.125   0         0         0
dmu:store_D     1         1       0         1         0
dmu:store_E     1         1       0         0         0

                ref:      ref:      islack:     islack:   oslack:
                store_D   store_E   i_employee  i_area    o_sales
dmu:store_A     0         0         0           0         0
dmu:store_B     0         0         0           0         0
dmu:store_C     0         1         0           0         0
dmu:store_D     1         0         0           0         0
dmu:store_E     0         1         0           0         0

                oslack:
                o_profits
dmu:store_A     0
dmu:store_B     0
dmu:store_C     0
dmu:store_D     0
dmu:store_E     0
```

Result Window 2.3

As another example, we can estimate the FDH efficiency score for the data taken from Kim et al. (2022, pp.9-11, Table 1). The data consist of 107 DMUs that use two inputs (Price, Body weight) to produce 9 outputs (Network band, Screen size, Resolution, Sensors, Network speed, CPU speed, Camera Performance, Battery Capacity, WLAN generation).

. use "D:\data\ lee_table1.dta"

You can estimate the FDH model for year 2020 with input-oriented two stage using the following command to get the results shown in Result Window 2.4:

. dea price = scrnsize if year==2020, fdh ort(in)

```
options: ORT(IN) STAGE(2)
FDH-INPUT Oriented DEA Efficiency Results:
```

dmu:	rank	theta	ref: Mi_10_Pro_5G	ref: Reno4_5G
Mi_10_Pro_5G	4	.94086	0	0
Reno4_5G	1	1	0	1
Xperia_1_II	9	.38496	0	0
P40_Pro	5	.924703	0	0
V60_ThinQ_5G	1	1	0	0
Edge+	7	.583333	0	0
Galaxy_S2~5G	8	.548961	0	1
iPhone_SE_(2020)	6	.918114	0	1
X50_Pro	1	1	0	0

dmu:	ref: Xperia_1_II	ref: P40_Pro	ref: V60_ThinQ_5G	ref: Edge+
Mi_10_Pro_5G	0	0	1	0
Reno4_5G	0	0	0	0
Xperia_1_II	0	0	0	0
P40_Pro	0	0	1	0
V60_ThinQ_5G	0	0	1	0
Edge+	0	0	1	0
Galaxy_S2~5G	0	0	0	0
iPhone_SE_(2020)	0	0	0	0
X50_Pro	0	0	0	0

dmu:	ref: Galaxy_S2~5G	ref: iPhone_SE_(2020)	ref: X50_Pro	islack: price
Mi_10_Pro_5G	0	0	0	0
Reno4_5G	0	0	0	0
Xperia_1_II	0	0	1	0
P40_Pro	0	0	0	0
V60_ThinQ_5G	0	0	0	0
Edge+	0	0	0	0
Galaxy_S2~5G	0	0	0	0
iPhone_SE_(2020)	0	0	0	0
X50_Pro	0	0	1	0

dmu:	oslack: scrnsize
Mi_10_Pro_5G	.13
Reno4_5G	0
Xperia_1_II	.0599999
P40_Pro	.22
V60_ThinQ_5G	0
Edge+	.1
Galaxy_S2~5G	.23
iPhone_SE_(2020)	1.73
X50_Pro	0

Result Window 2.4

Result Window 2.4 shows the results of measuring efficiency by assuming input-oriented two-stage free-disposability, with price as the input and screen size as the output, for smartphones released in 2020. In Result Window 2.4, it can be seen that there are three DMUs with rank 1. While one may expect there to be only one first place, this may not be fully satisfying. In other words, it may be possible to improve in terms of discrimination power, which will be discussed partially in Chapter 9 on the Super-efficiency model.

2.4 Exercises

2.4.1 Solve the store example in Table 2.1 using the FDH model with output-oriented two stage and compare the results with Result Window 2.3.

2.4.2 In table 2.1, diagram the FDH production possibility set for stores with employee as input and sales as output.

2.4.3 For store C in table 2.1, diagram the output-oriented measure of FDH efficiency score with area as input and profits as output.

2.4.4 For the data in lee_table1.dta, solve the input-oriented FDH model with two inputs (Price, Body weight) to produce 9 outputs (Network band, Screen size, Resolution, Sensors, Network speed, CPU speed, Camera Performance, Battery Capacity, WLAN generation). If you get the efficiency scores all the same, explain why it happens in terms of model specification requirements.

2.5 References

Deprins, D., Simar, L., & H. Tulkens. (1984). Measuring Labor-efficiency in Post Offices. LIDAM Reprints Core 571.

Thrall, R. M. (1999). What Is the Economic Meaning of FDH?. Journal of Productivity Analysis, 11(3): 243–250.

Cherchye, L., Kuosmanen, T., & Post, T. (2000). What Is the Economic Meaning of FDH? A Reply to Thrall. Journal of Productivity Analysis, 13(3), 263–267.

Cooper, W., Seiford, L. M., & Tone, K. (2006). Introduction to Data Envelopment Analysis and Its Use. 233 Spring Street, New York, NY 10013, USA: Springer Science & Business Media, Inc.

Lee, Jeong-dong and Oh, Dong-hyun. (2012). Theory of efficiency analysis. Seoul, Korea: Jiphil Media.

3 THE CCR MODEL

The Charnes, Cooper, Rhodes model, CCR model, also called the primal model, is the first model amongst others to be considered DEA and proposes DMU efficiency measurements by finding an optimal ratio of weighted outputs to weighted inputs. In other words, it uses constant returns to scale (CRS) to construct the production possibility sets as shown in the Figure 2.1.

<Figure 3.1> shows the concepts of returns to scale (RTS) and Production Possibility Set (PPS). <Figure 3.1> shows the production activities of DMUs with single input X and single output Y. The frontier that passes through $O - C - E - NIRS$ can be called the NIRS (non-increasing returns to scales) Frontier, the CRS Frontier can be defined as extending the line $\overline{OC}$, and the NDRS (Non-Decreasing Returns to Scales) Frontier can be defined as extending CRS through $A_1 - A - C - NDRS$. In this case, since the PPS is the set below and to the right of the frontier, it can be seen that the area of the PPS is in the order of CRS>(NDRS, NIRS)>VRS. The CCR model is a method of defining the production possibility set using the CRS frontier and measuring efficiency using the distance from the frontier to the DMU.

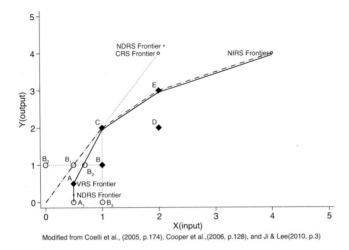

Modified from Coelli et al., (2005, p.174), Cooper et al.,(2006, p.128), and Ji & Lee(2010, p.3)

<Figure 3.1> Concepts of Returns to Scale and PPS

The CCR model can show the overall location of DMUs by pinpointing the outermost point of DMU, the frontier, and put across a line to consider all outcomes below the line as feasible. First, by using linear programming, the CCR model sets 'virtual' outputs and inputs to maximize the ratio between the two. The virtual input and virtual output are both achieved by adding each input or output mix quantity and multiply the sum by corresponding weight. By using this method, one can achieve same efficiency scores regardless of unit of input or output measurement.

Just like the FDH model, the CCR model can also be divided into two: the input-oriented and the output-oriented models. The input-oriented model focuses on reducing the input value as much as possible if the input can produce the same output value. The output-oriented CCR model increases the output value so long as the input stays the same.

From the input oriented/output oriented CCR model, we can learn that:

A. if all input values increase by x amount, the outcome becomes 1/x times less efficient and the same goes for when x is applied to all outputs.

B. Efficiency value can lie between 0 and 1 or 1 to infinity. In the 0 to 1 scale, the closer the value gets to 0, it gets less efficient and 1 being the most efficient. And in the scale of 1 to infinity, the value 1 is the most efficient and as it gets closer to infinity, it gets less and less efficient.

However, sometimes, even when the efficiency value is 1, the point might not be the most efficient one since there can be a point where less inputs can achieve the same output. This is called the "slack value". If the efficiency value is 1 and there is no slack for the DMU, as in other DMUs that share the same output value with the smaller input value, it's in the category of "strong efficiency". But if there lies another DMU that gives the same output with less input, then the DMU is in "weak" efficiency.

3.1 Data

Table 3.1 data was taken from Coelli et al. (2005, p.165, Table 6.1) for the CRS DEA analysis. The data consist of five firms that use two inputs (x1, x2) to produce single output (y).

<Table 3.1> Data of 5 Firms

Firm	y	x1	x2
A	1	2	5
B	2	2	4
C	3	6	6
D	1	3	2
E	2	6	2

3.2 Model Description

Input-oriented CCR model follows as below.

$$\min_{\theta,\lambda} \theta^k \qquad (2.1)$$

subject to $\quad \theta^k x_m^k \geq \sum_{j=1}^{J} x_m^j \lambda^j \quad (m = 1,2,\dots,M);$

$$y_n^k \leq \sum_{j=1}^{J} y_n^j \lambda^j \quad (n = 1,2,\dots,N);$$

$$\lambda^j \geq 0$$

Output-oriented CCR model follows as below.

$$\max_{\theta,\lambda} \theta^k \tag{2.2}$$

subject to $\quad x_m^k \geq \sum_{j=1}^{J} x_m^j \lambda^j \quad (m = 1,2,\dots,M);$

$$\theta^k y_n^k \leq \sum_{j=1}^{J} y_n^j \lambda^j \quad (n = 1,2,\dots,N);$$

$$\lambda^j \geq 0$$

3.3 CCR Analysis @Stata

The following command loads into memory the data set of 'coelli_table6.3a.dta', a Stata-format dataset previously saved by save command from your working directory. The data input and output follow the general data management of Stata, so for data input, data can be directly entered in the Stata window GUI or data in the form of a spreadsheet or statistical package can be saved in the Stata data format filename.dta in ASCII file form and read in.

. use "D:\data\ coelli_table6.3a.dta"

And you can use the command *list* to Result Window the values of variables(see Result Window 3.1).

. list

	dmu	y	x1	x2
1.	A	1	2	5
2.	B	2	2	4
3.	C	3	6	6
4.	D	1	3	2
5.	E	2	6	2

Result Window 3.1

The syntax of the *dea* command for CCR analysis is:

dea *inputvars(min=1)* = *outputvars(min=1)* *[if]* *[in]* [using/ *filename*], [ort(i|in|input|o|out|output) rts(crs|ccr) stage (integer 2) tol1(real 1e-14) tol2(real 1e-8) trace <u>saving</u>(*filename*) replace]

In command syntax, the terms i, in, and input have the same meaning for ort, and the other string variables such as crs and ccr should also be understood in the same way.

You can estimate the CCR model with input-oriented two stage using the following command to get the results shown in Result Window 3.2:

. dea x1 x2= y, ort(in) rts(crs) stage(2)

```
options: RTS(CRS) ORT(IN) STAGE(2)
CRS-INPUT Oriented DEA Efficiency Results:
                         ref:      ref:     ref:    ref:     ref:    islack:
           rank   theta   1         2        3       4        5       x1
dmu:1       5     .5       0        .5        0       0        0       0
dmu:2       1     1        0        1         0       0        0       0
dmu:3       3     .833333  0        1         0       0       .5       0
dmu:4       4     .714286  0       .214286    0       0      .285714   0
dmu:5       1     1        0        0         0       0        1       0


           islack:  oslack:
            x2        y
dmu:1       .5        0
dmu:2       0         0
dmu:3       0         0
dmu:4       0         0
dmu:5       0         0
```

Result Window 3.2

As the default command, you can get the same result by doing the following command.

. dea x1 x2= y

Also, it is possible to estimate the CCR model with output-oriented single stage using the following command to get the results shown in Result Window 3.3:

. dea x1 x2= y, ort(out) rts(crs) stage(1)

```
options: RTS(CRS) ORT(OUT) STAGE(1)
CRS-OUTPUT Oriented DEA Efficiency Results:
                        ref:   ref:   ref:   ref:   ref:  islack:
            rank  theta    1      2      3      4      5     x1
dmu:1         5      2      0      1      0      0      0      0
dmu:2         1      1      0      1      0      0      0      0
dmu:3         3    1.2      0    1.2      0      0     .6      0
dmu:4         4    1.4      0     .3      0      0     .4      0
dmu:5         1      1      0      0      0      0      1      0

            islack:  oslack:
              x2       y
dmu:1          1       0
dmu:2          0       0
dmu:3          0       0
dmu:4          0       0
dmu:5          0       0
```

Result Window 3.3

3.4 Exercises

3.4.1 Solve the firm example in Table 3.1 using the CCR model with output-oriented two stage and compare the results with Result Window 3.3.

3.3. Describe the values that should not change whether the stage option is set to 1 or 2.

3.4.2 In Table 3.1, diagram the CCR production possibility set for firms with x1 as input and y as output. In the CCR Model, describe the reason as to whether the efficiency score would change based on the ort option (set to input or output). Confirm if you can see the same efficiency score when there are multiple inputs or outputs.

3.4.3 For firm A in Table 3.1, diagram the output-oriented measure of CCR efficiency score with x2 as input and y as output.

3.4.4 In Table 3.1, diagram the production possibility set of the constant returns to scale and FDH returns to scale all together for stores with x1 as input and y as output.

3.5 References

Coelli, T.J., Rao, D.S.P., O'Donnell, C.J., & Battese, G.E. (2005). An Introduction to Efficiency and Productivity Analysis. Berlin, Germany: Springer Science & Business Media.

18

Cooper, W., Seiford, L. M., & Tone, K. (2006). Introduction to Data Envelopment Analysis and Its Use. 233 Spring Street, New York, NY 10013, USA: Springer Science & Business Media, Inc.

Ji, Y., & Lee, C. (2010). Data envelopment analysis. *The Stata Journal 10*(2): 267–280.

Lee, C. (2010). An Efficient Data Envelopment Analysis with a large Data Set in Stata. Boston, USA:BOS10 Stata Conference.

_____ (2011). Malmquist Productivity Analysis using DEA Frontier in Stata. Washington DC, USA:Chicago11 Stata Conference.

Lee, C., & Ji, Y. (2009). Data Envelopment Analysis in Stata. Washington DC, USA:DC09 Stata Conference.

Lee, Jeong-dong and Oh, Dong-hyun. (2012). Theory of efficiency analysis. Seoul, Korea: Jiphil Media.

4 THE BCC MODEL

The Banker, Charnes, Cooper (BCC) model was developed to improve upon the CCR model; it added a new separate variable to determine whether operations were conducted in regions of increasing, decreasing or constant returns to scale. This is the reason why it is called 'variable returns to scale'. On the increasing returns to scale in Figure 3.1, the BCC model shows increase in outputs as more inputs are put in. On the constant returns to scale in Figure 3.1, it's on its peak inputs, therefore no more increase in outputs. And finally, if it's on the decreasing returns to scale in Figure 3.1, output values do not increase, and more inputs would seem wasteful.

The BCC model also contains input-oriented and output-oriented models within itself, and it shares the same method with the CCR model. Production possibility sets are used to represent the potential outputs that a firm can produce given its available inputs and technology. There are several different models for representing production possibility sets, including the FDH (free disposability of the inputs), CCR (constant returns to scale and free disposability of the inputs), and BCC (variable returns to scale and free disposability of the inputs) models.

Efficiency is typically measured in relation to the production possibility frontier, which represents the maximum output that can be achieved for a given set of inputs and technology. The efficiency score is a measure of the relative distance of a firm's actual output from the production possibility frontier.

In the context of production possibility sets, "disposability" refers to the ability of a firm to vary the use of its inputs or outputs in the production process. "Returns to scale" refers to the relationship between the inputs used and the output produced, with constant returns to scale indicating that the output increases at the same rate as the inputs, and variable returns to scale indicating that the output increases at a different rate than the inputs.

4.1 Data

Table 3.1 data was taken from Coelli et al. (2005, p.165, Table 6.1) for the BCC DEA analysis. The data consist of five firms that use two inputs (x1, x2) to produce single output (y).

Table 4.1 Data of 5 Firms

Firm	y	x1	x2
A	1	2	5
B	2	2	4
C	3	6	6
D	1	3	2
E	2	6	2

4.2 Model Description

Input-oriented BCC model follows as below.

$$\min_{\theta,\lambda} \theta^k \tag{2.1}$$

subject to
$$\theta^k x_m^k \geq \sum_{j=1}^{J} x_m^j \lambda^j \quad (m = 1,2,\dots,M);$$

$$y_n^k \leq \sum_{j=1}^{J} y_n^j \lambda^j \quad (n = 1,2,\dots,N);$$

$$\sum \lambda^j = 1$$

Output-oriented BCC model is shown in equation (2.2).

$$\max_{\theta,\lambda} \theta^k \qquad (2.2)$$

subject to $\quad x_m^k \geq \sum_{j=1}^{J} x_m^j \lambda^j \quad (m = 1,2,\dots,M);$

$$\theta^k y_n^k \leq \sum_{j=1}^{J} y_n^j \lambda^j \quad (n = 1,2,\dots,N);$$

$$\sum \lambda^j = 1$$

4.3 BCC Analysis @Stata

The following command loads into memory the data set of 'coelli_table6.3.dta', a Stata-format dataset previously saved by *save* command from your working directory.

. use "D:\data\ coelli_table6.3.dta"

And you can use the command *list* to Result Window the values of variables(see Result Window 4.1).

. list

dmu	y	x1	x2
1. A	1	2	5
2. B	2	2	4
3. C	3	6	6
4. D	1	3	2
5. E	2	6	2

Result Window 4.1

The syntax of the **dea** command for BCC analysis is:

dea *inputvars(min=1)* = *outputvars(min=1)* *[if]* *[in]* [using/ *filename*], [ort(i|in|input|o|out|output) rts(bcc|vrs) stage (integer 2) tol1(real 1e-14) tol2(real 1e-8) trace saving(*filename*) replace]

You can estimate the BCC model with input-oriented two stage using the following command to get the results shown in Result Window 4.2:

. dea x1 x2= y, ort(in) rts(vrs) stage(2)

```
options: RTS(VRS) ORT(IN) STAGE(2)
VRS-INPUT Oriented DEA Efficiency Results:
                            ref:     ref:     ref:     ref:    ref: islack:
            rank    theta     A        B        C        D       E      x1
dmu:A         5       1       0        1        0        0       0       0
dmu:B         1       1       0        1        0        0       0       0
dmu:C         1       1       0        0        1        0       0       0
dmu:D         1       1       0        0        0        1       0       0
dmu:E         1       1       0        0        0        0       1       0

            islack:  oslack:
              x2       y
dmu:A          1       1
dmu:B          0       0
dmu:C          0       0
dmu:D          0       0
dmu:E          0       0


VRS Frontier(-1:drs, 0:crs, 1:irs)
            CRS_TE       VRS_TE       DRS_TE        SCALE         RTS
dmu:A     0.500000     1.000000     0.500000     0.500000     1.000000
dmu:B     1.000000     1.000000     1.000000     1.000000     0.000000
dmu:C     0.833333     1.000000     1.000000     0.833333    -1.000000
dmu:D     0.714286     1.000000     0.714286     0.714286     1.000000
dmu:E     1.000000     1.000000     1.000000     1.000000     0.000000


VRS Frontier:
```

	dmu	y	x1	x2	CRS_TE	VRS_TE	SCALE	RTS
1.	A	1	2	5	0.500000	1.000000	0.500000	irs
2.	B	2	2	4	1.000000	1.000000	1.000000	–
3.	C	3	6	6	0.833333	1.000000	0.833333	drs
4.	D	1	3	2	0.714286	1.000000	0.714286	irs
5.	E	2	6	2	1.000000	1.000000	1.000000	–

Result Window 4.2

It is possible that in Result Window 4.2, all DMUs (decision making units) have an efficiency score of 1, but DMU A has a ranking of 5th place. This may be because the characteristics of the DMU and the estimated results from the model are considered in determining the ranking.

Specifically, if the output-oriented VRS (variable returns to scale) or NIRS (non-increasing returns to scale) frontier is applied to estimate the efficiency of DMU D in Figure 4.1, it will have an efficiency score of 1, which indicates that it is efficient. DMU C will also have an efficiency score of 1. Although the efficiency scores of DMUs C and D are both 1, when determining the ranking, DMU D may be given a lower ranking because it can maintain the same efficiency score of 1 even if the input level is reduced from 2 to 1, while maintaining the same level of output. This means that DMU D has slack, or unused capacity, in its inputs, while DMUs C and others do not have slack. In Result Window 4.2, DMUs that do not have slack are given a higher ranking than DMU A, which does have slack.

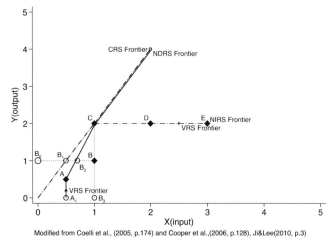

Modified from Coelli et al., (2005, p.174) and Cooper et al.,(2006, p.128), Ji&Lee(2010, p.3)

<Figure 4.1> Returns to Scale and Frontier of PPS

Figure 4.2 represents an activity that produces the same output y using two inputs. All production sets on the line connecting A-B-C-D-E-F in the figure are efficiently producing the output. In contrast, DMUs G and H are relatively inefficient because they produce the same output using more inputs. However, DMUs A, B, E, and F are also efficient in their production activities, but can produce the same output even if they reduce their input levels. In this case, the analysis may show a slack value greater than 0, so it may be possible to differentiate the ranks and assign them accordingly.

The production sets on the line connecting C-D in Figure 4.2 can change their production levels by increasing or decreasing their inputs. However, DMUs C and D have the same efficiency score of

1. One approach to differentiating their ranks could be to use the super-efficiency model, which has been proposed academically as a method for analyzing efficiency in such cases(see Chapter 9). It may also be possible to consider whether DMUs C and D are self-referencing in the analysis before applying the super-efficiency model. In Result Window 4.2, DMUs B, C, D, and E are all self-referencing, so it may be possible to consider the application of the super-efficiency model. Another approach could be to consider the effect of changing options such as RTS (returns to scale) and orientation on the result values.

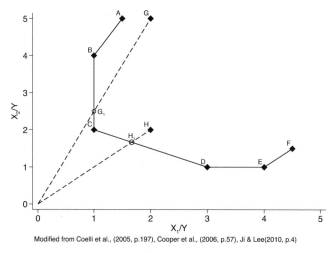

Modified from Coelli et al., (2005, p.197), Cooper et al., (2006, p.57), Ji & Lee(2010, p.4)

<Figure 4.2> Two inputs case PPS Frontier

As the default command, you can get the same result by doing the following command.
. dea x1 x2= y, rts(vrs)

Also, it is easy to estimate the BCC model with output-oriented single stage using the following command to get the results shown in Result Window 4.3:
. dea x1 x2= y, ort(out) rts(vrs) stage(1)

In this analysis, it is determined that DMU A is inefficient in terms of efficiency value, while all other DMUs are efficient, when the options for the analysis are changed. In other words, while all

DMUs had the same efficiency value in the input-oriented model, DMU A is considered inefficient in the output-oriented model. Therefore, it may be possible to consider this when determining the rank of DMUs.

```
options: RTS(VRS) ORT(OUT) STAGE(1)
VRS-OUTPUT Oriented DEA Efficiency Results:
                           ref:    ref:    ref:    ref:    ref: islack:
            rank    theta    A       B       C       D       E      x1
dmu:A        5        2       0       1       0       0       0       0
dmu:B        1        1       0       1       0       0       0       0
dmu:C        1        1       0       0       1       0       0       0
dmu:D        1        1       0       0       0       1       0       0
dmu:E        1        1       0       0       0       0       1       0

            islack:  oslack:
              x2        y
dmu:A         1         0
dmu:B         0         0
dmu:C         0         0
dmu:D         0         0
dmu:E         0         0


VRS Frontier(-1:drs, 0:crs, 1:irs)
            CRS_TE      VRS_TE      DRS_TE      SCALE       RTS
dmu:A      2.000000    2.000000    2.000000    1.000000    0.000000
dmu:B      1.000000    1.000000    1.000000    1.000000    0.000000
dmu:C      1.200000    1.000000    1.000000    1.200000   -1.000000
dmu:D      1.400000    1.000000    1.400000    1.400000    1.000000
dmu:E      1.000000    1.000000    1.000000    1.000000    0.000000


VRS Frontier:

     | dmu   y    x1   x2     CRS_TE      VRS_TE      SCALE    RTS
  1. | A     1    2    5     2.000000    2.000000    1.000000    -
  2. | B     2    2    4     1.000000    1.000000    1.000000    -
  3. | C     3    6    6     1.200000    1.000000    1.200000   drs
  4. | D     1    3    2     1.400000    1.000000    1.400000   irs
  5. | E     2    6    2     1.000000    1.000000    1.000000    -
```

Result Window 4.3

Result Window 4.3 shows that when the VRS option is selected, it presents results not only for CRS and VRS technical efficiency, but also for DRS technical efficiency, scale efficiency, and returns to scale. Scale efficiency is obtained by dividing the CRS efficiency score by the VRS efficiency score and returns to scale is determined by finding out which returns to scale the specific DMU is in and presenting the result. DMU C,D are respectively in DRS, IRS states.

4.4 Exercises

4.4.1 Solve the firm example in Table 4.1 using the BCC model with output-oriented two stage and compare the results with Result Window 4.3.

4.4.2 In Table 4.1, diagram the BCC production possibility set for firms with x1 as input and y as output.

4.4.3 For firm A in table 4.1, diagram the output-oriented measure of BCC efficiency score with x2 as input and y as output.

4.4.4 In Table 4.1, diagram the production possibility set of the constant returns to scale, variable returns to scale, and FDH returns to scale all together for stores with x1 as input and y as output.

4.4.5 In the above 4.4.4 diagram solution, discuss about the definition of returns to scale and formulate it using PPS, the sum of reference weight, and slope parameter.

4.5 References

Banker, R.D., Charnes, A., & Cooper, W.W. (1984). Some Models for Estimating Technical and Scale Inefficiencies in Data Envelopment Analysis. *Management Science 30*(9): 1078-1092.

Cooper, W., Seiford, L. M., & Tone, K. (2006). Introduction to Data Envelopment Analysis and Its Use. 233 Spring Street, New York, NY 10013, USA: Springer Science & Business Media, Inc.

Ji, Y., & Lee, C. (2010). Data envelopment analysis. *The Stata Journal 10*(2): 267–280.

Lee, Jeong-dong and Oh, Dong-hyun. (2012). Theory of efficiency analysis. Seoul, Korea: Jiphil Media.

5 THE SBM MODEL

The Slack Based Model (SBM) uses slacks and can compare DMUs from different datasets regardless of their unit of measurement; it gets rid of the unit by dividing the slack applied input and output values by the corresponding original input or output value. This was a constraint for CCR and BCC models; they couldn't compare DMUs that were measured in different units.

The Slack Based model shows the information on possible adjustments to individual DMUs and catch any further inefficiencies in DMUs that other models had not found; however, this does not reclassify any DMU from efficient to inefficient.

By using slack, the SBM ranks DMUs for how close it is to the frontier value; it compares each DMUs with the DMU that lies on the frontier and generate different slack values for each DMUs. In the input oriented SBM, this is called "the input slack" and in the output oriented SBM, this is called "the output slack". Let's say that the range of efficiency ratio is set to zero to one, as it can also range from one to infinity. For the input oriented SBM, as the input slack gets closer to zero, it gets closer to the frontier, thus zero being the DMU with the most efficiency. In the output oriented SBM, as the output slack gets closer to one, it gets closer to the frontier, stronger efficiency.

5.1 Data

Table 5.1 data was taken from Cooper, Seiford, and Tone (2006, p.75, Table 3.7) for the SBM analysis. The data consist of five stores that use two inputs (employee, area) to produce two outputs (sales, profits).

Table 5.1 Data of 5 Stores

Store	Employee	Area	Sales	Profits
A	10	20	70	6
B	15	15	100	3
C	20	30	80	5
D	25	15	100	2
E	12	9	90	8

5.2 Model Description

According to the notation of Lee & Oh (2012), a general VRS-SBM model is as follows:

$$\theta_{SBM}^{k*} = \frac{min}{\lambda, s^+, s^-} \left(\frac{1}{M}\sum_{m=1}^{M}\frac{x_m^k - s_m^-}{x_m^k}\right) / \left(\frac{1}{N}\sum_{1}^{N}\frac{y_n^k + s_n^+}{y_n^k}\right) \tag{5.1}$$

subject to

$$x_m^k = \sum_{j=1}^{J} x_m^j \lambda^j + s_m^- \ (m = 1,2,\dots,M);$$

$$y_n^k = \sum_{j=1}^{J} y_n^j \lambda^j - s_n^+ \ (n = 1,2,\dots,N);$$

$$\sum_{j=1}^{J} \lambda^j = 1; \tag{5.2}$$

$$\lambda^j \geq 0 \ (j = 1,2,\dots,J);$$
$$s_m^- \geq 0 \ (m = 1,2,\dots,M);$$
$$s_n^+ \geq 0 \ (n = 1,2,\dots,N)$$

If we relax the constraint in Equation 5.2 in VRS-SBM, we can obtain the CRS-SBM model as in Equation 5.3.

$$\theta_{SBM}^{k*} = \frac{min}{\lambda, s^+, s^-} \left(\frac{1}{M}\sum_{m=1}^{M}\frac{x_m^k - s_m^-}{x_m^k}\right) / \left(\frac{1}{N}\sum_{1}^{N}\frac{y_n^k + s_n^+}{y_n^k}\right) \tag{5.3}$$

subject to

$$x_m^k = \sum_{j=1}^{J} x_m^j \lambda^j + s_m^- \ (m = 1,2,\dots,M);$$

$$y_n^k = \sum_{j=1}^{J} y_n^j \lambda^j - s_n^+ \ (n = 1,2,\dots,N);$$

$$\lambda^j \geq 0 \ (j = 1,2,\dots,J);$$
$$s_m^- \geq 0 \ (m = 1,2,\dots,M);$$
$$s_n^+ \geq 0 \ (n = 1,2,\dots,N)$$

The definition and generalized model of SBM can be found in the description by Cooper et al. (2006, pp.95-102).

5.3 SBM Analysis @Stata
The following command loads into memory the data set of 'cooper_table3.7.dta', a Stata-format dataset previously saved by *save* command from your working directory.

. use "D:\data\ cooper_table3.7.dta"

And you can use the command *list* to Result Window the values of variables(see Result Window 5.1).

. list

	dmu	i_empl~e	i_area	o_sales	o_prof~s
1.	store A	10	20	70	6
2.	store B	15	15	100	3
3.	store C	20	30	80	5
4.	store D	25	15	100	2
5.	store E	12	9	90	8

Result Window 5.1

The syntax of the *dea_sbm* command for SBM analysis is:

dea_sbm inputvars(min=1) = outputvars(min=1) [if] [in] [using/ filename], rts,[{crs|ccr} | {bcc|vrs}] [ort(i|in|input|o|out|output) stage (integer 2) tol1(real 1e-14) tol2(real 1e-8) trace saving(filename)]

You can estimate the SBM with input-oriented using the

following command to get the results shown in Result Window 5.2:

. dea_sbm i_employee i_area= o_sales o_profits , ort(in)

```
options: RTS(CRS) ORT(IN)
CRS DEA-SBM Efficiency Results:
                                      ref:       ref:       ref:
                 rank      theta    store_A    store_B    store_C
dmu:store_A        3     .641667         0          0          0
dmu:store_B        2     .777778         0          0          0
dmu:store_C        5        .4           0          0          0
dmu:store_D        4        .6           0          0          0
dmu:store_E        1         1           0          0          0

                  ref:       ref:    islack:    islack:    oslack:
               store_D    store_E  i_employee   i_area    o_sales
dmu:store_A        0     .777778    .666667        13          0
dmu:store_B        0    1.11111    1.66667          5          0
dmu:store_C        0    .888889    9.33333         22          0
dmu:store_D        0    1.11111    11.6667          5          0
dmu:store_E        0         1          0           0          0

               oslack:
              o_profits
dmu:store_A    .222222
dmu:store_B    5.88889
dmu:store_C    2.11111
dmu:store_D    6.88889
dmu:store_E          0
```

Result Window 5.2

As the default command, you can get the same result by doing the following command.
. dea_sbm i_employee i_area= o_sales o_profits

As shown in Result Window 5.2, the analysis results of SBM can be compared to the results obtained using the CCR and BCC models introduced in Chapters 3 and 4. It can be seen that the rankings of DMUs do not necessarily match when compared using the same criteria. This is because there is a difference between the SBM model, which is classified as a non-radial model, and the CCR and BCC models, which are classified as radial models. On the other hand, SBM is more advantageous in terms of ranking DMUs because there is a difference in efficiency values for each DMU.

Also, it is easy to estimate the SBM with output-oriented using the following command to get the results shown in Result Window 5.3:
. dea_sbm i_employee i_area= o_sales o_profits , ort(out)

```
options: RTS(CRS) ORT(OUT)
CRS DEA-SBM Efficiency Results:
                                    ref:        ref:        ref:
                  rank     theta   store_A     store_B     store_C
dmu:store_A         4     1.09127       0           0           0
dmu:store_B         3     2.22917       0           0           0
dmu:store_C         2     2.27083       0           0           0
dmu:store_D         1     4.08333       0           0           0
dmu:store_E         5       1           0           0           0


                  ref:        ref:     islack:     islack:     oslack:
                store_D     store_E   i_employee    i_area     o_sales
dmu:store_A         0     .833333        0          12.5          5
dmu:store_B         0      1.25          0          3.75        12.5
dmu:store_C         0     1.66667        0          15           70
dmu:store_D         0     1.66667        5           0           50
dmu:store_E         0       1            0           0            0


                oslack:
                o_profits
dmu:store_A     .666667
dmu:store_B        7
dmu:store_C     8.33333
dmu:store_D     11.3333
dmu:store_E        0
```

Result Window 5.3

5.4 Exercises

5.4.1 In Table 5.1, diagram the SBM production possibility set for store with employee as input and sales as output.

5.4.2 For Store A in table 5.1, diagram the output-oriented measure of SBM efficiency score with area as input and profit as output.

5.5 References

Lee, Jeong-dong and Oh, Dong-hyun. 2012. Theory of efficiency analysis. Seoul, Korea: Jiphil Media.

Cooper, W., L. M. Seiford, and K. Tone. 2006. Introduction to Data Envelopment Analysis and Its Use. 233 Spring Street, New York, NY 10013, USA: Springer Science & Business Media, Inc.

6 THE COST EFFICIENCY MODEL

The Cost Efficiency Model(CEM) introduced the concept of allocative efficiency and uses cost data as well as the quantity data. The goal for CEM is to find the point where one can minimize the cost and achieve most amounts of output. The concept works as follows:

A. Determine the frontier, find all possible inputs and outputs.

B. Apply cost to all DMUs and draw a line where most cost can be saved (cost effective).

C. Determine the distance from the chosen DMU that you'd like to investigate to the origin.

D. Determine where the DMU must be in order for it to be most cost effective; in other words, where the DMU intersects with the cost-effective line.

E. Divide the outcome of D with the outcome of C.

6.1 Data

Table 6.1 data was taken from Jeong-dong Lee and Dong-hyun Oh (2012, p.155, Table 8.1) for the CEM analysis. The data consist of seven DMUs that use two inputs-x1 with unit input cost 1 and x2 with unit input cost 2- to produce single output (y).

Table 6.1 Data of 7 Stores

DMU	A	B	C	D	E	F	G
x1	2	3	5	9	6	3	8
x2	8	6	3	2	7	9	4
y	1	1	1	1	1	1	1
c1	1	1	1	1	1	1	1
c2	2	2	2	2	2	2	2
p	3	3	3	3	3	3	3

6.2 Model Description

C. Lee (2012) and Lee & Oh (2012, p.151) describe the concept of input allocative efficiency as shown in Figure 6.1. Let's say that there are DMUs A, B, C, D, E that produce input y using input elements x1, x2. The production cost of DMU K can be expressed as a cost function $k_j = c_1 x_1 + c_2 x_2$, where c_1 and c_2 are the unit costs of x_1 and x_2, respectively.

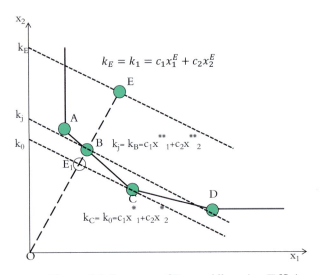

Figure 6.1 Concept of Input Allocative Efficiency

Further we define Overall Efficiency(OE)

$$0 \leq \frac{k_0}{k_1} = \frac{\sum_{i=1}^{M} c_i x_i^*}{\sum_{i=1}^{M} c_i x_i} = \frac{d(O,E_1)}{d(O,E)} \leq 1; \qquad (6.1)$$

Technical Efficiency(TE)

$$0 \leq \frac{k_j}{k_1} = \frac{\sum_{i=1}^{M} c_i x_i^{**}}{\sum_{i=1}^{M} c_i x_i} = \frac{d(O,B)}{d(O,E)} \leq 1; \qquad (6.2)$$

Allocative Efficiency(AE)

$$0 \leq \frac{k_0}{k_j} = \frac{\sum_{i=1}^{M} c_i x_i^{*}}{\sum_{i=1}^{M} c_i x_i^{**}} = \frac{d(O,E_1)}{d(O,B)} \leq 1. \qquad (6.3)$$

Then, we can find the minimum cost mix by solving the following cost minimization problem.

$$k_0 = cx^* = \min_{x,\lambda} \sum_{i=1}^{M} c_i x_i \qquad (6.4)$$

subject to

$$x_i \geq \sum_{j=1}^{J} x_m^j \lambda^j \text{ (input } m = 1,2, \dots, M)$$

$$y_0 \leq \sum_{j=1}^{J} y_n^j \lambda^j \text{ (output } n = 1,2, \dots, N)$$

$$\lambda^j \geq 0 (j = 1,2, \dots, J),$$

where c_i is unit input price or unit cost of i_{th} input.

Substituting x^* obtained from equation (6.4) into equations (6.1), (6.2), and (6.3) allows us to find OE, TE, and AE.

6.3 CEM Analysis @Stata

The following command loads into memory the data set of 'lee_table8.1.dta', a Stata-format dataset previously saved by *save* command from your working directory.

. use "D:\data\ lee_table8.1.dta"

And you can use the command *list* to Result Window the values of variables(see Result Window 6.1).

. list

	dmu	x1	x2	y	c1	c2	p
1.	A	2	8	1	1	2	3
2.	B	3	6	1	1	2	3
3.	C	5	3	1	1	2	3
4.	D	9	2	1	1	2	3
5.	E	6	7	1	1	2	3
6.	F	3	9	1	1	2	3
7.	G	8	4	1	1	2	3

Result Window 6.1

The syntax of the *dea_allocative* command for CEM analysis is:

dea_allocative *inputvars(min=1)* = *outputvars(min=1)* *[if]* *[in]* [using/ *filename*][, model(cost) values(numlist>0) unitvars(varlist numeric) rts,[{crs|ccr} | {bcc|vrs}] saving(*filename*)]

where
model(string) specifies the cost ;
rts(string) specifies crs or vrs returns to scale. The default option is crs ;
values and unitvars are case sensitive ;
val(numlist) specifies the common unit cost or price ;
and unit(varlist) specifies the variables that contain the unit cost or price to be used.

You can estimate the CEM with input-oriented constant returns to scale using the following command to get the results shown in Result Window 6.2:

. dea_allocative x1 x2 = y, mod(c) unitvars(c1 c2) sav(alloc_cost_exam1.dta)

```
options: RTS(CRS)
CRS DEA-Cost Efficiency Results:
          CUR:    CUR:    CUR:    TECH:    TECH:    TECH:    TECH:    MIN:
          x1      x2      cost    theta    x1       x2       cost     x1
dmu:A     2       8       18      1        2        8        18       5
dmu:B     3       6       15      1        3        6        15       5
dmu:C     5       3       11      1        5        3        11       5
dmu:D     9       2       13      1        9        2        13       5
dmu:E     6       7       20      .65625   3.9375   4.59375  13.125   5
dmu:F     3       9       21      .8       2.4      7.2      16.8     5
dmu:G     8       4       16      .708333  5.66667  2.83333  11.3333  5

          MIN:    MIN:
          x2      cost    OE       AE       TE
dmu:A     3       11      .611111  .611111  1
dmu:B     3       11      .733333  .733333  1
dmu:C     3       11      1        1        1
dmu:D     3       11      .846154  .846154  1
dmu:E     3       11      .55      .838095  .65625
dmu:F     3       11      .52381   .654762  .8
dmu:G     3       11      .6875    .970588  .708333
```

Result Window 6.2

DMUs A, B, and D have TE equal to 1, but have values of OE and AE that are less than 1, so it is necessary to improve allocative efficiency through adjustment of the input mix.

Also, it is easy to estimate the Allocative model with VRS using the following command to get the results shown in Result Window 6.3:

. dea_allocative x1 x2 = y, mod(c) unitvars(c1 c2) rts(vrs)

```
options: RTS(VRS)
VRS DEA-Cost Efficiency Results:
          CUR:    CUR:    CUR:    TECH:    TECH:    TECH:    TECH:    MIN:
          x1      x2      cost    theta    x1       x2       cost     x1
dmu:A     2       8       18      1        2        8        18       5
dmu:B     3       6       15      1        3        6        15       5
dmu:C     5       3       11      1        5        3        11       5
dmu:D     9       2       13      1        9        2        13       5
dmu:E     6       7       20      .65625   3.9375   4.59375  13.125   5
dmu:F     3       9       21      .8       2.4      7.2      16.8     5
dmu:G     8       4       16      .708333  5.66667  2.83333  11.3333  5

          MIN:    MIN:
          x2      cost    OE       AE       TE
dmu:A     3       11      .611111  .611111  1
dmu:B     3       11      .733333  .733333  1
dmu:C     3       11      1        1        1
dmu:D     3       11      .846154  .846154  1
dmu:E     3       11      .55      .838095  .65625
dmu:F     3       11      .52381   .654762  .8
dmu:G     3       11      .6875    .970588  .708333
```

Result Window 6.3

37

The results in Result Window 6.3 indicate that the setting of RTS does not affect the results when compared to the results in Result Window 6.2.

It can also be analyzed by specifying the unit price of the input element as an option as shown below.

. dea_allocative x1 x2 = y, mod(c) rts(crs) val(1 2)

```
options: RTS(CRS)
CRS DEA-Cost Efficiency Results:
            CUR:     CUR:     CUR:    TECH:    TECH:    TECH:    TECH:     MIN:
            x1       x2       cost    theta    x1       x2       cost      x1
dmu:A        2        8       18        1       2        8       18        5
dmu:B        3        6       15        1       3        6       15        5
dmu:C        5        3       11        1       5        3       11        5
dmu:D        9        2       13        1       9        2       13        5
dmu:E        6        7       20      .65625  3.9375  4.59375  13.125      5
dmu:F        3        9       21       .8       2.4      7.2     16.8       5
dmu:G        8        4       16     .708333 5.66667  2.83333  11.3333      5


            MIN:     MIN:
            x2       cost      OE       AE       TE
dmu:A        3        11    .611111  .611111      1
dmu:B        3        11    .733333  .733333      1
dmu:C        3        11        1        1        1
dmu:D        3        11    .846154  .846154      1
dmu:E        3        11      .55    .838095   .65625
dmu:F        3        11    .52381   .654762     .8
dmu:G        3        11     .6875   .970588  .708333
```

Result Window 6.4

Result Window 6.4 shows the results of finding TE, AE, and OE through the setting of unit prices using the dea_allocative command.

6.4 Exercises

6.4.1 In Table 6.1, diagram the CEM production possibility set in the input dimension for DMUs with x1 and x2 as inputs.

6.4.2 For DMU A in Table 6.1, diagram the CEM efficiency estimate with x1 as input and y as output.

6.4.3 Estimate the CEM with output-oriented variable returns to scale using the data of Table 6.2.

Table 6.2 Data of 7 Stores

DMU	A	B	C	D	E	F	G
x1	2	3	5	9	6	3	8
x2	8	6	3	2	7	9	4
y	1	1	1	1	1	1	1
c1	2	2	2	2	2	2	2
c2	1	1	1	1	1	1	1
p	3	3	3	3	3	3	3

6.5 References

Cooper, W., Seiford, L. M., & Tone, K. (2006). Introduction to Data Envelopment Analysis and Its Use. 233 Spring Street, New York, NY 10013, USA: Springer Science & Business Media, Inc.

Lee, C.(2012). Allocative Efficiency Analysis using Stata. San Diego, USA:2012 San Diego Stata Conference.

Lee, Jeong-dong and Oh, Dong-hyun. (2012). Theory of efficiency analysis. Seoul, Korea: Jiphil Media.

7 THE REVENUE EFFICIENCY MODEL

The Revenue Efficiency Model (REM) has a goal of maximizing the output with a set amount of price, thereby called "Revenue Efficiency" Model. REM also shares similar concept with the CEM:

A. Determine the frontier, find all possible inputs and outputs.

B. Apply price to all DMUs and draw a line where most output can be drawn (revenue effective).

C. Determine the distance from the chosen DMU that you'd like to investigate to the origin.

D. Determine where the DMU has to be in order for it to produce most output while making most out of the revenue; in other words, where the DMU intersects with the revenue effective line.

E. Divide the outcome of D from the outcome of C.

7.1 Data
Table 7.1 data was taken from Jeong-dong Lee and Dong-hyun Oh (2012, p.155, Table 8.1) for the REM analysis. The data consist of seven DMUs that use two inputs-x1 with unit input cost 1 and x2 with unit input cost 2- to produce single output (y).

<Table 7.1> Data of seven DMUs with two inputs and single output

DMU	A	B	C	D	E	F	G
x1	2	3	5	9	6	3	8
x2	8	6	3	2	7	9	4
y	1	1	1	1	1	1	1
c1	1	1	1	1	1	1	1
c2	2	2	2	2	2	2	2
p	3	3	3	3	3	3	3

7.2 Model Description

C. Lee (2012) and Lee & Oh (2012, p.151) describe the concept of output revenue efficiency as shown in Figure 7.1. Let's assume that there is a production activity that generates revenue by producing two products y_1 and y_2. The revenue of DMU K can be expressed as a revenue function $R_K = p_1 y_1 + p_2 y_2$, where p_1 and y_1 are the unit prices of y_1 and y_2, respectively.

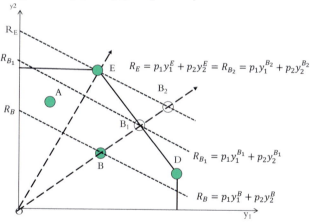

<Figure 7.1> Concept of Output Revenue Efficiency

Further we define Overall Efficiency(OE)

$$0 \leq OE = \frac{R_B}{R_{B_2}} = \frac{\sum_{j=1}^{N} p_j y_j}{\sum_{j=1}^{N} p_j y_j^2} = \left(\frac{\sum_{j=1}^{N} p_j y_j}{\sum_{j=1}^{N} p_j y_j^1}\right) \cdot \left(\frac{\sum_{j=1}^{N} p_j y_j^1}{\sum_{j=1}^{N} p_j y_j^2}\right) = TE \cdot AE \leq 1; \quad (7.1)$$

Then, we can find the maximum revenue mix by solving the following revenue maximization problem.

$$R = py^* = \max_{y,\lambda} \sum_{n=1}^{N} p_n y_n \qquad (7.2)$$

subject to

$$x_i \geq \sum_{j=1}^{J} x_m^j \lambda^j \quad (\text{input } m = 1,2,\dots,M)$$

$$y_0 \leq \sum_{j=1}^{J} y_n^j \lambda^j \quad (\text{output } n = 1,2,\dots,N)$$

$$\lambda^j \geq 0 (j = 1,2,\dots,J),$$

where p_n is unit price of n_{th} output.

Substituting y^* obtained from equation (7.2) into equation (7.1) allows us to find OE, TE, and AE.

7.3 REM Analysis @Stata

The following command loads into memory the data set of 'lee_table8.1.dta', a Stata-format dataset previously saved by *save* command from your working directory.

. use "D:\data\ lee_table8.1.dta"

And you can use the command *list* to Result Window the values of variables(see Result Window 7.1).

. list

	dmu	x1	x2	y	c1	c2	p
1.	A	2	8	1	1	2	3
2.	B	3	6	1	1	2	3
3.	C	5	3	1	1	2	3
4.	D	9	2	1	1	2	3
5.	E	6	7	1	1	2	3
6.	F	3	9	1	1	2	3
7.	G	8	4	1	1	2	3

Result Window 7.1

The syntax of the *dea_allocative* command for REM analysis is:

dea_allocative inputvars(min=1) = outputvars(min=1) [if] [in] [using/ filename][, model(revenue) values(numlist>0) unitvars(varlist numeric)

42

<u>rts</u>,[{crs|ccr} | {bcc|vrs}] <u>saving</u>(*filename*)]
where model(string) specifies the <u>r</u>evenue.

You can estimate the REM with input-oriented constant returns to scale using the following command to get the results shown in Result Window 7.2:

. dea_allocative x1 x2 = y, mod(r) unitvars(p)

```
options: RTS(CRS)
CRS DEA-Revenue Efficiency Results:
          CUR:     CUR:    TECH:    TECH:    TECH:    MAX:     MAX:
          y        price   eta      y        price    y        price    OE
dmu:A     1        3       1        1        3        1        3        1
dmu:B     1        3       1        1        3        1        3        1
dmu:C     1        3       1        1        3        1        3        1
dmu:D     1        3       1        1        3        1        3        1
dmu:E     1        3       1.52381  1.52381  4.57143  1.52381  4.57143  .65625
dmu:F     1        3       1.25     1.25     3.75     1.25     3.75     .8
dmu:G     1        3       1.41176  1.41176  4.23529  1.41176  4.23529  .708333


          AE       TE
dmu:A     1        1
dmu:B     1        1
dmu:C     1        1
dmu:D     1        1
dmu:E     1        .65625
dmu:F     1        .8
dmu:G     1        .708333
```

Result Window 7.2

We can calculate revenue efficiency using the VRS option as follows.
. dea_allocative x1 x2 = y, mod(r) unitvars(p) rts(vrs)

```
options: RTS(VRS)
VRS DEA-Revenue Efficiency Results:
          CUR:   CUR:    TECH:  TECH:  TECH:  MAX:   MAX:
          y      price   eta    y      price  y      price   OE   AE   TE
dmu:A     1      3       1      1      3      1      3       1    1    1
dmu:B     1      3       1      1      3      1      3       1    1    1
dmu:C     1      3       1      1      3      1      3       1    1    1
dmu:D     1      3       1      1      3      1      3       1    1    1
dmu:E     1      3       1      1      3      1      3       1    1    1
dmu:F     1      3       1      1      3      1      3       1    1    1
dmu:G     1      3       1      1      3      1      3       1    1    1
```

Result Window 7.3

It can also be analyzed by specifying the unit price of the output element as an option as shown below.

43

. dea_allocative x1 x2 = y, mod(r) val(3)

```
options: RTS(CRS)
CRS DEA-Revenue Efficiency Results:
              CUR:     CUR:    TECH:    TECH:    TECH:     MAX:     MAX:
                y     price     eta       y     price       y      price      OE
dmu:A           1        3       1        1        3        1        3         1
dmu:B           1        3       1        1        3        1        3         1
dmu:C           1        3       1        1        3        1        3         1
dmu:D           1        3       1        1        3        1        3         1
dmu:E           1        3  1.52381  1.52381  4.57143  1.52381  4.57143   .65625
dmu:F           1        3     1.25     1.25     3.75     1.25     3.75       .8
dmu:G           1        3  1.41176  1.41176  4.23529  1.41176  4.23529  .708333


               AE       TE
dmu:A           1        1
dmu:B           1        1
dmu:C           1        1
dmu:D           1        1
dmu:E           1    .65625
dmu:F           1       .8
dmu:G           1  .708333
```

Result Window 7.4

7.4 Exercises

7.4.1 Estimate the REM with variable returns to scale using the data of lee_table8.1.dta shown in result window 7.1.

7.4.2 For DMU A in Table 7.1, diagram the REM efficiency estimate with x1 as input and y as output.

7.5 References

Cooper, W., Seiford, L. M., & Tone, K. (2006). Introduction to Data Envelopment Analysis and Its Use. 233 Spring Street, New York, NY 10013, USA: Springer Science & Business Media, Inc.

Lee, C.(2012). Allocative Efficiency Analysis using Stata. San Diego, USA:2012 San Diego Stata Conference.

Lee, Jeong-dong and Oh, Dong-hyun. (2012). Theory of efficiency analysis. Seoul, Korea: Jiphil Media.

8 THE PROFIT EFFICIENCY MODEL

The Profit Efficiency Model (PEM) is a calculation that compares the profit currently being obtained from a combination of inputs and outputs to the potential profit that could be obtained from the optimal combination of inputs and outputs. It measures the difference between the two. Profit Efficiency Model (PEM) is a mixture of REM and CEM where various combinations of cost and revenue applied DMUs are being compared to find the most effective way to bring about most profit for the target DMU; in another words, it's about getting the best out of the least amounts of input(cost) for the most amounts of output(revenue).

8.1 Data

Table 8.1 data was taken from Jeong-dong Lee and Dong-hyun Oh (2012, p.155, Table 8.1) for the PEM analysis. The data consist of seven DMUs that use two inputs-x1 with unit input cost 1 and x2 with unit input cost 2- to produce single output (y).

<Table 8.1> Data of seven DMUs for PEM analysis

DMU	A	B	C	D	E	F	G
x1	2	3	5	9	6	3	8
x2	8	6	3	2	7	9	4
y	1	1	1	1	1	1	1
c1	1	1	1	1	1	1	1
c2	2	2	2	2	2	2	2
p	3	3	3	3	3	3	3

8.2 Model Description

If the unit price of the n-th output and the unit cost of the m-th input are given, you can use equation (8.1) to find the inputs and outputs that maximize profit.

$$\pi^* = py^* - cx^* = \max_{x,y,\lambda}(\sum_{n=1}^{N} p_n y_n - \sum_{m=1}^{M} c_m x_m) \qquad (8.1)$$

subject to

$$x_i \geq \sum_{j=1}^{J} x_m^j \lambda^j \ (\text{input } m = 1,2,\dots,M)$$

$$y_0 \leq \sum_{j=1}^{J} y_n^j \lambda^j \ (\text{output } n = 1,2,\dots,N)$$

$$\lambda^j \geq 0 (j = 1,2,\dots,J),$$

where p_n is unit price of n_{th} output and c_m is unit cost of m_{th} input.

If profit efficiency is defined as in equation (8.2), then the values of OE, TE, and AE can be obtained by substituting the optimal inputs and outputs found in equation (8.1) into equation (8.2). Again, it is not clear from the given information what equation (8.2) is or how it relates to equations (8.1) and the calculation of OE, TE, and AE. Equation 8.1 can be solved while controlling the input and output simultaneously.

$$OE_\pi = \frac{\pi}{\pi^*} = \frac{\sum_{n=1}^{N} p_n y_n - \sum_{m=1}^{M} c_m x_m}{\sum_{n=1}^{N} p_n y_n^* - \sum_{m=1}^{M} c_m x_m^*} = TE_\pi \cdot AE_\pi \qquad (8.2)$$

8.3 PEM Analysis @Stata

The following command loads into memory the data set of 'lee_table8.1.dta', a Stata-format dataset previously saved by *save* command from your working directory.

. use "D:\data\ lee_table8.1.dta"

And you can use the command list to Result Window the values of variables(see Result Window 7.1).

. list

	dmu	x1	x2	y	c1	c2	p
1.	A	2	8	1	1	2	3
2.	B	3	6	1	1	2	3
3.	C	5	3	1	1	2	3
4.	D	9	2	1	1	2	3
5.	E	6	7	1	1	2	3
6.	F	3	9	1	1	2	3
7.	G	8	4	1	1	2	3

Result Window 8.1

The syntax of the ***dea_allocative*** command for PEM analysis is:

dea_allocative *inputvars(min=1)* = *outputvars(min=1)* *[if]* *[in]* [using/ *filename*][, model(profit) values(numlist>0) unitvars(varlist numeric) rts,[{crs|ccr}|{bcc|vrs}] saving(*filename*)]

where model(string) specifies the profit.

You can estimate the PEM with constant returns to scale using the following command to get the results shown in Result Window 8.2:

. dea_allocative x1 x2 = y, mod(p) unitvars(c1 c2 p)

```
options: RTS(CRS)
CRS DEA-Profit Efficiency Results:
          MAX_H:    MAX:   MIN_H:   MIN_H:     MIN:    MAX:    CUR:
             y    revenue     x1       x2      cost   profit  profit      OE
dmu:A        1       3        2        8        18     -15     -15         1
dmu:B        1       3        3        6        15     -12     -12         1
dmu:C        1       3        5        3        11      -8      -8         1
dmu:D        1       3        9        2        13     -10     -10         1
dmu:E        1       3        5        3        11      -8     -17     2.125
dmu:F        1       3        3        6        15     -12     -18       1.5
dmu:G        1       3        5        3        11      -8     -13     1.625
```
Result Window 8.2

By specifying the options for variable returns to scale, it is possible to analyze them as follows:

dea_allocative x1 x2 = y, mod(p) unitvars(c1 c2 p) rts(vrs)

```
options: RTS(VRS)
VRS DEA-Profit Efficiency Results:
          MAX_H:    MAX:   MIN_H:   MIN_H:     MIN:    MAX:    CUR:
             y    revenue     x1       x2      cost   profit  profit      OE
dmu:A        1       3        2        8        18     -15     -15         1
dmu:B        1       3        3        6        15     -12     -12         1
dmu:C        1       3        5        3        11      -8      -8         1
dmu:D        1       3        9        2        13     -10     -10         1
dmu:E        1       3        5        3        11      -8     -17     2.125
dmu:F        1       3        3        6        15     -12     -18       1.5
dmu:G        1       3        5        3        11      -8     -13     1.625
```
Result Window 8.3

It can also be analyzed by specifying the unit price of the output element as an option as shown below.

. dea_allocative x1 x2 = y, mod(p) val(1 2 3)

```
options: RTS(CRS)
CRS DEA-Profit Efficiency Results:
          MAX_H:    MAX:   MIN_H:   MIN_H:     MIN:    MAX:    CUR:
             y    revenue     x1       x2      cost   profit  profit      OE
dmu:A        1       3        2        8        18     -15     -15         1
dmu:B        1       3        3        6        15     -12     -12         1
dmu:C        1       3        5        3        11      -8      -8         1
dmu:D        1       3        9        2        13     -10     -10         1
dmu:E        1       3        5        3        11      -8     -17     2.125
dmu:F        1       3        3        6        15     -12     -18       1.5
dmu:G        1       3        5        3        11      -8     -13     1.625
```
Result Window 8.4

8.4 Exercises

8.4.1 Estimate the PEM with the data of table 8.2 and compare the results of Result Window 8.2. Explain the difference in terms of translation invariant.

Table 8.2 Data of seven DMUs for exercise 8.4.1

DMU	A	B	C	D	E	F	G
x1	2	3	5	9	6	3	8
x2	8	6	3	2	7	9	4
y	3	3	3	3	3	3	3
c1	1	1	1	1	1	1	1
c2	2	2	2	2	2	2	2
p	3	3	3	3	3	3	3

8.4.2 Estimate the PEM with the data of table 8.3 and compare the results of exercise 8.4.1. Explain the difference in terms of translation invariant.

Table 8.3 Data of seven DMUs for exercise 8.4.2

DMU	A	B	C	D	E	F	G
x1	4	5	7	11	8	5	10
x2	10	8	5	4	9	11	6
y	3	3	3	3	3	3	3
c1	1	1	1	1	1	1	1
c2	2	2	2	2	2	2	2
p	3	3	3	3	3	3	3

8.5 References

Cooper, W., Seiford, L. M., & Tone, K. (2006). Introduction to Data Envelopment Analysis and Its Use. 233 Spring Street, New York, NY 10013, USA: Springer Science & Business Media, Inc.

Lee, C.(2012). Allocative Efficiency Analysis using Stata. San Diego, USA:2012 San Diego Stata Conference.

Lee, Jeong-dong and Oh, Dong-hyun. (2012). Theory of efficiency analysis. Seoul, Korea: Jiphil Media.

9 THE SUPER-EFFICIENCY MODEL

After a while, people realized that there are sometimes not one, but a lot of DMUs that lie in the frontier. The Super Efficiency Model (SEM) allows the user to figure out which one of these DMUs are the most effective out of all DMUs that share the same efficiency score by testing DMUs one at a time:

A. Pick one of the DMUs that lie on the frontier and measure the distance between the chosen DMU from the origin.

B. Recalculate the production possibility set and frontier line excluding the one that is being examined and measure the new distance that had been created. If the new frontier line is where the original frontier line had been, then the DMU is not the most effective one.

C. Divide the new distance (without the chosen DMU) by the original distance (with the chosen DMU).

D. Do the same for all other DMUs that lie on the frontier line.

E. Compare them all and the most efficient DMU can be found. When comparing the scores, the value should be the biggest of them all when input orientation is concerned, and the value should be the smallest when output orientation concerned.

When calculating super-efficiency score with the VRS option, it is necessary to note that depending on the location of the observation being analyzed, the solution of the super-efficiency model may not be obtained.

9.1 Data

Table 9.1 data was taken from Cooper et al. (2006, p.303, Table 10.1) for the Radial Super-Efficiency Model analysis. The data consist of six DMUs that use two inputs (x1, x2) to produce single output (y).

Table 9.1 Data of 5 DMUs

DMU	y	x1	x2
A	1	2	12
B	1	2	8
C	1	5	5
D	1	10	4
E	1	10	6
F	1	3.5	6.5

9.2 Model Description

Super-efficiency models can be divided into radial and non-radial models.

Radial CRS Input-oriented Super-efficiency Model:

$$\theta^* = \underset{\theta,\lambda,s-,s+}{min} \theta - \varepsilon(\sum_{m=1}^{M} s_m^- + \sum_{n=1}^{N} s_n^+) \qquad (9.1)$$

subject to

$$\theta x_m^k = \sum_{j=1, j\neq k}^{J} x_m^j + s_m^- \ (m=1, 2,...,M);$$

$$y_n^k = \sum_{j=1, j\neq k}^{J} y_n^j \lambda_j - s_n^+ \ (n=1, 2, ..., N);$$

$$\lambda_j \geq 0 \ (j = 1,2,...,J, j \neq k)$$

Radial VRS Input-oriented Super-efficiency Model:

$$\theta^* = \underset{\theta,\lambda,s-,s+}{min} \theta - \varepsilon(\sum_{m=1}^{M} s_m^- + \sum_{n=1}^{N} s_n^+) \qquad (9.2)$$

subject to

$$\theta x_m^k = \sum_{j=1, j\neq k}^{J} x_m^j + s_m^- \ (m=1, 2,...,M);$$

$$y_n^k = \sum_{j=1, j\neq k}^{J} y_n^j \lambda_j - s_n^+ \ (n=1, 2, ..., N);$$

$$\sum_{j=1, j\neq k}^{J} \lambda^j = 1, \ \lambda_j \geq 0 \ (j = 1,2,...,J, j \neq k)$$

Radial CRS Input-oriented Super-efficiency SBM:

$$\delta^k = \min_{\emptyset,\lambda}(1 + \frac{1}{m}\sum_{i=1}^{M}\phi_i) \tag{9.3}$$

subject to

$$\sum_{j=1,j\neq k}^{N} x_{i,j} - x_i\emptyset_i \leq x_i \quad (i = 1,2,\dots,M)$$

$$\sum_{j=1,j\neq k}^{N} y_{r,j}\lambda_j \geq y_r \quad (r = 1,2,\dots,S)$$

$$\emptyset_i \geq 0 \; (\forall i), \lambda_j \geq 0 \; (\forall j)$$

The radial CRS Output-oriented Super-efficiency SBM also can be defined as like the above program.

In cases where the radial model is unable to find a feasible solution in the VRS option, several models have been proposed to solve this problem. One example of a well-known model is the Non-radial VRS SBM Super-efficiency Model, which is always feasible and has a finite optimum, in contrast to the radial super-efficiency model (Cooper et al, 2007, p.319; Lee & Oh, 2012, p.294).

$$\delta^k = \min \left(\frac{1}{M}\sum_{m=1}^{M} \bar{x}_m \middle/ x_m^k\right) \middle/ \left(\frac{1}{N}\sum_{n=1}^{N} \bar{y}_n \middle/ y_n^k\right) \tag{9.4}$$

subject to

$$\bar{x}_m \geq \sum_{j=1,j\neq k}^{j} x_m^j\lambda^j \quad (m = 1,2,\dots,M),$$

$$\bar{y}_n \leq \sum_{j=1,j\neq k}^{J} y_n^j\lambda^j \quad (n = 1,2,\dots,N)$$

$$\bar{x}_m \geq x_m^k \; and \; \bar{y}_n \leq y_n^k,$$

$$\sum_{j=1,j\neq k}^{J} \lambda^j = 1,$$

$$\lambda_j \geq 0 (j = 1,2,\dots,J, j \neq k)$$

9.3 Super-Efficiency Model Analysis @Stata

The following command loads into memory the data set of 'cooper_table10.1.dta', a Stata-format dataset previously saved by *save* command from your working directory.

. use "D:\data\ cooper_table10.1.dta"

And you can use the command *list* to Result Window the values of variables(see Result Window 9.1).

. list

dmu	y	x1	x2
1.	A	1	2	12
2.	B	1	2	8
3.	C	1	5	5
4.	D	1	10	4
5.	E	1	10	6
6.	F	1	3.5	6.5

Result Window 9.1

The syntax of the *dea_supereff* command for DEA Super-efficiency analysis is:

dea_supereff *inputvars(min=1)* = *outputvars(min=1)* *[if]* *[in]* [using/ *filename*][, rts(string) ort(string) stage(integer 2) saving(*filename*)]

You can estimate the DEA Super-efficiency with constant returns to scale using the following command to get the results shown in Result Window 9.2:

. dea_supereff x1 x2 = y

```
options: RTS(CRS) ORT(IN) STAGE(2)
CRS-INPUT Oriented DEA Efficiency Results:
                          ref:     ref:     ref:     ref:     ref:     ref:
            rank    theta    A        B        C        D        E        F
dmu:A        5       1       0        1        0        0        0        0
dmu:B        1    1.26087  .652174    0        0        0        0     .347826
dmu:C        3    1.13333    0        0        0     .333333    0     .666667
dmu:D        2    1.25       0        0        1        0        0        0
dmu:E        6     .75       0        0       .5       .5        0        0
dmu:F        4       1       0       .5       .5        0        0        0

            islack:  islack:  oslack:
              x1       x2       y
dmu:A          0        4        0
dmu:B          0        0        0
dmu:C          0        0        0
dmu:D        7.5        0        0
dmu:E          0        0        0
dmu:F          0        0        0
```

Result Window 9.2

By specifying the options for variable returns to scale, it is possible to analyze them as follows:

. dea_supereff x1 x2= y, rts(vrs)

```
options: RTS(VRS) ORT(IN) STAGE(2)
VRS-INPUT Oriented DEA Efficiency Results:
                           ref:     ref:     ref:     ref:     ref:     ref:
            rank    theta    A        B        C        D        E        F
dmu:A        5        1       0        1        0        0        0        0
dmu:B        1     1.26087  .652174    0        0        0        0     .347826
dmu:C        3     1.13333    0        0        0     .333333     0     .666667
dmu:D        2      1.25      0        0        1        0        0        0
dmu:E        6       .75      0        0       .5       .5        0        0
dmu:F        4        1       0       .5       .5        0        0        0


            islack:  islack:  oslack:
              x1       x2       y
dmu:A          0        4        0
dmu:B          0        0        0
dmu:C          0        0        0
dmu:D         7.5       0        0
dmu:E          0        0        0
dmu:F          0        0        0



VRS Frontier(-1:drs, 0:crs, 1:irs)
            CRS_TE     VRS_TE     DRS_TE     SCALE      RTS
dmu:A     1.000000   1.000000   1.000000   1.000000   0.000000
dmu:B     1.260870   1.260870   1.260870   1.000000   0.000000
dmu:C     1.133333   1.133333   1.133333   1.000000   0.000000
dmu:D     1.250000   1.250000   1.250000   1.000000   0.000000
dmu:E     0.750000   0.750000   0.750000   1.000000   0.000000
dmu:F     1.000000   1.000000   1.000000   1.000000   0.000000


VRS Frontier:


      dmu    y    x1    x2     CRS_TE      VRS_TE      SCALE     RTS

 1.    A    1    2    12    1.000000    1.000000    1.000000     -
 2.    B    1    2     8    1.260870    1.260870    1.000000     -
 3.    C    1    5     5    1.133333    1.133333    1.000000     -
 4.    D    1   10     4    1.250000    1.250000    1.000000     -
 5.    E    1   10     6    0.750000    0.750000    1.000000     -

 6.    F    1   3.5   6.5   1.000000    1.000000    1.000000     -
```

Result Window 9.3

Result Window 9.4 shows that calculating super-efficiency with the VRS option may not be able to solve the super-efficiency model depending on the location of the observed object to analysis.

. dea_supereff x1 x2 = y, rts(vrs) ort(out)

```
No Solution(No more candidate for entering variable):[DMUi=2][LOOP=5]VRS-OUT-SI
> -PI
No Solution(No more candidate for entering variable):[DMUi=3][LOOP=5]VRS-OUT-SI
> -PI
No Solution(No more candidate for entering variable):[DMUi=4][LOOP=3]VRS-OUT-SI
> -PI

options: RTS(VRS) ORT(OUT) STAGE(2)
VRS-OUTPUT Oriented DEA Efficiency Results:
                            ref:    ref:     ref:     ref:    ref:    ref:
            rank    theta     A       B        C        D       E       F
dmu:A        2        1       0       1        0        0       0       0
dmu:B        .        .       .       .        .        .       .       .
dmu:C        .        .       .       .        .        .       .       .
dmu:D        .        .       .       .        .        .       .       .
dmu:E        3        1       0  .333333  .666667       0       0       0
dmu:F        1        1       0      .5       .5         0       0       0


           islack:  islack:  oslack:
             x1       x2        y
dmu:A         0        4        0
dmu:B         .        .        .
dmu:C         .        .        .
dmu:D         .        .        .
dmu:E         6        0        0
dmu:F         0        0        0


VRS Frontier(-1:drs, 0:crs, 1:irs)
           CRS_TE     VRS_TE      DRS_TE      SCALE        RTS
dmu:A    1.000000   1.000000    1.000000   1.000000   0.000000
dmu:B    0.793103       .        0.793103       .      1.000000
dmu:C    0.882353       .        0.882353       .      1.000000
dmu:D    0.800000       .        0.800000       .      1.000000
dmu:E    1.333333   1.000000    1.000000   1.333333  -1.000000
dmu:F    1.000000   1.000000    1.000000   1.000000   0.000000


VRS Frontier:
```

dmu	y	x1	x2	CRS_TE	VRS_TE	SCALE	RTS
1.	A	1	2	12	1.000000	1.000000	1.000000	–
2.	B	1	2	8	0.793103	.	.	irs
3.	C	1	5	5	0.882353	.	.	irs
4.	D	1	10	4	0.800000	.	.	irs
5.	E	1	10	6	1.333333	1.000000	1.333333	drs
6.	F	1	3.5	6.5	1.000000	1.000000	1.000000	–

Result Window 9.4

Input-oriented VRS radial SBM is applied to obtain super-efficiency solutions and the result is shown in Result Window 9.5.

. dea_supersbm x1 x2 = y, rts(vrs) ort(in)

```
options: RTS(VRS) ORT(IN)
VRS DEA-SUPER-SBM Efficiency Results:
                  ref:    ref:    ref:    ref:    ref:    ref:  islack:
          theta     A       B       C       D       E       F     x1
dmu:A       1       0       1       0       0       0       0      0
dmu:B     1.25      1       0       0       0       0       0      0
dmu:C   1.09231     0       0       0    .230769    0    .769231   0
dmu:D    1.125      0       0       1       0       0       0      0
dmu:E       1      .25      0       0      .75      0       0      0
dmu:F       1       0      .5      .5       0       0       0      0


          islack:  oslack:
            x2       y
dmu:A        0       0
dmu:B        4       0
dmu:C    .923077     0
dmu:D        1       0
dmu:E        0       0
dmu:F        0       0
```

Result Window 9.5

Result Window 9.6 shows that even for radial super-efficiency SBM, the super-efficiency solution is not found for this case.

. dea_supersbm x1 x2= y, rts(vrs) ort(out)

```
No Solution(No more candidate for entering variable):[DMUi=2][LOOP=6]VRS-OUT-PI
No Solution(No more candidate for entering variable):[DMUi=3][LOOP=6]VRS-OUT-PI
No Solution(No more candidate for entering variable):[DMUi=4][LOOP=4]VRS-OUT-PI

options: RTS(VRS) ORT(OUT)
VRS DEA-SUPER-SBM Efficiency Results:
                  ref:    ref:    ref:    ref:    ref:    ref:  islack:
          theta     A       B       C       D       E       F     x1
dmu:A       1       0       1       0       0       0       0      0
dmu:B       .       .       .       .       .       .       .      .
dmu:C       .       .       .       .       .       .       .      .
dmu:D       .       .       .       .       .       .       .      .
dmu:E       1      .25      0       0      .75      0       0      0
dmu:F       1       0      .5      .5       0       0       0      0


          islack:  oslack:
            x2       y
dmu:A        0       0
dmu:B        .       .
dmu:C        .       .
dmu:D        .       .
dmu:E        0       0
dmu:F        0       0
```

Result Window 9.6

9.4 Exercises

9.4.1 Define the Radial VRS output-oriented Super-efficiency Model in mathematical form.

9.4.2 Define the non-Radial CRS output-oriented Super-efficiency Model in mathematical form.

9.4.3 Table 9.2 data was taken from Cooper et al. (2007, p.320, Table 10.4) for the Super-Efficiency Model analysis. The data consist of six DMUs that use two inputs (x1, x2) to produce two outputs (y1, y2). Solve the VRS input-oriented Super-SBM model.

Table 9.2 Data for Super-efficiency model analysis

DMU	x1	x2	y1	y2
A	2	12	4	1
B	2	8	3	1
C	5	5	2	1
D	10	4	2	1
E	10	6	1	1
F	3.5	6.5	1	1

9.4.4 Define the Non-Radial CRS Super-efficiency Model that is always feasible and has a finite optimum. Discuss the limitation of the model in real case application.

9.5 References

Coelli, T.J., Rao, D.S.P., O'Donnell, C.J., & Battese, G.E. (2005). An Introduction to Efficiency and Productivity Analysis. Berlin, Germany: Springer Science & Business Media.

Cooper, W., Seiford, L. M., & Tone, K. (2006). Introduction to Data Envelopment Analysis and Its Use. 233 Spring Street, New York, NY 10013, USA: Springer Science & Business Media, Inc.

_____. (2007). Data Envelopment Analysis: A Comprehensive Text with Models, Applications, References and DEA-Solver Software. 233 Spring Street, New York, NY 10013, USA: Springer Science & Business Media, Inc.

Ji, Y., & Lee, C. (2010). Data envelopment analysis. *The Stata Journal 10*(2): 267–280.

Lee, C. (2010). An Efficient Data Envelopment Analysis with a large Data Set in Stata. Boston, USA:BOS10 Stata Conference.

_____ (2011). Malmquist Productivity Analysis using DEA Frontier in Stata. Washington DC, USA:Chicago11 Stata Conference.

Lee, C., & Ji, Y. (2009). Data Envelopment Analysis in Stata. Washington DC, USA:DC09 Stata Conference.

Lee, Jeong-dong and Oh, Dong-hyun. (2012). Theory of efficiency analysis. Seoul, Korea: Jiphil Media.

10 THE ADDITIVE MODEL

The Additive DEA Model (ADM) attempts to find most efficient solution for the designated DMU by trying out various mixtures of inputs and outputs that bring out the DMU to the frontier line. This is quite similar to what SBM is doing yet they are not the same; while SBM does not have a unit of measurement and it is simply a ratio between the slack applied DMU with the original DMU, ADM has a unit of measurement since it's taking the existing DMUs and figure out where they'd have to end up becoming most efficient.

10.1 Data
Table 10.1 data was taken from Jeong-dong Lee and Dong-hyun Oh (2012, p.120, Table 7.1) for the ADM analysis. The data consist of seven DMUs that use single input x1 to produce single output y.

Table 10.1 Data for Additive DEA Model

DMU	A	B	C	D	E	F	G
x	3	2	6	4	8	8	10
y	1	2	4	6	7	9	9

10.2 Model Description
Lee et al.(2012) describes the following additive models among several types of additive models.

VRS Additive Model

$$\theta^{k^*} = \max_{\lambda, s^+, s^-} \left(\sum_{m=1}^{M} s_m^- + \sum_{n=1}^{N} s_n^+\right) \qquad (10.1)$$

subject to

$$x_m^k = \sum_{j=1}^{J} x_m^j \lambda^j + s_m^- \quad (m = 1,2, \dots, M);$$

$$y_n^k = \sum_{j=1}^{J} y_n^j \lambda^j - s_n^+ \quad (n = 1,2, \dots, N);$$

$$\sum_{j=1}^{J} \lambda^j = 1;$$

$$\lambda^j \geq 0 \ (j = 1,2, \dots, J);$$

$$s_m^- \geq 0 \ (m = 1,2, \dots, M);$$

$$s_n^+ \geq 0 \ (n = 1,2, \dots, N);$$

10.3 ADM Analysis @Stata

The following command loads into memory the data set of 'lee_table7.1.dta', a Stata-format dataset previously saved by save command from your working directory.

. use "D:\data\ lee_table7.1.dta"

And you can use the command *list* to Result Window the values of variables(see Result Window 10.1).

. list

Result Window 10.1

The syntax of the **dea_additive** command for DEA Additive efficiency analysis is:

dea_additive *inputvars(min=1)* = *outputvars(min=1)* [if] [in] [using/ filename][, rts(string) ort(string) stage(integer 2) saving(filename)]

You can estimate the ADM with constant returns to scale using the following command to get the results shown in Result Window 10.2:

. dea_additive x= y

```
options: RTS(CRS)
CRS DEA-Additive Efficiency Results:
```

	rank	theta	ref: A	ref: B	ref: C	ref: D	ref: E	ref: F
dmu:A	.	3.5	0	0	0	.75	0	0
dmu:B	.	1	0	0	0	.5	0	0
dmu:C	.	5	0	0	0	1.5	0	0
dmu:D	.	0	0	0	0	1	0	0
dmu:E	.	5	0	0	0	2	0	0
dmu:F	.	3	0	0	0	2	0	0
dmu:G	.	6	0	0	0	2.5	0	0

	ref: G	islack: x	oslack: y
dmu:A	0	0	3.5
dmu:B	0	0	1
dmu:C	0	0	5
dmu:D	0	0	0
dmu:E	0	0	5
dmu:F	0	0	3
dmu:G	0	0	6

Result Window 10.2

By specifying the options for variable returns to scale, it is possible to analyze them as follows:

. dea_additive x= y, rts(vrs)

A Handbook of Data Envelopment Analysis @ Stata

```
options: RTS(VRS)
VRS DEA-Additive Efficiency Results:
                         ref:   ref:   ref:   ref:   ref:   ref:
          rank   theta    A      B      C      D      E      F
dmu:A       .      3      0     .5      0     .5      0      0
dmu:B       .      0      0      1      0      0      0      0
dmu:C       .      4      0      0      0      1      0      0
dmu:D       .      0      0      0      0      1      0      0
dmu:E       .  2.66667     0      0      0  .666667    0  .333333
dmu:F       .      0      0      0      0      0      0      1
dmu:G       .      2      0      0      0      0      0      1

          ref:  islack:  oslack:
           G      x        y
dmu:A      0      0        3
dmu:B      0      0        0
dmu:C      0      2        2
dmu:D      0      0        0
dmu:E      0  2.66667      0
dmu:F      0      0        0
dmu:G      0      2        0
```

Result Window 10.3

It is important to note that the results given in the Result Window do not include information about rank. The additive model measures efficiency by adding slack to the values of inputs and outputs, regardless of the units used for these values. Therefore, it is possible to evaluate whether an additive model is efficient or inefficient, but it is not appropriate to use an additive model to rank the efficiency of different models. This is because the model does not consider the units of inputs and outputs when measuring efficiency.

10.4 Exercises

10.4.1 Apply the VRS Additive DEA Model to Table 10.2 data and compare with the BCC Output-oriented Model.

Table 10.2 Data for Additive DEA Model

DMU	A	B	C	D	E	F	G
x	4	2	6	4	10	8	8
y	2	1	4	6	8	9	7

10.4.2 Apply the Additive DEA Model to Table 10.3 and Table 10.4 data and compare with the results of the Table 10.2.

62

Table 10.3 Data for Additive DEA Model

DMU	A	B	C	D	E	F	G
x	8	4	12	8	20	16	16
y	2	1	4	6	8	9	7

Table 10.4 Data for Additive DEA Model

DMU	A	B	C	D	E	F	G
x	8	6	10	8	14	12	12
y	2	1	4	6	8	9	7

10.5 References

Coelli, T.J., Rao, D.S.P., O'Donnell, C.J., & Battese, G.E. (2005). An Introduction to Efficiency and Productivity Analysis. Berlin, Germany: Springer Science & Business Media.

Cooper, W., Seiford, L. M., & Tone, K. (2006). Introduction to Data Envelopment Analysis and Its Use. 233 Spring Street, New York, NY 10013, USA: Springer Science & Business Media, Inc.

_____. (2007). Data Envelopment Analysis: A Comprehensive Text with Models, Applications, References and DEA-Solver Software. 233 Spring Street, New York, NY 10013, USA: Springer Science & Business Media, Inc.

Ji, Y., & Lee, C. (2010). Data envelopment analysis. *The Stata Journal 10*(2): 267–280.

Lee, C. (2010). An Efficient Data Envelopment Analysis with a large Data Set in Stata. Boston, USA:BOS10 Stata Conference.

_____ (2011). Malmquist Productivity Analysis using DEA Frontier in Stata. Washington DC, USA:Chicago11 Stata Conference.

Lee, C., & Ji, Y. (2009). Data Envelopment Analysis in Stata. Washington DC, USA:DC09 Stata Conference.

Lee, Jeong-dong and Oh, Dong-hyun. (2012). Theory of efficiency analysis. Seoul, Korea: Jiphil Media.

11 THE TFDEA MODEL

We can use DEA to forecast technological change for the future. The Technology Forecasting using DEA(TFDEA) model was first proposed in 2001 by Anderson et al and it uses the rate of change from the previous technological advancement to predict the future technological advancement. For example, for the given datasets of 5 consecutive years, if the user would like to predict the frontier for the 10th year, it begins by drawing the frontier for each year, while logging every process of change for each year, and calculate where the frontier would end up for the 10th year by calculating the rate of change from all DMUs that contributed for change. This model, however, does not predict any abrupt changes in technological advancement, but the State Of the Art (SOA) technologies that are progressive, and therefore, those that are more measurable and predictable.

11.1 Data

The data was taken from Kim et al. (2022, pp.9-11, Table 1) for the TFDEA analysis. The data consist of 107 DMUs that use single two inputs(Price, Body weight) to produce 9 outputs(Network band, Screen size, Resolution, Sensors, Network speed, CPU speed, Camera Performance, Battery Capacity, WLAN generation).

11.2 Model Description

Anderson et al.(2001) first introduced the Technology Forecasting using Data Envelopment Analysis (TFDEA) at the PICMET 01 Conference. TFDEA estimates the technological frontier using DEA and measures a change of frontiers as new DMUs appear. Rate of change (ROC) is obtained from the efficiency changes of DMUs that existed in the frontier when it appeared but later became inefficient as new frontier appeared. The process of TFDEA is first to estimate the technological frontier using DEA and ROC of the frontier, and then to forecast a technology at the certain point of time using ROC. Kim et al. (2022) describes the details of TFDEA methodology.

11.3 TFDEA Analysis @Stata

The following command loads into memory the data set of 'lee_table1.dta', a Stata-format dataset previously saved by *save* command from your working directory.

. use "D:\data\ lee_table1.dta"

And you can use the command *describe* to produce a summary of the dataset in memory or of the data stored in a Stata-format dataset(see Result Window 11.1).

. describe

```
 obs:           107
 vars:           15                   23 Dec 2022 08:01
 size:         7,062

                storage   display    value
variable name   type      format     label      variable label

oem             str8      %9s
dmu             str20     %20s
year            int       %8.0g
price           int       %8.0g
bdywgt          float     %8.0g
ntwk            byte      %8.0g
scrnsize        float     %8.0g
resolution      long      %8.0g
sensors         byte      %8.0g
ntwk1           float     %8.0g                 ntwk.1
cpuspeed        int       %8.0g
pcr             float     %8.0g
prmycamperf     float     %8.0g
btrycpcty       int       %8.0g
comlev          float     %8.0g
```

Result Window 11.1

The syntax of the *tfdea* command for Technology Forecasting using DEA is:

tfdea inputvars(min=1) = outputvars(min=1) [if] [in] [using/ filename][, rts(string) ort(string) tf(string) dmu(varname) model(string) tk(varname) saving(filename)]

where tf(string) sets the current year as the last year for computing rate of change; dmu(varname) specifies the dmu variable name; model(string) choose the forecasting model; tk(name) specifies the first year of DMU appearance.

You can estimate the TFDEA with output-oriented variable returns to scale using the following command to get the results shown in Result Window 11.2-3:

. tfdea price bdywgt= ntwk scrnsize resolution sensors ntwk1 cpuspeed pcr prmycamperf btrycpcty comlev, tf(2017)

```
TFDEA Forecasting Results:
                year    SE_tf    tf_eff    tf_exp
   Galaxy_S9    2018       .8    2016.5    2020.1
 Mate_20_Pro    2018  .796895   2016.82   2020.49
        Mi_8    2018   .91099         .         .
      Moto_G6    2018  .843693   2014.89   2017.64
         R15    2018  .956796      2017   2017.71
   V40_ThinQ    2018       .8         .         .
         X23    2018  .937566      2017   2018.04
  Xperia_XZ2    2018  .919516   2014.82   2016.17
   iPhone_XR    2018  .888889   2015.82   2017.72
 Galaxy_S1~5G    2019  .741327   2015.53   2020.36
  Mi_9_Pro_5G    2019  .823067   2014.33   2017.48
 Moto_G7_Po~r    2019  .650667   2016.33   2023.27
      P30_Pro    2019  .796895   2016.82   2020.82
    Reno3_5G    2019       .8    2015.5    2019.1
 V50_ThinQ_5G    2019  .788628   2015.52   2019.35
         X30    2019  .874398   2015.54   2017.71
    Xperia_1    2019  .675182      2017   2023.34
   iPhone_11    2019  .869088   2015.48   2017.74
        Edge+    2020  .744795   2015.28   2020.04
 Galaxy_S2~5G    2020  .615385   2016.31   2024.15
 Mi_10_Pro_5G    2020  .803399   2016.58   2020.11
      P40_Pro    2020  .753978   2016.83   2021.39
    Reno4_5G    2020       .8    2015.5    2019.1
 V60_ThinQ_5G    2020  .666667      2016   2022.55
      X50_Pro    2020   .85712   2015.98   2018.47
 Xperia_1_II    2020  .629737      2017   2024.47
  iPhone_SE_(
       2020)    2020       .8   2016.43   2020.03
```

Result Window 11.2

```
DEA Options: RTS(VRS) ORT(OUT)

Rate of Change (ROC) calculation Results:
                    tk    theta_tk    theta_tf    tk_eff        ROC
         A1200    2005           1     1.78371   2012.17    1.08411
      RAZR_V3xx    2006          1     1.32312   2008.59    1.11417
           U830    2006          1           1   2015.59          .
    i607_Black~k    2006         1     1.26419   2009.11    1.07819
       RIZR_Z10    2007          1     1.42625   2010.87     1.0962
           U960    2007          1           1      2007          .
           i780    2007          1     1.19883   2011.49    1.04121
         iPhone    2007          1     1.55714   2015.81    1.05154
     KF900_Prada    2008         1         1.5   2013.33    1.07899
      RAZR2_V9x     2008         1      1.5578   2010.25    1.21786
     i900_Omnia     2008        1       1.315   2012.07    1.06967
     iPhone_3G      2008        1     1.05907   2009.97    1.02955
          GM750     2009        1     1.49173   2013.04    1.10405
    I7500_Galaxy    2009        1     1.05208   2010.68    1.03068
          U8220     2009        1     1.55714   2015.81    1.06717
          XT701     2009        1     1.49611      2016    1.05925
     iPhone_3GS     2009        1     1.22578   2011.49    1.08509
   DROID_PR~610     2010        1           1      2010          .
   M110S_Gala~S     2010        1        1.18      2013    1.05672
     Optimus_2X     2010        1     1.20877   2013.95    1.04912
  U9000_IDEO~6      2010        1           1      2010          .
     iPhone_4       2010        1     1.44837   2014.38    1.08815
   I9100_Gala~I     2011        1           1      2011          .
   M886_Mercury     2011        1           1      2011          .
   Optimus_~935     2011        1     1.21067   2015.8     1.04063
    RAZR_XT910      2011        1     1.17023    2014.2    1.05035
     iPhone_4s      2011        1     1.15455   2013.95       1.05
   Ascend_P1_~E     2012        1           1      2012          .
  DROID_RAZR~D      2012        1           1   2015.71          .
           Find     2012        1           1      2012          .
   I9300_Gala~I     2012        1     1.00803   2013.05    1.00762
           Mi_2     2012        1     1.08333   2002.33    .991754
   Optimus~100S     2012        1     1.08647   2015.66    1.02291
    Xperia_T_LTE    2012        1        1.04   2015.98    1.00989
     iPhone_5       2012        1           1      2013          .
     Ascend_P6      2013        1           1   2008.15          .
             G2     2013        1           1      2013          .
   I9502_Gala~4     2013        1           1      2013          .
           Mi_3     2013        1           1      2013          .
         Moto_X     2013        1           1   2094.64          .
       R1_R829T     2013        1     1.05952    2015.6    1.02253
      Xperia_Z1     2013        1           1    2016.1          .
            Y15     2013        1           1      2013          .
     iPhone_5s      2013        1           1      2013          .
   Ascend_Mat~h     2014        1           1      2014          .
             G3     2014        1           1      2014          .
      Galaxy_S5     2014        1           1      2014          .
       Mi_4_LTE     2014        1           1      2014          .
       Nexus_6      2014        1           1      2014          .
             R5     2014        1     1.11631    2016.1    1.04315
             X5     2014        1     1.05786   2015.14    1.05056
      Xperia_Z3     2014        1           1      2014          .
     iPhone_6       2014        1           1      2014          .
   Droid_Turb~2     2015        1           1      2015          .
      Galaxy_S6     2015        1           1      2015          .
           Mi_4i    2015        1           1      2015          .
         P8lite     2015        1           1      2015          .
             R7     2015        1     1.10119   2016.01    1.09994
            V10     2015        1           1      2015          .
             X6     2015        1     1.01393   2015.26    1.05415
      Xperia_Z5     2015        1           1      2015          .
     iPhone_6s      2015        1           1      2015          .
      Galaxy_S7     2016        1           1      2016          .
          Mi_5s     2016        1           1      2016          .
         Moto_Z     2016        1           1      2016          .
        P9_lite     2016    1.01072     1.01072   2014.83          .
            R9s     2016        1           1   2017.63          .
            V20     2016        1           1      2016          .
             X9     2016        1     1.02849   2016.22    1.13473
     Xperia_XZ      2016        1           1      2016          .
     iPhone_7       2016        1           1      2016          .
      Galaxy_S8     2017        1           1      2017          .
    Mate_10_Pro     2017        1           1      2017          .
           Mi_6     2017        1           1    2018.5          .
      Moto_G5S      2017        1           1      2017          .
           R11s     2017        1           1      2017          .
            V30     2017        1           1      2017          .
            X20     2017        1           1      2017          .
     Xperia_XZ1     2017        1           1      2017          .
     iPhone_8       2017        1           1      2017          .

Annual Rate of Change (AROC) is: 1.0638689(31 DMU chosen)
```

Result Window 11.3

You can estimate the TFDEA with input-oriented constant returns to scale using the following command to get the results shown in Result Window 11.4-5:

. tfdea price bdywgt= ntwk scrnsize resolution sensors ntwk1 cpuspeed pcr prmyc amperf btrycpcty comlev, tf(2017) rts(crs) ort(in)

```
TFDEA Forecasting Results:
                  year     SE_tf     tf_eff     tf_exp
   Galaxy_S9      2018   1.08892    5541.75    5540.38
 Mate_20_Pro      2018   1.04497    6545.31     6544.6
        Mi_8      2018   .969612    5808.15    5808.65
     Moto_G6      2018   1.11605    6391.87    6390.11
         R15      2018   .910494    5158.53    5160.03
   V40_ThinQ      2018   1.02758    4362.68    4362.24
         X23      2018   1.00694    4744.44    4744.32
  Xperia_XZ2      2018    .81049    3532.82     3536.2
   iPhone_XR      2018   .803601    3397.07    3400.59
 Galaxy_S1~5G     2019   1.13097    5822.82    5820.84
  Mi_9_Pro_5G     2019   .954815    4069.57    4070.32
 Moto_G7_Po~r     2019   1.30485    3754.04    3749.77
      P30_Pro     2019   1.01693    4990.87     4990.6
    Reno3_5G      2019   1.06634    4265.02    4263.98
 V50_ThinQ_5G     2019   1.06371    4552.31    4551.31
         X30      2019   .947625    4144.09    4144.95
    Xperia_1      2019   1.27538    3543.88    3539.97
   iPhone_11      2019   .834948    1541.21    1544.11
       Edge+      2020     1.095    4061.69    4060.23
 Galaxy_S2~5G     2020   1.35966    3702.11    3697.17
 Mi_10_Pro_5G     2020   .952002    3149.67    3150.46
      P40_Pro     2020   .976196    4033.79    4034.17
    Reno4_5G      2020    1.0507    3042.34    3041.55
 V60_ThinQ_5G     2020   1.12094    3391.51    3389.67
      X50_Pro     2020   1.03051    3279.71    3279.23
  Xperia_1_II     2020   1.28026    4298.05    4294.08
 iPhone_SE_(
       2020)      2020   1.15656     2886.8    2884.46
```

Result Window 11.4

```
DEA Options: RTS(CRS) ORT(IN)

Rate of Change (ROC) calculation Results:
                    tk  theta_tk   theta_tf    tk_eff        ROC
        A1200     2005         1    1.94122   2014.49    1.07242
    RAZR_V3xx     2006         1    1.86941   2015.18    1.07056
        U830      2006         1    1.70956      2016    1.05509
   i607_Black~k   2006         1   -.132642         .          .
     RIZR_Z10     2007         1    1.80786   2014.65    1.08043
        U960      2007         1          1      2007          .
        i780      2007         1    1.57531   2016.41    1.04947
      iPhone      2007         1    1.55987      2016    1.05064
   KF900_Prada    2008         1    1.50612   2013.26    1.08097
    RAZR2_V9x     2008   1.13676    1.71478   2012.14          .
    i900_Omnia    2008         1    1.45548   2014.87    1.05616
    iPhone_3G     2008         1    1.08878   2010.28    1.03798
       GM750      2009   1.02828    1.60277   2015.81          .
  I7500_Galaxy    2009         1    1.34606   2014.87    1.05192
       U8220      2009   1.05766    1.55987      2016          .
       XT701      2009         1    1.53021      2016    1.06266
    iPhone_3GS    2009         1    1.23522   2011.64    1.08337
  DROID_PR~610    2010         1          1      2010          .
  M110S_Gala~S    2010         1    1.22335      2016    1.03417
   Optimus_2X     2010         1    1.22413   2012.16    1.09827
  U9000_IDEO~6    2010         1          1      2010          .
    iPhone_4      2010         1    1.45062   2014.26    1.09117
  I9100_Gala~I    2011         1          1      2011          .
  M886_Mercury    2011         1          1      2011          .
  Optimus_~935    2011         1    1.21324      2016    1.03942
    RAZR_XT910    2011   1.00417    1.19443      2016          .
    iPhone_4s     2011         1    1.16429   2013.81    1.05554
   Ascend_P1_~E   2012         1          1      2012          .
  DROID_RAZR~D    2012         1    1.05165   2015.89    1.01303
        Find      2012         1          1      2012          .
  I9300_Gala~I    2012         1    1.01048   2012.23    1.04573
        Mi_2      2012         1    1.21761   2013.41    1.14969
  Optimus~100S    2012    1.0643    1.23674   2015.17          .
  Xperia_T_LTE    2012   1.04099    1.16102      2013          .
    iPhone_5      2012         1          1      2013          .
    Ascend_P6     2013         1          1      2013          .
         G2       2013         1          1      2013          .
  I9502_Gala~4    2013         1          1      2013          .
        Mi_3      2013         1    1.00114    2014.2    1.00095
       Moto_X     2013         1          1      2013          .
     R1_R829T     2013   1.01523    1.07692      2015          .
    Xperia_Z1     2013         1    1.16781   2015.71    1.05882
        Y15       2013         1          1      2013          .
    iPhone_5s     2013         1          1      2013          .
  Ascend_Mat~h    2014         1    1.08293      2015    1.08293
         G3       2014         1          1      2014          .
    Galaxy_S5     2014         1          1      2014          .
    Mi_4_LTE      2014         1          1      2014          .
      Nexus_6     2014   1.09364    1.13175    2014.4          .
         R5       2014   1.09589    1.17069    2015.4          .
         X5       2014   1.02001    1.07869    2014.7          .
    Xperia_Z3     2014         1          1      2014          .
    iPhone_6      2014         1    1.00243   2013.41     .99592
  Droid_Turb~2    2015         1          1      2015          .
    Galaxy_S6     2015         1          1      2015          .
       Mi_4i      2015         1          1      2015          .
      P8lite      2015         1          1      2015          .
         R7       2015   1.13077    1.13077      2015          .
        V10       2015         1    1.00724   2016.39    1.00522
         X6       2015         1    1.01703   2015.08    1.24553
    Xperia_Z5     2015   1.01247    1.01247   2013.85          .
    iPhone_6s     2015   1.05413    1.07777   2014.13          .
    Galaxy_S7     2016         1          1      2016          .
       Mi_5s      2016         1          1      2016          .
       Moto_Z     2016         1          1      2016          .
      P9_lite     2016   1.01795    1.01795   2014.81          .
        R9s       2016   1.00387    1.00433   2016.28          .
        V20       2016    1.1074     1.1149   2015.62          .
         X9       2016   1.10146    1.10146   2015.43          .
    Xperia_XZ     2016   1.04502    1.04502   2013.87          .
    iPhone_7      2016         1          1      2016          .
    Galaxy_S8     2017         1          1      2017          .
   Mate_10_Pro    2017   1.01452    1.01452   2015.13          .
        Mi_6      2017   1.07261    1.07261   2015.22          .
     Moto_G5S     2017         1          1      2017          .
        R11s      2017         1          1      2017          .
        V30       2017         1          1      2017          .
        X20       2017    1.0457     1.0457   2015.53          .
   Xperia_XZ1     2017   1.00131    1.00131   2014.54          .
    iPhone_8      2017   1.05367    1.05367    2015.6          .

Annual Rate of Change (AROC) is: 1.0641549(26 DMU chosen)
```

Result Window 11.5

69

11.4 Exercises

11.4.1 Obtain ROC using Kim et al.(2022)' Table 1 data with the tf(2016) specification and compare with the tf(2017) specification.

11.4.2 Discuss about the reason the VRS TFDEA Model may suffer from infeasible solution under the certain conditions.

11.4.3 Is it the same with the reason why VRS Super-efficiency Model may not have a feasible solution?

11.5 References

Anderson, T., Hollingsworth, K., & Inman, L. (2001). Assessing the rate of change in the enterprise database system market over time using DEA. *Proceedings of PICMET '01. Portland International Conference on Management of Engineering and Technology 2.*

Inman, O.L. (2004). Technology Forecasting Using Data Envelopment Analysis. PhD dissertations, Portland State University, Portland, OR, USA.

Inman, O.L., Anderson, T.R., & Harmon, R.R. (2006). Predicting U.S. jet fighter aircraft introductions from 1944 to 1982: A dogfight between regression and TFDEA. *Technological Forecasting and Social Change 73*(9) 1178-1187.

Jung, B.K., Kim, H.C., & Lee, C. (2016). A Study on Technology Forecasting of Unmanned Aerial Vehicles (UAVs) using TFDEA. *Journal of Korea Technology Innovation Society 19*, 799-821.

Kim, S., Jung, B., Han, D., & Lee, C. (2022). Technology Prediction for Acquiring a Must-Have Mobile Device for Military Communication Infrastructure. *Applied Sciences 12*(6). https://doi.org/10.3390/app12063207

Lee, C. (2022). Data Envelopment Analysis using Stata. Retrieved from https://sourceforge.net/p/deas/code/HEAD/tree/trunk/ (accessed on December 26, 2022).

Lee, Jeong-dong and Oh, Dong-hyun. (2012). Theory of efficiency analysis. Seoul, Korea: Jiphil Media.

12 THE MALMQUIST PRODUCTIVITY INDEX USING DEA MODEL

In Economics, Malmquist means "the rate of change in productivity" and therefore, this model measures just that. To measure Malmquist Productivity Index value, we must:

A. Get Efficiency score for the t year

Thus, from Figure 12.1, find the efficiency score of A, B, C, D, E at CRS Frontier at Year_t.

B. Get Efficiency score for the t+1 year

Thus, from Figure 12.1, find the efficiency score of A1, B1, C1, D1, E1 at CRS Frontier at Year_t using t+1

C. Compare t year frontier line with t+1 year DMU

Thus, from Figure 12.1 find the efficiency score of A, B, C, D, E at CRS Frontier at Year_t+1 using t+1.

D. Compare t+1 year frontier line with the t year DMU

Thus, from Figure 12.1, find the efficiency score of A1, B1, C1, D1, E1 at CRS Frontier at Year_t using t+1.

E. Using the DEA model, create a model for DMU changes (see 12.2 model description).

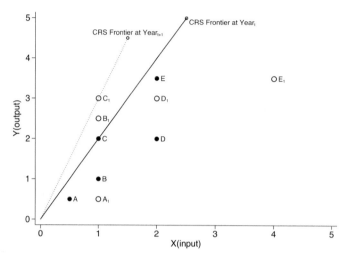

<Figure 12.1> Concept of MPI measurement

12.1 Data

The data was taken from Kim et al. (2022, pp.9-11, Table 1) for the MPI analysis. The data consist of 107 DMUs that use single two inputs(Price, Body weight) to produce 9 outputs(Network band, Screen size, Resolution, Sensors, Network speed, CPU speed, Camera Performance, Battery Capacity, WLAN generation).

12.2 Model Description

The Malmquist productivity index (MPI) measures the productivity changes along with time variations and can be expressed in terms of distance function. Fare, Grosskopf, Norris, and Zhang (1994) provided the formal derivation of the MPI, and it is the most popular method among the various methods that have been developed to estimate a production technology(2005).

Equation (12.1) shows the geometric mean of the MPI is the multiplication of technical change (TECHCH) and efficiency change (EFFCH):

$$MPI^G = EFFCH \cdot TECHCH^G = (\frac{\theta^{t+1}(x^{t+1},y^{t+1})}{\theta^t(x^t,y^t)}) \cdot$$

$$[(\frac{\theta^t(x^t,y^t)}{\theta^{t+1}(x^t,y^t)}) \cdot (\frac{\theta^t(x^{t+1},y^{t+1})}{\theta^{t+1}(x^{t+1},y^{t+1})})]^{1/2} \qquad (12.1)$$

And further the technical efficiency can be decomposed into scale efficiency and pure technical efficiency components. A scale efficiency change (SECH) is given as below:

$$SECH = [(\frac{E_{vrs}^{t+1}(x^{t+1},y^{t+1})/E_{crs}^{t+1}(x^{t+1},y^{t+1})}{E_{vrs}^{t+1}(x^t,y^t)/E_{crs}^{t+1}(x^t,y^t)}) \cdot$$
$$(\frac{E_{vrs}^t(x^{t+1},y^{t+1})/E_{crs}^t(x^{t+1},y^{t+1})}{E_{vrs}^t(x^t,y^t)/E_{crs}^t(x^t,y^t)})]^{1/2} \qquad (12.2)$$

A pure efficiency change (PECH) is given as below:
$$PECH = \frac{E_{vrs}^{t+1}(x^{t+1},y^{t+1})}{E_{crs}^t(x^t,y^t)} \qquad (12.3)$$

We can obtain the global Malmquist productivity index(GMPI) from the production changes using the pooled data over the period.
$$MPI_G^{t,t+1} = \frac{\theta^G(x^{t+1},y^{t+1})}{\theta^G(x^t,y^t)} \qquad (12.4)$$

12.3 MPI Analysis @Stata
The syntax of the *malmq* command for Malmquist Productivity Index using DEA Frontier is:

malmq inputvars(min=1) = outputvars(min=1) [if] [in] [using/ *filename*][, period(name) gml rts(string) ort(string) saving(*filename*)]

where period(name) specifies the year variable; gml specifies the global Malmquist-Luenburger application.

You can estimate the MPI with output-oriented variable returns to scale using the following command to get the results shown in Result Window 12.1-2:

. malmq price bdywgt = ntwk cpuspeed prmycamperf sensors btrycpcty if year>2012, ort(out) rts(bcc) period(year) sav(lee_tfdea.dta)

A Handbook of Data Envelopment Analysis @ Stata

```
Cross CRS-DEA Result:
                      from    thru        t        t1
          dmu:Y15     2013    2014  .912159   .916667
     dmu:R1_R829T     2013    2014  .990846   .984781
    dmu:iPhone_5s     2013    2014  .925906   .868217
    dmu:Ascend_P6     2013    2014  .876471   1.06919
           dmu:G2     2013    2014  1.02222   .802857
       dmu:Moto_X     2013    2014  .748042   .909091
dmu:I9502_Galaxy_S4   2013    2014  .659686   .910345
   dmu:Xperia_Z1     2013    2014  1.19231   1.14976
         dmu:Mi_3     2013    2014  .842932   .980382
          dmu:Y15     2014    2015  .973332   1.06801
     dmu:R1_R829T     2014    2015   .87919   .811399
    dmu:iPhone_5s     2014    2015  1.09445   1.08293
    dmu:Ascend_P6     2014    2015  .854814   .903511
           dmu:G2     2014    2015  .951724   1.02932
       dmu:Moto_X     2014    2015  1.03902   .816928
dmu:I9502_Galaxy_S4   2014    2015   1.0388   .654545
   dmu:Xperia_Z1     2014    2015  .953615   1.19231
         dmu:Mi_3     2014    2015  .864294   .799498
          dmu:Y15     2015    2016   .81558   1.02541
     dmu:R1_R829T     2015    2016  .922727   .772727
    dmu:iPhone_5s     2015    2016  1.13788    .98536
    dmu:Ascend_P6     2015    2016  .691925   .998386
           dmu:G2     2015    2016  .964206   .907895
       dmu:Moto_X     2015    2016  .990676   .916667
dmu:I9502_Galaxy_S4   2015    2016  .856354   1.08088
   dmu:Xperia_Z1     2015    2016    1.016   .996324
         dmu:Mi_3     2015    2016  .737202   .904033
          dmu:Y15     2016    2017  1.05003   .843865
     dmu:R1_R829T     2016    2017  .940141   .919331
    dmu:iPhone_5s     2016    2017  1.03901   1.08491
    dmu:Ascend_P6     2016    2017  .980871   .642851
           dmu:G2     2016    2017     .625   .922288
       dmu:Moto_X     2016    2017  .906433   .985297
dmu:I9502_Galaxy_S4   2016    2017   .94721   .947712
   dmu:Xperia_Z1     2016    2017  1.07428   1.05545
         dmu:Mi_3     2016    2017  1.04487   .706499
          dmu:Y15     2017    2018  1.09867   1.02575
     dmu:R1_R829T     2017    2018  1.14569   .845936
    dmu:iPhone_5s     2017    2018  .993394   .904255
    dmu:Ascend_P6     2017    2018  .939421   .942802
           dmu:G2     2017    2018  .666164   .833333
       dmu:Moto_X     2017    2018  .835326   .840308
dmu:I9502_Galaxy_S4   2017    2018  1.15224   .819015
   dmu:Xperia_Z1     2017    2018  1.02092   .970141
         dmu:Mi_3     2017    2018  .965906   .963362
          dmu:Y15     2018    2019  .981618   1.01702
     dmu:R1_R829T     2018    2019  .861965   1.09391
    dmu:iPhone_5s     2018    2019   1.1683   .949732
    dmu:Ascend_P6     2018    2019  1.01218   .930785
           dmu:G2     2018    2019  .938355   .627178
       dmu:Moto_X     2018    2019  .694038   .731762
dmu:I9502_Galaxy_S4   2018    2019   .81279   1.05023
   dmu:Xperia_Z1     2018    2019  .919305   .969588
         dmu:Mi_3     2018    2019  .887118   .893825
          dmu:Y15     2019    2020  1.04462   1.03427
     dmu:R1_R829T     2019    2020  .910661   1.00798
    dmu:iPhone_5s     2019    2020  .795381   1.20471
    dmu:Ascend_P6     2019    2020  .998344   1.06028
           dmu:G2     2019    2020  .971417   1.08433
       dmu:Moto_X     2019    2020   .92581   .454054
dmu:I9502_Galaxy_S4   2019    2020  .822285   .512715
   dmu:Xperia_Z1     2019    2020  .789443   1.00965
         dmu:Mi_3     2019    2020  .965148   1.01617
```

Result Window 12.1

74

Malmquist efficiency OUTPUT Oriented DEA Results:

	year	dmu	CRS_eff	VRS_eff
1.	2013	Y15	1	1
2.	2013	R1_R829T	1.01659	1
3.	2013	iPhone_5s	1	1
4.	2013	Ascend_P6	1.0196	1
5.	2013	G2	1	1
6.	2013	Moto_X	1	1
7.	2013	I9502_Galaxy_S4	1	1
8.	2013	Xperia_Z1	1.06656	1
9.	2013	Mi_3	.999967	1
10.	2014	Y15	1	1
11.	2014	R1_R829T	1	1
12.	2014	iPhone_5s	1	1
13.	2014	Ascend_P6	1.00773	1
14.	2014	G2	1.08522	1
15.	2014	Moto_X	1	1
16.	2014	I9502_Galaxy_S4	1	1
17.	2014	Xperia_Z1	1.09309	1
18.	2014	Mi_3	1	1
19.	2015	Y15	1	1
20.	2015	R1_R829T	1	1
21.	2015	iPhone_5s	1	1
22.	2015	Ascend_P6	1	1
23.	2015	G2	1	1
24.	2015	Moto_X	1	1
25.	2015	I9502_Galaxy_S4	1.13077	1
26.	2015	Xperia_Z1	1.13821	1
27.	2015	Mi_3	1	1
28.	2016	Y15	1	1
29.	2016	R1_R829T	1	1
30.	2016	iPhone_5s	1.14652	1
31.	2016	Ascend_P6	1	1
32.	2016	G2	1	1
33.	2016	Moto_X	1	1
34.	2016	I9502_Galaxy_S4	1.02005	1
35.	2016	Xperia_Z1	1.07881	1
36.	2016	Mi_3	1	1
37.	2017	Y15	1	1
38.	2017	R1_R829T	1	1
39.	2017	iPhone_5s	1	1
40.	2017	Ascend_P6	1	1
41.	2017	G2	1	1
42.	2017	Moto_X	1	1
43.	2017	I9502_Galaxy_S4	1	1
44.	2017	Xperia_Z1	1.01481	1.01226
45.	2017	Mi_3	1.00209	1
46.	2018	Y15	1.032	1.01084
47.	2018	R1_R829T	1.19018	1
48.	2018	iPhone_5s	1	1
49.	2018	Ascend_P6	1	1
50.	2018	G2	1	1
51.	2018	Moto_X	1	1
52.	2018	I9502_Galaxy_S4	1.15796	1.0274
53.	2018	Xperia_Z1	1	1
54.	2018	Mi_3	1	1
55.	2019	Y15	1	1
56.	2019	R1_R829T	1	1
57.	2019	iPhone_5s	1.05402	1.03364
58.	2019	Ascend_P6	1	1
59.	2019	G2	1	1
60.	2019	Moto_X	1	1
61.	2019	I9502_Galaxy_S4	.999984	1
62.	2019	Xperia_Z1	1	1
63.	2019	Mi_3	1.05297	1.01432
64.	2020	Y15	1.1231	1.00231
65.	2020	R1_R829T	1	1
66.	2020	iPhone_5s	1	1
67.	2020	Ascend_P6	1.07279	1
68.	2020	G2	1.02972	1
69.	2020	Moto_X	1	1
70.	2020	I9502_Galaxy_S4	1	1
71.	2020	Xperia_Z1	1	1
72.	2020	Mi_3	1	1

Result Window 12.2

If you specified the sav(lee_tfdea.dta) execution command option, the resulting file saved to your system will contain the same information as shown in Result Window 12.3.

Malmquist productivity index Output Oriented DEA Results:

period	dmu	tfpch	effch	techch	pech	sech
2013~2014	Y15	0.998	1.000	0.998	1.000	1.000
2013~2014	R1_R829T	0.995	0.984	1.011	1.000	0.984
2013~2014	iPhone_5s	1.033	1.000	1.033	1.000	1.000
2013~2014	Ascend_P6	0.900	0.988	0.911	1.000	0.988
2013~2014	G2	1.175	1.085	1.083	1.000	1.085
2013~2014	Moto_X	0.907	1.000	0.907	1.000	1.000
2013~2014	I9502_Galaxy_S4	0.851	1.000	0.851	1.000	1.000
2013~2014	Xperia_Z1	1.031	1.025	1.006	1.000	1.025
2013~2014	Mi_3	0.927	1.000	0.927	1.000	1.000
2014~2015	Y15	0.955	1.000	0.955	1.000	1.000
2014~2015	R1_R829T	1.041	1.000	1.041	1.000	1.000
2014~2015	iPhone_5s	1.005	1.000	1.005	1.000	1.000
2014~2015	Ascend_P6	0.969	0.992	0.976	1.000	0.992
2014~2015	G2	0.923	0.921	1.002	1.000	0.921
2014~2015	Moto_X	1.128	1.000	1.128	1.000	1.000
2014~2015	I9502_Galaxy_S4	1.340	1.131	1.185	1.000	1.131
2014~2015	Xperia_Z1	0.913	1.041	0.876	1.000	1.041
2014~2015	Mi_3	1.040	1.000	1.040	1.000	1.000
2015~2016	Y15	0.892	1.000	0.892	1.000	1.000
2015~2016	R1_R829T	1.093	1.000	1.093	1.000	1.000
2015~2016	iPhone_5s	1.151	1.147	1.004	1.000	1.147
2015~2016	Ascend_P6	0.832	1.000	0.832	1.000	1.000
2015~2016	G2	1.031	1.000	1.031	1.000	1.000
2015~2016	Moto_X	1.040	1.000	1.040	1.000	1.000
2015~2016	I9502_Galaxy_S4	0.845	0.902	0.937	1.000	0.902
2015~2016	Xperia_Z1	0.983	0.948	1.037	1.000	0.948
2015~2016	Mi_3	0.903	1.000	0.903	1.000	1.000
2016~2017	Y15	1.115	1.000	1.115	1.000	1.000
2016~2017	R1_R829T	1.011	1.000	1.011	1.000	1.000
2016~2017	iPhone_5s	0.914	0.872	1.048	1.000	0.872
2016~2017	Ascend_P6	1.235	1.000	1.235	1.000	1.000
2016~2017	G2	0.823	1.000	0.823	1.000	1.000
2016~2017	Moto_X	0.959	1.000	0.959	1.000	1.000
2016~2017	I9502_Galaxy_S4	0.990	0.980	1.010	1.000	0.980
2016~2017	Xperia_Z1	0.978	0.941	1.040	1.012	0.929
2016~2017	Mi_3	1.217	1.002	1.215	1.000	1.002
2017~2018	Y15	1.051	1.032	1.019	1.011	1.021
2017~2018	R1_R829T	1.270	1.190	1.067	1.000	1.190
2017~2018	iPhone_5s	1.048	1.000	1.048	1.000	1.000
2017~2018	Ascend_P6	0.998	1.000	0.998	1.000	1.000
2017~2018	G2	0.894	1.000	0.894	1.000	1.000
2017~2018	Moto_X	0.997	1.000	0.997	1.000	1.000
2017~2018	I9502_Galaxy_S4	1.276	1.158	1.102	1.027	1.127
2017~2018	Xperia_Z1	1.018	0.985	1.033	0.988	0.997
2017~2018	Mi_3	1.000	0.998	1.002	1.000	0.998
2018~2019	Y15	0.967	0.969	0.998	0.989	0.979
2018~2019	R1_R829T	0.814	0.840	0.968	1.000	0.840
2018~2019	iPhone_5s	1.139	1.054	1.080	1.034	1.020
2018~2019	Ascend_P6	1.043	1.000	1.043	1.000	1.000
2018~2019	G2	1.223	1.000	1.223	1.000	1.000
2018~2019	Moto_X	0.974	1.000	0.974	1.000	1.000
2018~2019	I9502_Galaxy_S4	0.818	0.864	0.947	0.973	0.887
2018~2019	Xperia_Z1	0.974	1.000	0.974	1.000	1.000
2018~2019	Mi_3	1.022	1.053	0.971	1.014	1.038
2019~2020	Y15	1.065	1.123	0.948	1.002	1.121
2019~2020	R1_R829T	0.950	1.000	0.950	1.000	1.000
2019~2020	iPhone_5s	0.791	0.949	0.834	0.967	0.981
2019~2020	Ascend_P6	1.005	1.073	0.937	1.000	1.073
2019~2020	G2	0.960	1.030	0.933	1.000	1.030
2019~2020	Moto_X	1.428	1.000	1.428	1.000	1.000
2019~2020	I9502_Galaxy_S4	1.266	1.000	1.266	1.000	1.000
2019~2020	Xperia_Z1	0.884	1.000	0.884	1.000	1.000
2019~2020	Mi_3	0.950	0.950	1.000	0.986	0.963

Result Window 12.3

12.4 Exercises

12.4.1 Describe the meaning of MPI > 1.

12.4.2 The MPI values calculated using panel data and Equation (12.1) are known to not satisfy the property of transitivity. Describe the reason and use models that satisfy transitivity as examples.

12.4.3 From Equation(12.2-3) efficiency change, what does it mean for technology change > 1?

12.5 References

Kim, S., Jung, B., Han, D., & Lee, C. (2022). Technology Prediction for Acquiring a Must-Have Mobile Device for Military Communication Infrastructure. *Applied Sciences* *12*(6). https://doi.org/10.3390/app12063207

Lee, C. (2011). Malmquist Productivity Analysis using DEA Frontier in Stata. Washington DC, USA:Chicago11 Stata Conference.

Lee, C. (2022). Data Envelopment Analysis using Stata. Retrieved from https://sourceforge.net/p/deas/code/HEAD/tree/trunk/ (accessed on December 26, 2022).

Lee, Jeong-dong and Oh, Dong-hyun. (2012). Theory of efficiency analysis. Seoul, Korea: Jiphil Media.

13 THE STATISTICAL INFERENCE FOR DEA ESTIMATES USING BOOTSTRAP

Non-statistic and non-parametric characteristics are endogenous vulnerabilities in Data Envelopment Analysis(DEA). Many papers have tried to overcome this problem and bootstrap method is also one of this purpose. In this chapter, we suggest a user written package to estimate statistical inference and confidential intervals. We first describe a basic concept of DEA and the efficiency estimates. And introduce bootstrap procedures to inference statistical estimates using smoothed frontiers according to Simar and Wilson (2007, 2011) and data generating processes(DGPs) for bootstrap method and truncated regression for censored data.

DEA is most famous and useful productivity and efficiency estimates tool with strength to deal with multi-input and multi-output capability. And it doesn't need to assume the distribution of sample data due to its non-parametric and non-statistic characteristics. DEA inference the estimates with enveloping observed data and draw a frontier with it. To do so it can inference the relative efficiency of each decision making units (Dmus) according to frontiers. But because of these characteristics, the DEA estimates have an endogenous vulnerability with statistical explanation and measuring the influence of environmental factors which affects to efficiency.

To overcome this problem many literatures study about this. For efficiency estimates only, Simar and Wilson (1998), Badin and Simar (2004), Simar and Wilson (2011), Simar et al. (2013) are using bootstrap method for directional DEA models. And for Free Disposal Hull(FDH) models order-m and order-quantile methods are suggested by Simar and Zelenyuk (2011) and Simar et al. (2013). For environmental influence on the efficiency, Fried et al. (2002) suggested three-stage approach and Tsionas and Papadakis (2010) use Bayesian method. But mostly used bootstrap approach. According to Kneip et al. (2008), bootstrap method is based on the asymptotic distribution of DEA estimates. And regress the estimates on environmental factors to inference the influence. Hoff(2007) and McDonald (2009) use Tobit regression model because the efficiency estimates are censored. And Simar et al. (2013) suggest truncated regression model because the Tobit model is improper to efficiency data.

13.1 Data

The 1978 automobile data is a dataset provided as system data in Stata that can be used for various analyses.

13.2 Model Description

In the two-stage bootstrap method, it needs more assumption besides the basic assumption of DEA, free disposability and convexity.

First, the samples are independently and identically distributed observations with probability density function which support the population.

Second, the efficiency estimates are operated through the function, $\theta_i = \theta(x_i, y_i) = \beta_i z_i + \varepsilon_i \geq 1$, where β_i is parameters, z_i is environmental variables, and ε_i is an error term.

And third, the error terms ε_i is a $iid \sim N(0, \sigma_\varepsilon^2)$ with left-truncated at $1 - \beta_i z_i$ for each i. These assumptions provide a rational to DGP through bootstrapping procedures. For the details, see Simar and Wilson(2007) and Simar et al.(2013). With assumption described previous, the user-written code follows the two-stage bootstrap algorithm suggested by Simar and Wilson (2007).

13.3 Statistical Inference @Stata

. sysuse auto
(1978 Automobile Data)

. describe

```
Contains data from /Applications/Stata/ado/base/a/auto.dta
  obs:            74                          1978 Automobile Data
  vars:           12                          13 Apr 2018 17:45
                                              (_dta has notes)

              storage   display    value
variable name   type    format     label      variable label

make            str18   %-18s                 Make and Model
price           int     %8.0gc                Price
mpg             int     %8.0g                 Mileage (mpg)
rep78           int     %8.0g                 Repair Record 1978
headroom        float   %6.1f                 Headroom (in.)
trunk           int     %8.0g                 Trunk space (cu. ft.)
weight          int     %8.0gc                Weight (lbs.)
length          int     %8.0g                 Length (in.)
turn            int     %8.0g                 Turn Circle (ft.)
displacement    int     %8.0g                 Displacement (cu. in.)
gear_ratio      float   %6.2f                 Gear Ratio
foreign         byte    %8.0g      origin     Car type

Sorted by: foreign
```

dea_ci calculates a bias-corrected efficiency estimates and a confidential interval of influence of environmental variables on efficiency estimates. The inputvars and outputvars are the input and output variables for computing DEA for the efficiency estimates of observations. And envars(varlist) is environmental variables for the truncated regression. This program uses *dea*.ado for calculating DEA and *truncreg* for calculating truncated regression. For the statistical inference, assumed error terms in Data Generating Process as normality with left-truncation at $1 - \beta_i z_i$ for each i.

The syntax of the *dea_ci* command for the statistical inference for DEA estimates using bootstrap is:

dea_ci inputvars(min=1) = outputvars(min=1) [if] [in] [using/ filename][, envars(varlist) [level(#) reps1(#) reps2(#) rts(string) ort(string) nolaptime stage(#) trace separator(#)]

where

envars(varlist) is an environmental variable which the users want to analyze the influence on the firm's efficiency. The number of environmental variables is not limited but must consider the validation of regression model.

level(#) sets confidence level for the truncated regression and confidence interval, respectively. The default is level(95).

reps1(#) is an integer number of iteration of first stage for computing bootstrap efficiency estimates of DMUs. The purpose of first stage is to get bias-corrected efficiency estimates. The default number of iteration is 100 as recommended by Simar and Wilson (2007).

reps2(#) is an integer number of iteration of second stage for computing bootstrap influence estimates of environmental variables on efficiency estimates. The purpose of second stage is to get confidential interval of influence estimates. The default number of iteration is 2,000 as recommended by Simar and Wilson (2007).

rts(string) specifies the returns to scale. There are two types of rts, constant returns to scale (rts(crs)) and variable returns to scale(rts(vrs)). The default is rts(crs).

ort(string) specifies the orientation for radial models. There are two types of ort, ort(in) means input-oriented analysis, ort(out) means output-oriented analysis. The default is ort(in).

nolaptime shows the time spent for each stage, that is, laptime 1 displays an elapsed time for first stage, computing bias-corrected efficiency estimates, and laptime 2 displays an elapsed time for second stage, inferencing the influence of environmental variables and confidential interval of them. The default is a showing laptime. If you want to not show the laptime, type nolaptime.

stage(#) is an integer 1 or 2 which specifies the way of computing DEA with Simplex linear programming (LP). stage(1) means to calculate a minimizing (or maximizing) the original problem. And stage(2) means to maximizing (or minimizing) the sum of slacks adding to the stage(1). The default is stage(1).

trace let all sequences and results displayed in the result window which saved in the "dea_ci.log" file.

separator(#) draw separator line after every #variables. The default is 5.

You can estimate the Statistical Inference of DEA estimates with output-oriented constant returns to scale using the following command to get the results shown in Result Window 13.1:

. dea_ci length displacement = price mpg, envars(weight) rts(crs) ort(out) stage(1)

```
crs-OUTPUT Oriented DEA Efficiency Results:
          theta_h    theta_hs      bias    theta_hh
dmu:dmu1   1.90184    1.30384    -.598004   2.49984      dmu:dmu37   2.1292    1.24053   -.888667   3.01787
dmu:dmu2   1.96413    1.22238    -.741745   2.70587      dmu:dmu38   2.36895   1.29399   -1.07496   3.44391
dmu:dmu3   1.818      1.2229     -.595098   2.4131       dmu:dmu39   2.27898   1.3049    -.974074   3.25305
dmu:dmu4   2.03505    1.24282    -.792228   2.82728      dmu:dmu40   1.7901    1.23634   -.553759   2.34386
dmu:dmu5   1.9786     1.14005    -.838549   2.81715      dmu:dmu41   1.48356   1.06599   -.417568   1.90113
dmu:dmu6   2.1182     1.25379    -.864407   2.98261      dmu:dmu42   1.47867   1.3859    -.0927663  1.47867
dmu:dmu7   1.57314    1.12549    -.447656   2.0208       dmu:dmu43   1.15229   1.03095   -.121335   1.27362
dmu:dmu8   1.98192    1.22598    -.755938   2.73785      dmu:dmu44   1.51167   1.13939   -.372276   1.88395
dmu:dmu9   1.34981    1.1315     -.218307   1.56811      dmu:dmu45   1.32655   1.13349   -.19306    1.51961
dmu:dmu10  2.30362    1.30417    -.999447   3.30307      dmu:dmu46   2.39061   1.29944   -1.09117   3.48178
dmu:dmu11  1.51353    1.07778    -.435744   1.94927      dmu:dmu47   2.08522   1.25899   -.826227   2.91144
dmu:dmu12  1.09697    1.0242     -.0727652  1.09697      dmu:dmu48   2.14364   1.25574   -.887896   3.03154
dmu:dmu13  1          1.07177    .0717702   1            dmu:dmu49   2.05881   1.18828   -.870524   2.92933
dmu:dmu14  1.48676    1.07452    -.412243   1.89901      dmu:dmu50   2.14214   1.2082    -.933939   3.07608
dmu:dmu15  2.20943    1.20182    -1.00761   3.21704      dmu:dmu51   2.25398   1.29049   -.963492   3.21748
dmu:dmu16  1.96102    1.28618    -.674835   2.63585      dmu:dmu52   1.78402   1.2273    -.556728   2.34075
dmu:dmu17  1.92109    1.2464     -.674689   2.59578      dmu:dmu53   1.08695   1.07202   -.0149281  1.08695
dmu:dmu18  1.87343    1.27249    -.600947   2.47438      dmu:dmu54   1.15457   1.0683    -.0862664  1.15457
dmu:dmu19  2.30098    1.33394    -.967039   3.26802      dmu:dmu55   1         1.04795   .0479472   1
dmu:dmu20  1.43301    1.07664    -.356375   1.78939      dmu:dmu56   1.3431    1.08135   -.261751   1.60485
dmu:dmu21  2.46397    1.34678    -1.11719   3.58116      dmu:dmu57   1.10635   1.0866    -.0197505  1.10635
dmu:dmu22  2.13852    1.158      -.98052    3.11904      dmu:dmu58   1.49799   1.09989   -.398101   1.8961
dmu:dmu23  2.02515    1.24234    -.782812   2.80796      dmu:dmu59   1.27281   1.08504   -.187773   1.46059
dmu:dmu24  1.29952    1.03647    -.263048   1.56257      dmu:dmu60   1.63635   1.07427   -.562086   2.19844
dmu:dmu25  1.89933    1.18136    -.717964   2.61729      dmu:dmu61   1.32732   1.09577   -.231549   1.55887
dmu:dmu26  1.58016    1.16627    -.41389    1.99405      dmu:dmu62   1.28452   1.03504   -.249481   1.534
dmu:dmu27  1.3192     1.15564    -.163567   1.48277      dmu:dmu63   1.29664   1.07971   -.216923   1.51356
dmu:dmu28  1.12596    1.04307    -.0828893  1.12596      dmu:dmu64   1         1.03936   .0393617   1
dmu:dmu29  1.8366     1.18033    -.648269   2.48487      dmu:dmu65   1.27581   1.05907   -.216737   1.49255
dmu:dmu30  2.5562     1.24106    -1.31514   3.87134      dmu:dmu66   1.23945   1.06936   -.17009    1.40954
dmu:dmu31  2.19822    1.14022    -1.058     3.25622      dmu:dmu67   1.57096   1.02926   -.541702   2.11266
dmu:dmu32  2.23975    1.25313    -.986618   3.22637      dmu:dmu68   1.40791   1.11689   -.29102    1.69893
dmu:dmu33  2.27284    1.19446    -1.07837   3.35121      dmu:dmu69   1.61226   1.12254   -.489715   2.10197
dmu:dmu34  2.38007    1.26583    -1.11424   3.4943       dmu:dmu70   1.04656   1.05721   .0106511   1.04656
dmu:dmu35  1.60873    1.19347    -.41526    2.02399      dmu:dmu71   1         1.06146   .0614614   1
dmu:dmu36  2.03797    1.20978    -.828191   2.86617      dmu:dmu72   1.28416   1.08193   -.202227   1.48638
                                                         dmu:dmu73   1.0613    1.026     -.0352918  1.0613
                                                         dmu:dmu74   1.04331   1.03142   -.0118982  1.04331
```

Truncated regression on Efficiency estimate:

Variable	Obs	Coef.	Std. Err.	[95% Conf. Interval]	
weight	2000	.0011229	2.86e-07	.0011223	.0011234
sigma_hh	2000	.4888172	.0010114	.4868337	.4908008

```
laptime: 1 is dea, 2 is truncated regression
   1:     14.81 /      1 =    14.8150
   2:     71.31 /      1 =    71.3130
```

Result Window 13.1

13.4 Exercises

13.4.1 Analyze the result of Result Window 13.1.

13.4.2 Describe Simar and Wilson (2007) two-stage bootstrap algorithm.

13.5 References

Fried, H.O., Lovell, C.A.K., Schmidt, S.S., & Yaisawarng, S. (2002). Accounting for environmental effects and statistical noise in Data Envelopment Analysis. *Journal of Productivity Analysis 17*(1-2): p. 157-174.

Kneip, A., Simar, L. & Wilson, P. W. (2008). Asymptotic and consistent bootstraps for DEA estimators in nonparametric frontier models. *Econometric Theory 24*(06): 1663~1697.

McDonald, J. (2009). Using least squares and Tobit in second stage DEA efficiency analyses. *European Journal of Operational Research 197*(2): 792~798.

Simar, L., & Wilson, P. W. (1998). Sensitivity analysis of efficiency scores: How to bootstrap in nonparametric frontier models. *Management science 44*(1): 49~61.

_____. (2000). Statistical inference in nonparametric frontier models: The state of the art. *Journal of productivity analysis 13*(1): 49~78.

_____. (2007). Estimation and inference in two-stage, semi-parametric models of production processes. *Journal of Econometrics 136*(1): 31~64.

_____. (2011). Performance of the Bootstrap for DEA Estimators and Iterating the Principle, International Series in Operations Research & Management Science, in: William W. Cooper & Lawrence M. Seiford & Joe Zhu (ed.), Handbook on Data Envelopment Analysis, chapter 0, pages 241-271, Springer.

Simar, L., Wilson, P. W., & Kiviet, J. F. (2013). Estimation and inference in non-parametric frontier models: Recent developments and perspectives. Now Publishers Incorporated.

Simar, L., & Zelenyuk, V. (2011). Stochastic FDH/DEA estimators for frontier analysis. *Journal of Productivity Analysis 36*(1): 1~20.

Tone, K. (2002). A slacks-based measure of super-efficiency in data envelopment analysis. *European Journal of Operational Research 143*(1): 32 ~41.

Tsionas, E. G., & Papadakis, E. N. (2010). A Bayesian approach to statistical inference in stochastic DEA. *Omega 38*(5): 309~314.

14 LINEAR PROGRAMMING: THE MATCHING PROBLEM

This chapter introduces the basic form of linear programming, which is a key tool when trying to obtain answers to DEA from a computer and explains how to implement it in Stata using the kidney matching problem as an example.

In 2018, 21,167 and 2,855 people in the United States and South Korea underwent kidney transplants surgery, respectively. According to daily statistics, 58 people received a Kidney transplant. However, 103,029 people in the United States and 23,591 in South Korea are waiting for kidney transplants. The waiting list is more than the provider. In 2014, 4,537 people died waiting for a kidney transplant, 13 people lost their lives every day.

Kidney exchange is a living donor kidney matching problem between recipient and doners. it requires that all surgeries must be executed simultaneously. Compatibility between transplantable people is also an issue.

This chapter introduces the highlights of Lee & Cho (2019), which we hope will serve as a reference for those who want to study extended topics using Stata.

The kidney exchange problem can be approached in various ways, such as K-way exchange and chain exchange. <Figure 14.1> illustrates the most basic model, the two-way exchange. The purpose of the program is to write an algorithm to find the Pair that is the match shown in the figure. When donors and patients are unbalanced and complex considerations such as Kidney's compatibility and preference are included, it will be difficult to get an easy answer. Therefore, we want to solve complex problems using the computational power of computers to solve them in real time so that there are the best beneficiaries.

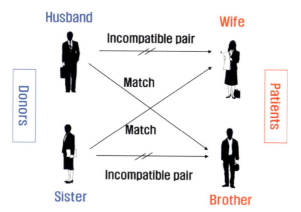

<Figure 14.1> illustration of two-way exchange problem
Source: Lee&Cho(2019)

14.1 Data

<Table 14.1> is imaginary data created to illustrate a matching problem using LP.

<Table 14.1> Data for illustration of matching problem-solving

x12	x21	x23	x32	x31	rel	rhs
1	0	0	0	0	<=	1
0	1	1	0	0	<=	1
0	0	0	1	1	<=	1
-1	1	0	0	1	=	0
1	-1	-1	1	0	=	0
0	0	1	-1	-1	=	0
1	0	1	0	1	<=	2
1	1	0	0	0	<=	2
0	0	1	1	0	<=	2

14.2 Model Description

For formal definition and problem statements, see Roth et al. (2004, 2005, 2007) and Grotschel & Holland (1985). In this chapter, through the implementation of the basic model, we will present the possibility of expanding research on complex application problems in Stata, leaving the rest to the researcher. The problem illustrated in this chapter is a modification of Lee & Cho(2019) 's content.

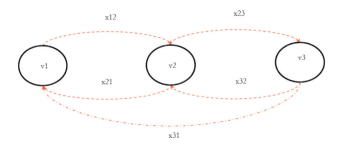

<Figure 14.1> Kidney matching problem illustration

Notes : v is incompatible doner-patient pair, x_{ij} or x_{ji} takes value 1 if matched in cycle otherwise 0 value. k is the maximum number of cycles allowed.

Equation(14.1) show the problem considered.

$$\text{Max} \sum_{i,j \in N} x_{i,j} \qquad (14.1)$$

subject to

$$\sum_{j \in N} x_{i,j} \leq 1 \quad \forall i, j \in N$$
$$\sum_{j \in N} x_{i,j} = \sum_{j \in N} x_{j,i} \; \forall i \in N$$
$$x_{i1i2} + x_{i2i3} + \ldots + x_{ikik+1} \leq k - 1$$

Equation(14.1) can be transformed into the following standard form of linear programming:

$$\max z = x_{12} + x_{21} + x_{23} + x_{32} + x_{31} \qquad (14.2)$$

subject to

$$x_{12} \leq 1$$
$$x_{21} + x_{23} \leq 1$$
$$x_{32} + x_{31} \leq 1$$
$$x_{21} + x_{31} = x_{12}$$

$$x_{12} + x_{32} = x_{21} + x_{23}$$
$$x_{32} = x_{32} + x_{31}$$
$$x_{12} + x_{23} + x_{31} \leq 2$$
$$x_{12} + x_{21} \leq 2$$
$$x_{23} + x_{32} \leq 2$$

14.3 Kidney Matching Problem @Stata

The following command loads into memory the data set of 'kidney_matching.dta', a Stata-format dataset previously saved by *save* command from your working directory.

. use "D:\data\ kidney_matching.dta"

And you can use the command *describe* to produce a summary of the dataset in memory or of the data stored in a Stata-format dataset(see Result Window 14.1).

. describe

```
    obs:            9
    vars:           7                         22 Jan 2018 01:21
    size:         234

              storage    display    value
variable name   type     format     label     variable label

x12            float     %9.0g
x21            float     %9.0g
x23            float     %9.0g
x32            float     %9.0g
x31            float     %9.0g
rel            str2      %9s
rhs            float     %9.0g
```

Result Window 14.1

lp solves the optimization problem using the simplex method. The syntax of the *lp* command for the paired live Kidney Exchange problem:

lp varlists [if] [in] [using/] [, rel(*varname*) rhs(*varname*) min max intvars(*varlist*) tol1(real) tol2(real) saving(*filename*)]

where
rel(*varname*) specifies the variable with the relationship symbols. The default option is rcl.

rhs(*varname*) specifies the variable with constants in the right hand side of equation. The default option is rhs.

min and max are case sensitive. min(max) is to minimize(maximize) the objective function.

intvars(*varlist*) specifies variables with integer value.

tol1(real) sets the tolerance of pivoting value. The default value is 1e-14. tol2(*real*) sets the tolerance of matrix inverse. The default value is 2.22e-12.

You can obtain the solution of the linear program using the following command to get the results shown in Result Window 14.2-3:

. lp x12 x21 x23 x32 x31, max intvars(x12 x21 x23 x32 x31) rel(rel) rhs(rhs)

```
MILP L0 Input Values:

        x12   x21   x23   x32   x31   rel   rhs

  1.     1     0     0     0     0    <=     1
  2.     0     1     1     0     0    <=     1
  3.     0     0     0     1     1    <=     1
  4.    -1     1     0     0     1     =     0
  5.     1    -1    -1     1     0     =     0

  6.     0     0     1    -1    -1     =     0
  7.     1     0     1     0     1    <=     2
  8.     1     1     0     0     0    <=     2
  9.     0     0     1     1     0    <=     2

       z  x12  x21  x23  x32  x31  s1  s2  s3  s4  s5  a1  a2  a3  rhs
  r1   1    1    0    0    0    0   0   0   0   0   0   1   1   1    1
  r2   0    0    1    1    0    0   1   0   0   0   0   0   0   0    1
  r3   0    0    0    0    1    1   0   1   0   0   0   0   0   0    1
  r4   0   -1    1    0    0    1   0   0   0   0   0   1   0   0    0
  r5   0    1   -1   -1    1    0   0   0   0   0   0   0   1   0    0
  r6   0    0    0    1   -1   -1   0   0   0   0   0   0   0   1    0
  r7   0    1    0    1    0    1   0   0   1   0   0   0   0   0    2
  r8   0    1    1    0    0    0   0   0   0   1   0   0   0   0    2
  r9   0    0    0    1    1    0   0   0   0   0   1   0   0   0    2


MILP L0 Results: options(max)
        c1   c2   c3   c4   c5   c6   c7   c8   c9  c10  c11
  r1     1    1    1    0    0    0    0    1    1    0    2
```

Result Window 14.2

```
Input Values:
     z  x12  x21  x23  x32  x31  s1  s2  s3  s4  s5  a1  a2  a3  rhs
r1   1   1    0    0    0    0    0   0   0   0   0   1   1   1   1
r2   0   0    1    1    0    0    1   0   0   0   0   0   0   0   1
r3   0   0    0    0    1    1    0   1   0   0   0   0   0   0   1
r4   0  -1    1    0    0    1    0   0   0   0   0   1   0   0   0
r5   0   1   -1   -1    1    0    0   0   0   0   0   0   1   0   0
r6   0   0    0    1   -1   -1    0   0   0   0   0   0   0   1   0
r7   0   1    0    1    0    1    0   0   1   0   0   0   0   0   2
r8   0   1    1    0    0    0    0   0   0   1   0   0   0   0   2
r9   0   0    0    1    1    0    0   0   0   0   1   0   0   0   2


LP Results: options(max)
         z  x12  x21  x23  x32  x31  s1  s2  s3  s4  s5
opt_val  1   1    1    0    0    0    0   1   1   0   2
```

Result Window 14.3

Result Window 14. The opt_val in 3 tells us that the optimal solution is for doner pair 1 to share to 2 and 2 to 1. This result is possible because compatibility is set in the entered data. If kidney compatibility is uncertain or multiple responses, the complexity of the problem increases. However, a basic approach to the problem is possible as shown in this example. Choi et al. (2022) would be an example.

14.4 Exercises

14.4.1 Result Window 14. 2 Use the data to find the optimal solution and interpret the meaning.

<Table 14.2> Data for exercise

x12	x21	x23	x32	x31	rel	rhs
1	0	0	1	0	<=	1
0	1	1	0	0	<=	1
0	0	0	1	1	<=	1
-1	1	0	0	1	=	0
1	-1	-1	1	0	=	0
0	0	1	-1	-1	=	0
1	0	1	0	1	<=	2
1	1	0	0	0	<=	2
0	0	1	1	0	<=	2

14.4.2 We will try to solve the linear program problem using the data in table 14.2 presented in problem 14.4.3. Write a linear program in standard form.

14.5 References

Choi, E., Lee, C., Kim, S., & Cho, N. (2022). An Algorithm for Exchanging Target Asset Pairs using the Kidney Exchange Model. *Defence Science Journal 72*(6), 846-853. https://doi.org/10.14429/dsj.72.1841

Grotschel, M., & Holland, O. (1985). Solving Matching Problems with Linear Programming. *Mathematical Programming 33*:243-259.

Roth, A. E., Sommez, T., & Unver, M. U. (2004). Kidney Exchange. *Quarterly Journal of Economics 119*(2): 457-88.

_____ (2005). Pairwise Kidney Exchange. *Journal of Economic Theory 125*(2): 151–188.

_____ (2007). Efficient Kidney Exchange: Coincidence of Wants in Markets with Compatibility-Based Preferences. *The American Economic Review 97*(3): 828-851.

15 THE VIRTUAL PRICE MODEL

Charnes, Cooper, and Rhodes (1978) proposed the basic DEA model using the concepts of virtual input and output weights to determine the weight using linear programming to maximize the ratio of 'virtual output' over 'virtual input'. Where 'virtual input' equals to the sum of each input mix quantity multiplied by corresponding weight(v) and 'virtual output' equals to the sum of each output mix quantity multiplied by corresponding weight(μ).

15.1 Data

For comparison of the results, <Table 15.1> data is taken from Lee & Oh(2012, p.50).

<Table 15.1> Data for six DMUs

DMU	A	B	C	D	E	F
x1	1	3	6	2	5	9
x2	4	1	1	8	5	2
y	1	1	1	1	1	1

15.2 Model Description

Equation (15.1) imports the formulation from Cooper, Seiford, and Tone (2006) and Lee & Oh(2012).

$$\max \frac{\sum_{j=1}^{s} u_j y_{jo}}{\sum_{i=1}^{m} v_i y_{io}} \qquad (15.1)$$

subject to

$$\frac{\sum_{j=1}^{s} u_j y_{jk}}{\sum_{i=1}^{m} v_i y_{ik}} \leq 1 (k = 1, \dots, n)$$

$$v_i \geq 0 \text{ for } \forall i$$

$$u_j \geq 0 \text{ for } \forall j$$

Charnes and Cooper (1962) introduced the transformation for linear fractional programming to obtain a representative solution. Equation (15.1) can be transformed to Equation (15.2).

$$\max \sum_{r=1}^{s} \mu_r y_{rk} \tag{15.2}$$

subject to

$$\sum_{r=1}^{s} \mu_r y_{rj} - \sum_{i=1}^{m} v_i x_{ij} \leq 0$$

$$\sum_{i=1}^{m} v_i x_{ik} = 1$$

$$\mu_r, v_i \geq 0$$

The efficiency scores obtained by the 'Virtual Price Model' is 'unit invariant', which means that we will get the same efficiency scores regardless the unit of input or output measurement. And the solution of weights is interpreted as the relative importance of the corresponding input or output factors, so the model names after the characteristic of virtual price(Cooper, 2006).

15.3 The Virtual Price Model @Stata

The following command loads into memory the data set of 'dea_vprice_in_1.dta', a Stata-format dataset previously saved by *save* command from your working directory.

. use "D:\data\ dea_vprice_in_1.dta"

And you can use the command list to Result Window the values of variables(see Result Window 15.1).

. list

```
      dmu   in1   in2   out1

1.     A     1     4      1
2.     B     3     1      1
3.     C     6     1      1
4.     D     2     8      1
5.     E     5     5      1

6.     F     9     2      1
```

Result Window 15.1

The syntax of the *dea_vprice* command for the virtual price model is:
dea_vprice inputvars(*min*=1) = outputvars(*min*=1) [*if*][*in*] [using/
filename], [ort(i│in│input│o│out│output) stage(*integer* 2) tol1(real 1e-
14) tol2(real 1e-8) trace saving(*filename*) replace]

where *inputvars* and *outputvars* mean input and output variable lists,
respectively.
dea_vprice requires the user to select the input and output variables
from the user designated data file and solves Virtual Price model
by options specified.
The *dea_vprice* program requires initial data set that contains the
input and output variables for observed production units.
Variable names must be identified by *inputvars* for input variable and
by *outputvars* for output variables to allow that *dea_vprice* program
can identify and handle the multiple input-output data set. And the
variable name of production units or DMUs may be specified by
"dmu" or leave it Stata generate them for the analysis.

Result Window 15.2 shows the result of Input-oriented Virtual Price
model with the following command.

. dea_vprice in1 in2= out1

```
options: ORT(IN)
DEA-Virtual Price Efficiency Results:
          oweight:  iweight:   iweight:
          out1       in1        in2
dmu:A     1         .272727    .181818
dmu:B     1         .272727    .181818
dmu:C     1          0          1
dmu:D     .5        .136364    .0909091
dmu:E     .44        .12        .08
dmu:F     .5          0         .5
```

Result Window 15.2

15.4 Exercises
15.4.1 Result Window 15. Interpret the result of step 2.
15.4.2 Analyze the output-oriented Virtual Price model.

15.5 References
Charnes, A., Cooper, W.W., & Rhodes, E. (1978). Measuring the efficiency of decision making units. *European Journal of Operational Research 2*(6), 429-444.

Cooper, W., Seiford, L. M., & Tone, K. (2006). Introduction to Data Envelopment Analysis and Its Use. 233 Spring Street, New York, NY 10013, USA: Springer Science & Business Media, Inc.

Lee, Jeong-dong and Oh, Dong-hyun. (2012). Theory of efficiency analysis. Seoul, Korea: Jiphil Media.

16 THE IMPRECISE DEA(IDEA) MODEL

Cooper and Yu (1999) developed models to use the imprecise data in DEA and Zhu (2004) provided the simplified procedure to solve the IDEA model. Their models permit the imprecise data given only within specified bounds or known in terms of ordinal relations. IDEA model is useful alternative when the basic DEA models are not appropriate due to the implicit data. This chapter shows the basic IDEA model and illustration of the Stata command.

16.1 Data

For illustration and comparison of the results, <Table 16.1-4> data are taken from Lee & Oh(2012, pp.189-209) and Zhu(2004).

<Table 16.1> Data for five DMUs

DMU	A	B	C	D	E
y1	1	4	3	2	1
y2(bounded)	[3,4]	[3,3]	[2,2]	[1,1]	[5,6]
x1	1	3	4	5	2

<Table 16.2> Data in ordinal value for five DMUs

DMU	A	B	C	D	E
y1	3	3	2	2	4
y2	2	1	3	4	5
x1	3	2	1	5	4

16.2 Model Description

Lee&Oh(2012, p.205) provides the basic form of IDEA as shown in Equation (16.1). It shows the input oriented IDEA model formulation.

$$\min \theta^k \qquad\qquad (16.1)$$

subject to

$$\sum_{j \neq k} \lambda^j \, \bar{x}_m^j + \lambda^k \underline{x}_m^k \leq \theta^k \underline{x}_m^k, m \in BI;$$

$$\sum_{j=1}^{J} \lambda^j x_m^j \leq \theta^k x_m^k, m \notin BI;$$

$$\sum_{j \neq k} \lambda^j \underline{y}_n^j + \lambda^k \overline{y}_n^k \geq \overline{y}_n^k, n \in BO;$$

$$\sum_{j=1}^{J} \lambda^j y_n^j \geq y_n^j, m \notin BO;$$

$$\lambda^j \geq 0, j = 1,2, \dots, J.$$

The original data will be transformed to new sets of data according to Zhu (2004). The following states the brief procedure of the data transformation. For the bounded variables, the overlined variable takes the upper limit value and underlined variable takes the lower limit value in the Equation (16.1). For the ordinal variables, the output value will be replaced with unity if it is equal to or larger than the value of production unit interested and others with zero. And the input value will be replaced with zero if the rank is lower than itself and others with unity. And then analyze the transformed data using the basic DEA models.

16.3 Imprecise DEA @Stata

The following command loads into memory the data set of 'dea_interval.dta', a Stata-format dataset previously saved by *save* command from your working directory.

. use "D:\data\ dea_interval.dta"

And you can use the command list to Result Window the values of variables(see Result Window 16.1).

. list

	dmu	y1	y2	x1
1.	A	1	[3, 4]	1
2.	B	4	[3, 3]	3
3.	C	3	[2,2]	4
4.	D	2	[1,1]	5
5.	E	1	[5,6]	2

Result Window 16.1

The syntax of the **dea** command for the Imprecise DEA model is: **dea** inputvars(min=1) = outputvars(min=1) [if][in] [using/ filename], [ort(i|in|input|o|out|output) bounded(varlist) ordinal(varlist) categorical(varlist) stage(integer 2) tol1(real 1e-14) tol2(real 1e-8) trace saving(filename) replace]

You can apply the bounded Imprecise DEA model to estimate efficiency scores of five DMUs in Table16.1.

. dea x1= y2 y1,b(y2)

```
options: RTS(CRS) ORT(IN) STAGE(2)
CRS-INPUT Oriented DEA Efficiency Results:
                       ref:    ref:    ref:    ref:    ref:  islack:
          rank   theta    A       B       C       D       E      x1
dmu:A      1      1       1       0       0       0       0       0
dmu:B      1      1       0       1       0       0       0       0
dmu:C      4     .5625    0      .75      0       0       0       0
dmu:D      5     .3       0      .5       0       0       0       0
dmu:E      3      1       2       0       0       0       0       0

         oslack:  oslack:
            y2       y1
dmu:A        0        0
dmu:B        0        0
dmu:C      .25        0
dmu:D      .5         0
dmu:E        0        1
```

Result Window 16.2

Variable Returns to Scale IDEA model will result the following.

. dea x1= y2 y1,b(y2) rts(vrs)

```
options: RTS(VRS) ORT(IN) STAGE(2)
VRS-INPUT Oriented DEA Efficiency Results:
                            ref:     ref:     ref:     ref:     ref:  islack:
           rank    theta      A        B        C        D        E      x1
dmu:A        1       1        1        0        0        0        0       0
dmu:B        1       1        0        1        0        0        0       0
dmu:C        4    .5625       0      .75        0        0        0       0
dmu:D        5      .3        0       .5        0        0        0       0
dmu:E        1       1        0        0        0        0        1       0

          oslack:  oslack:   slack:
            y2       y1     slack_1
dmu:A        0        0        0
dmu:B        0        0        0
dmu:C      .25        0      .25
dmu:D       .5        0       .5
dmu:E        0        0        0


VRS Frontier(-1:drs, 0:crs, 1:irs)
           CRS_TE      VRS_TE      DRS_TE      SCALE       RTS
dmu:A    1.000000    1.000000    1.000000    0.000000    0.000000
dmu:B    1.000000    1.000000    1.000000    0.000000    0.000000
dmu:C    0.562500    0.583333    0.562500    0.000000    1.000000
dmu:D    0.300000    0.333333    0.300000    0.000000    1.000000
dmu:E    1.000000    1.000000    1.000000    0.000000    0.000000


VRS Frontier:

     dmu   y1      y2    x1     CRS_TE      VRS_TE      SCALE     RTS
1.    A    1    [3, 4]    1    1.000000    1.000000    0.000000    -
2.    B    4    [3, 3]    3    1.000000    1.000000    0.000000    -
3.    C    3    [2,2]     4    0.562500    0.583333    0.000000   irs
4.    D    2    [1,1]     5    0.300000    0.333333    0.000000   irs
5.    E    1    [5,6]     2    1.000000    1.000000    0.000000    -
```

Result Window 16.3

The following command loads into memory the data set of 'dea_ordinal.dta.dta', a Stata-format dataset previously saved by *save* command from your working directory.

. use "D:\data\ dea_ordinal.dta"

And you can use the command list to Result Window the values of variables(see Result Window 16.4).

. list

	dmu	in1	out1	out2
1.	A	3	3	2
2.	B	2	3	1
3.	C	1	2	3
4.	D	5	2	4
5.	E	4	4	5

Result Window 16.4

You can apply the cardinal Imprecise DEA model to estimate efficiency scores of five DMUs in Table16.2.

. dea in1= out1 out2, ca(in1 out1 out2)

```
options: RTS(CRS) ORT(IN) STAGE(2)
CRS-INPUT Oriented DEA Efficiency Results:
                         ref:   ref:    ref:    ref:   ref: islack:
           rank   theta    A      B       C       D      E     in1
dmu:A       4      .5      0      0      1.5      0      0      0
dmu:B       2      .75     0      0      1.5      0      0      0
dmu:C       1      1       0      0       1       0      0      0
dmu:D       5    .266667   0      0     1.33333   0      0      0
dmu:E       3      .5      0      0       2       0      0      0

         oslack:  oslack:
          out1     out2
dmu:A       0      2.5
dmu:B       0      3.5
dmu:C       0       0
dmu:D    .666667    0
dmu:E       0       1
```

Result Window 16.5

16.4 Exercises
16.4.1 Apply the IDEA to the data in Table 16.3.

<Table 16.3> Data for eight

DMU	x1(ordinal)	x2	x3	y1(bounded)	y2	y3
A	5	124	18	[80,85]	26	90
B	7	95	9	[85,90]	18	100
C	3	92	8	[75,80]	10	87
D	1	61	6	[100,100]	8	99
E	2	63	5	[70,75]	7	96
F	6	50	4	[90,95]	6	86
G	4	40	4	[80,85]	2	71
H	8	16	1	[95,100]	3	98

16.4.2 If you have negative data, describe whether it can be analyzed in the IDEA model.

16.5 References
Cooper, William W., Park, K. S., & Yu, G. (1999). IDEA and AR-IDEA: Models for Dealing with Imprecise Data in DEA. *Management Science 45*(4):597-607.

Lee, Jeong-dong and Oh, Dong-hyun. 2012. Theory of efficiency analysis. Seoul, Korea: Jiphil Media.

Zhu, J. (2004). Imprecise DEA via standard linear DEA models with a revisit to a Korean mobile telecommunication company. *Operations Research, 52*(2):324-325.

17 THE INTERIOR POINT METHOD

The LinearProgram() class is available in Stata 16 version and after. It finds the parameter vector that minimizes or maximizes the linear objective function subject to some restrictions. The restrictions may be linear equality constraints, linear inequality constraints, lower bounds, or upper bounds. Stata describes LinearProgram() as "Mata class LinearProgram() solves linear programs. It uses Mehrotra's (1992) interior-point method, which is faster for large problems than the traditional simplex method". (https://www.stata.com/features/overview/linear-programming/. accessed Dec. 20, 2022)

17.1 Data
Stata provides a sample of 756 fictional firms producing a manufactured good with capital and labor. The inputs for the firms will be capital (lncapital) and labor (lnlabor); the output will be the manufactured good (lnoutput). You can download the data file from the following site.
https://www.stata-press.com/data/r17/frontier1

17.2 Model Description
You can use Stata's LinearProgram() to solve linear programs. For a detailed description of the model, see Mehrotra's (1992).

17.3 DEA using Interior Point Method @Stata

LinearProgram() can be run in Mata. The basic procedure for DEA analysis using LinearProgram(), introduced by the user's manual provided by Stata, is as follows.

First, read the data into Mata.
Second, generate an instance of the LinearProgram() class and store all the required information.
Third, set and execute the target DMU for efficiency calculation.

The following is an example of a program command.

Step 1: Read the data into Stata.

. use https://www.stata-press.com/data/r17/frontier1

Step 2: Read the data from Mata.

```
mata:
X = st_data(., ("lnlabor", "lncapital"))
Y = st_data(., "lnoutput")
n = rows(X)
m = cols(X)
p = cols(Y)
```

Step 3: When the linear program problem is developed in the standard form, specify the coefficients and constraints and set the ID of the DMU to be analyzed.

```
id = 8 //* id means dmu. user's choice.
c = (Y[id, .], J(1, m, 0))
Aec = (J(1, p, 0), X[id, .])
bec = 1
Aie = (Y, -X)
bie = J(n, 1, 0)
lowerbd = J(1, m + p, 0)
upperbd = J(1, m + p, .)
```

Step 4: Create an instance of the LinearProgram() class and store the necessary information.

q = LinearProgram()
q.setCoefficients(c)
q.setEquality(Aec, bec)
q.setInequality(Aie, bie)
q.setBounds(lowerbd, upperbd)

Step 5: Run to calculate the efficiency of the specified DMU to be analyzed.

q.optimize()

17.4 Exercises

17.4.1 Run the DEA program on DMU 8 using the LinearProgram() described in 17.3. Make sure your efficiency is within what it allows. If efficiency is out of the range, explain why.

17.4.2 Analyze the data given in Table 17.1 with output-oriented VRS using LinearProgram().

Table 17.1 Data of 5 Firms

Firm	y	x1	x2
A	1	2	5
B	2	2	4
C	3	6	6
D	1	3	2
E	2	6	2

17.5 References

Mehrotra, S. (1992). On the implementation of a primal-dual interior point method. *SIAM Journal on Optimization 2*: 575–601.

https://www.stata.com/features/overview/linear-programming/. (accessed Dec. 20, 2022)

APPENDIX A: ANSWERS TO SELECTED EXERCISES

Chapter 2
2.4.1
. dea i_employee i_area= o_sales o_profits,fdh ort(out) stage(2)

```
options: ORT(OUT) STAGE(2)
FDH-OUTPUT Oriented DEA Efficiency Results:
                                    ref:       ref:       ref:
                  rank      theta    store_A   store_B    store_C
dmu:store_A         1         1         1         0          0
dmu:store_B         1         1         0         1          0
dmu:store_C         5       1.125       0         0          0
dmu:store_D         1         1         0         0          0
dmu:store_E         1         1         0         0          0

                    ref:      ref:     islack:    islack:    oslack:
                  store_D    store_E   i_employee  i_area    o_sales
dmu:store_A         0         0         0          0          0
dmu:store_B         0         0         0          0          0
dmu:store_C         0         1         8         21          0
dmu:store_D         1         0         0          0          0
dmu:store_E         0         1         0          0          0

                  oslack:
                  o_profits
dmu:store_A         0
dmu:store_B         0
dmu:store_C       2.375
dmu:store_D         0
dmu:store_E         0
```

- rank and efficiency scores match.
- slack scores mismatch because the algorithm changed.

Chapter 3

3.4.1

. dea x1 x2= y,ort(out) rts(ccr) stage(2)

```
options: RTS(CRS) ORT(OUT) STAGE(2)
CRS-OUTPUT Oriented DEA Efficiency Results:
                        ref:    ref:    ref:    ref:    ref:  islack:
            rank   theta   A       B       C       D       E      x1
dmu:A        5       2     0       1       0       0       0       0
dmu:B        1       1     0       1       0       0       0       0
dmu:C        3      1.2    0      1.2      0       0      .6       0
dmu:D        4      1.4    0      .3       0       0      .4       0
dmu:E        1       1     0       0       0       0       1       0

           islack:  oslack:
            x2        y
dmu:A        1        0
dmu:B        0        0
dmu:C        0        0
dmu:D        0        0
dmu:E        0        0
```

- the results match. It is not generally true.

Chapter 4

4.4.1

. dea x1 x2= y,ort(out) rts(vrs) stage(2)

```
options: RTS(VRS) ORT(OUT) STAGE(2)
VRS-OUTPUT Oriented DEA Efficiency Results:
                     ref:      ref:      ref:      ref:      ref:  islack:
           rank    theta       A         B         C         D        E       x1
dmu:A        5        2        0         1         0         0         0        0
dmu:B        1        1        0         1         0         0         0        0
dmu:C        1        1        0         0         1         0         0        0
dmu:D        1        1        0         0         0         1         0        0
dmu:E        1        1        0         0         0         0         1        0

          islack:   oslack:
             x2        y
dmu:A         1        0
dmu:B         0        0
dmu:C         0        0
dmu:D         0        0
dmu:E         0        0


VRS Frontier(-1:drs, 0:crs, 1:irs)
           CRS_TE       VRS_TE       DRS_TE        SCALE          RTS
dmu:A    2.000000     2.000000     2.000000     1.000000     0.000000
dmu:B    1.000000     1.000000     1.000000     1.000000     0.000000
dmu:C    1.200000     1.000000     1.200000     1.200000    -1.000000
dmu:D    1.400000     1.000000     1.400000     1.400000     1.000000
dmu:E    1.000000     1.000000     1.000000     1.000000     0.000000


VRS Frontier:

      dmu    y    x1   x2      CRS_TE        VRS_TE        SCALE     RTS

 1.    A     1    2    5     2.000000      2.000000      1.000000     -
 2.    B     2    2    4     1.000000      1.000000      1.000000     -
 3.    C     3    6    6     1.200000      1.000000      1.200000    drs
 4.    D     1    3    2     1.400000      1.000000      1.400000    irs
 5.    E     2    6    2     1.000000      1.000000      1.000000     -
```

- the results match. It is not generally true.

Chapter 6
6.4.3
. dea_allocative x1 x2= y,mod(c) rts(vrs) val(2 1)

```
options: RTS(VRS)
VRS DEA-Cost Efficiency Results:
            CUR:      CUR:      CUR:     TECH:     TECH:     TECH:     TECH:      MIN:
             x1        x2       cost     theta       x1        x2       cost       x1
dmu:A         2         8        12        1         2         8        12         3
dmu:B         3         6        12        1         3         6        12         3
dmu:C         5         3        13        1         5         3        13         3
dmu:D         9         2        20        1         9         2        20         3
dmu:E         6         7        19     .65625    3.9375   4.59375   12.4688       3
dmu:F         3         9        15        .8       2.4       7.2        12         3
dmu:G         8         4        20    .708333   5.66667   2.83333   14.1667       3

            MIN:      MIN:
             x2       cost        OE        AE        TE
dmu:A         6        12         1         1         1
dmu:B         6        12         1         1         1
dmu:C         6        12    .923077   .923077        1
dmu:D         6        12        .6        .6         1
dmu:E         6        12    .631579   .962406    .65625
dmu:F         6        12        .8         1        .8
dmu:G         6        12        .6    .847059   .708333
```

Chapter 7
7.4.1
. dea_allocative x1 x2= y, mod(r) rts(vrs) unitvars(p)

```
options: RTS(VRS)
VRS DEA-Revenue Efficiency Results:
          CUR:   CUR:  TECH:  TECH:  TECH:   MAX:   MAX:
          y     price   eta    y     price    y     price    OE     AE     TE
dmu:A     1      3      1      1       3       1      3       1      1      1
dmu:B     1      3      1      1       3       1      3       1      1      1
dmu:C     1      3      1      1       3       1      3       1      1      1
dmu:D     1      3      1      1       3       1      3       1      1      1
dmu:E     1      3      1      1       3       1      3       1      1      1
dmu:F     1      3      1      1       3       1      3       1      1      1
dmu:G     1      3      1      1       3       1      3       1      1      1
```

Chapter 8
8.4.1
. dea_allocative x1 x2= y, mod(p) unitvars(c1 c2 p)

```
options: RTS(CRS)
CRS DEA-Profit Efficiency Results:
          MAX_H:   MAX:   MIN_H:  MIN_H:   MIN:    MAX:    CUR:
          y      revenue   x1      x2     cost    profit  profit    OE
dmu:A      3       9       2       8       18      -9      -9       1
dmu:B      3       9       3       6       15      -6      -6       1
dmu:C      3       9       5       3       11      -2      -2       1
dmu:D      3       9       9       2       13      -4      -4       1
dmu:E      3       9       5       3       11      -2     -11      5.5
dmu:F      3       9       3       6       15      -6     -12       2
dmu:G      3       9       5       3       11      -2      -7      3.5
```
- the model is not translation invariant

Chapter 9
9.4.3
. dea_supersbm x1 x2= y1 y2,rts(vrs)

```
options: RTS(VRS) ORT(IN)
VRS DEA-SUPER-SBM Efficiency Results:
                  ref:    ref:    ref:    ref:    ref:    ref:   islack:
         theta     A       B       C       D       E       F       x1
dmu:A      .       .       .       .       .       .       .       .
dmu:B    1.25      1       0       0       0       0       0       0
dmu:C  1.12414     0    .344828    0    .310345    0    .344828    0
dmu:D    1.125     0       0       1       0       0       0       0
dmu:E      1       0       0       0      .2       0      .8       0
dmu:F      1       0      .5      .5       0       0       0       0


         islack:  oslack:  oslack:
           x2       y1       y2
dmu:A       .        .        .
dmu:B       4        0        0
dmu:C    1.24138     0        0
dmu:D       1        0        0
dmu:E       0        0        0
dmu:F       0        0        0
```
- No solution for DMU A. Super-efficiency model with the

orientation option may not have a feasible solution.

Chapter 10
10.4.1
. dea_additive x= y,rts(vrs)

```
options: RTS(VRS)
VRS DEA-Additive Efficiency Results:
                            ref:    ref:    ref:    ref:    ref:    ref:
            rank    theta    A       B       C       D       E       F
dmu:A         .       4       0       0       0       1       0       0
dmu:B         .       0       0       1       0       0       0       0
dmu:C         .       4       0       0       0       1       0       0
dmu:D         .       0       0       0       0       1       0       0
dmu:E         .    3.33333    0       0       0   .333333     0    .666667
dmu:F         .       0       0       0       0       0       0       1
dmu:G         .    2.66667    0       0       0   .666667     0    .333333

            ref:   islack:  oslack:
             G       x        y
dmu:A        0       0        4
dmu:B        0       0        0
dmu:C        0       2        2
dmu:D        0       0        0
dmu:E        0     3.33333    0
dmu:F        0       0        0
dmu:G        0     2.66667    0
```

. dea x= y, ort(out) rts(vrs)

```
options: RTS(VRS) ORT(OUT) STAGE(2)
VRS-OUTPUT Oriented DEA Efficiency Results:
                          ref:    ref:    ref:    ref:    ref:    ref:
          rank    theta     A       B       C       D       E       F
dmu:A       7       3        0       0       0       1       0       0
dmu:B       1       1        0       1       0       0       0       0
dmu:C       6     1.875      0       0       0      .5       0      .5
dmu:D       1       1        0       0       0       1       0       0
dmu:E       4     1.125      0       0       0       0       0       1
dmu:F       1       1        0       0       0       0       0       1
dmu:G       5    1.28571     0       0       0       0       0       1

          ref:   islack: oslack:
           G       x       y
dmu:A       0       0       0
dmu:B       0       0       0
dmu:C       0       0       0
dmu:D       0       0       0
dmu:E       0       2       0
dmu:F       0       0       0
dmu:G       0       0       0


VRS Frontier(-1:drs, 0:crs, 1:irs)
          CRS_TE      VRS_TE      DRS_TE      SCALE       RTS
dmu:A    3.000000    3.000000    3.000000    1.000000    0.000000
dmu:B    3.000000    1.000000    3.000000    3.000000    1.000000
dmu:C    2.250000    1.875000    1.875000    1.200000   -1.000000
dmu:D    1.000000    1.000000    1.000000    1.000000    0.000000
dmu:E    1.875000    1.125000    1.125000    1.666667   -1.000000
dmu:F    1.333333    1.000000    1.000000    1.333333   -1.000000
dmu:G    1.714286    1.285714    1.285714    1.333333   -1.000000


VRS Frontier:
```

	dmu	x	y	CRS_TE	VRS_TE	SCALE	RTS
1.	A	4	2	3.000000	3.000000	1.000000	-
2.	B	2	1	3.000000	1.000000	3.000000	irs
3.	C	6	4	2.250000	1.875000	1.200000	drs
4.	D	4	6	1.000000	1.000000	1.000000	-
5.	E	10	8	1.875000	1.125000	1.666667	drs
6.	F	8	9	1.333333	1.000000	1.333333	drs
7.	G	8	7	1.714286	1.285714	1.333333	drs

- DMU B, C, and D are all efficient for both models.

Chapter 11
11.4.
. tfdea price bdywgt= ntwk scrnsize resolution sensors ntwk1 cpuspeed pcr prmycamperf btrycpcty comlev, tf(2017)
(Results Window : skip)

Chapter 14
14.4.1

MILP L0 Input Values:

	x12	x21	x23	x32	x31	rel	rhs
1.	1	0	0	1	0	<=	1
2.	0	1	1	0	0	<=	1
3.	0	0	0	1	1	<=	1
4.	-1	1	0	0	1	=	0
5.	1	-1	-1	1	0	=	0
6.	0	0	1	-1	-1	=	0
7.	1	0	1	0	1	<=	2
8.	1	1	0	0	0	<=	2
9.	0	0	1	1	0	<=	2

	z	x12	x21	x23	x32	x31	s1	s2	s3	s4	s5	a1	a2	a3	rhs
r1	1	1	0	0	1	0	0	0	0	0	0	1	1	1	1
r2	0	0	1	1	0	0	1	0	0	0	0	0	0	0	1
r3	0	0	0	0	1	1	0	1	0	0	0	0	0	0	1
r4	0	-1	1	0	0	1	0	0	0	0	0	1	0	0	0
r5	0	1	-1	-1	1	0	0	0	0	0	0	0	1	0	0
r6	0	0	0	1	-1	-1	0	0	0	0	0	0	0	1	0
r7	0	1	0	1	0	1	0	0	1	0	0	0	0	0	2
r8	0	1	1	0	0	0	0	0	0	1	0	0	0	0	2
r9	0	0	0	1	1	0	0	0	0	0	1	0	0	0	2

MILP L0 Results: options(max)

	c1	c2	c3	c4	c5	c6	c7	c8	c9	c10	c11
r1	1	1	1	0	0	0	0	1	1	0	2

Input Values:

	z	x12	x21	x23	x32	x31	s1	s2	s3	s4	s5	a1	a2	a3	rhs
r1	1	1	0	0	1	0	0	0	0	0	0	1	1	1	1
r2	0	0	1	1	0	0	1	0	0	0	0	0	0	0	1
r3	0	0	0	0	1	1	0	1	0	0	0	0	0	0	1
r4	0	-1	1	0	0	1	0	0	0	0	0	1	0	0	0
r5	0	1	-1	-1	1	0	0	0	0	0	0	0	1	0	0
r6	0	0	0	1	-1	-1	0	0	0	0	0	0	0	1	0
r7	0	1	0	1	0	1	0	0	1	0	0	0	0	0	2
r8	0	1	1	0	0	0	0	0	0	1	0	0	0	0	2
r9	0	0	0	1	1	0	0	0	0	0	1	0	0	0	2

LP Results: options(max)

	z	x12	x21	x23	x32	x31	s1	s2	s3	s4	s5
opt_val	1	1	1	0	0	0	0	1	1	0	2

APPENDIX B: PROGRAM CODES

B1.1 Figure 2.2: do file for <Figure 2.2> FDH production possibility sets and convexity assumption for two inputs (x1, x2)

```
clear
drop _all
input str2 label x1 x2
"A" 2 4
"B" 3 3
"C" 6 1
"D" 4 8
"E" 6 4
"F" 6 2

end

set scheme sj
local stairstep_coords "12 2 4 2 4 3 3 3 3 6 1 6 1 12"
local grid_coords
forvalues i = 1/12 {
    local grid_coords = "`grid_coords' 0 `i' 12 `i' `i' 0 `i' 12"
}

twoway scatteri `stairstep_coords', ///
        recast(area) lcolor(gs13) fcolor(gs13) base(12) ///
    || pcarrowi `grid_coords', ///
        mcolor(gs5) msize(0) barbsize(0) ///
        lpattern(tight_dot) lcolor(gs5) ///
    || scatteri `stairstep_coords', ///
        recast(line) lcolor(gs5) lwidth(medium) lpattern(solid) ///
    || line x2 x1 if label=="A" | label=="B" | label=="C", ///
        sort lcolor(gs1) lwidth(medium) lpattern(shortdash) ///
    || scatter x2 x1, ///
        msize(large) mcolor(gs5) msymbol(circle) mlabel(label) ///
        mlabsize(medlarge)    mlabcolor(gs5)    mlabposition(11)
mlabgap(tiny) ///
    || scatteri 0 0 8 4, ///
        recast(line)  lcolor(gs5)  lwidth(medium)  lpattern(solid)
///
    || scatteri 0 0 4 6, ///
        recast(line) lcolor(gs5) lwidth(medium) lpattern(solid) ///
```

|| scatteri 2.5 3.75 3 4.5, ///
    text(2.3 3.75 "E2" 3.8 4.5 "E1", ///
      place(s) size(medidum) color(gs5)) ///
    lwidth(medium) lpattern(solid) ///
    mcolor(gs5) msize(large) msymbol(circle_hollow) ///
    mlwidth(medium) ///
|| scatteri 0 0 2 6, ///
    recast(line) lcolor(gs5) lwidth(medium) lpattern(solid) ///
|| scatteri 1.67 5, ///
    text(1.47 5 "F1",place(s) size(medidum) color(gs5)) ///
    lwidth(medium) lpattern(solid) ///
    mcolor(gs5) msize(large) msymbol(circle_hollow) ///
    mlwidth(medium) ///
|| pcarrowi 0 0 0 12 (3) "x1" ///
        0 0 12 0 (12) "x2", ///
    text(0 0 "O", place(sw) size(medlarge)) headlabel ///
    msymbol(circle) mcolor(gs1) msize(2) barbsize(2) ///
    mlabsize(medlarge)   mlabcolor(gs1)   lwidth(medium)
lcolor(gs1) ///
    , ylabel(0(1)12, nogrid) ///
    xlabel(0(1)12, nogrid) ///
    yscale(off) xscale(off) legend(off) ///
    plotregion(margin(zero) fcolor(gs15) lcolor(gs15)) ///
    graphregion(margin(large)) aspect(1) ///
    name(fdh_example, replace)
  graph export fdh_example.eps, replace
  // graph drop _all
  exit

B1.2   Figure 2.1: do file for <Figure 2.1> (a) FDH production possibility sets, (b) production possibility sets comparison for RTS

```
clear
drop _all
input str2 label x y
"A" 2 2
"B" 3 6
"C" 6 7
"D" 7 10
"E" 5 3
"F" 8 4
"G" 10 10

end

set scheme sj
local stairstep_coords "0 2 2 2 2 3 6 3 6 6 7 6 7 7 10 7 10 12 0 12"
twoway scatteri `stairstep_coords', ///
        recast(area) lcolor(gs10) fcolor(gs10) fintensity(inten50) ///
    || pcarrowi 0 2 2 2     2 2 2 4 ///
            2 3 6 3      6 3 6 6 ///
            5 6 7 6      7 6 7 8 ///
            7 7 10 7    10 7 10 10 ///
            8 10 10 10   10 10 10 12 ///
            1 5 3 5      3 5 3 7 ///
            2 8 4 8      4 8 4 10 ///
            10 12 0 12 ///
        , lcolor(gs5) msize(0) barbsize(0) lwidth(medium) ///
    || scatter y x, ///
            msize(large) mcolor(gs5) msymbol(circle) mlabel(label) ///
            mlabsize(large) mlabcolor(gs5) mlabposition(11) mlabgap(tiny) ///
    || pcarrowi 0 0 0 13 (3) "x" ///
            0 0 12 0 (12) "y" ///
        , text(0 0 "0", place(sw) size(large)) headlabel ///
            mcolor(gs5) msize(2) barbsize(2) ///
            mlabsize(large) mlabcolor(gs5) lwidth(medium) ///
        , ylabel(0(1)12, valuelabel noticks nogrid) xlabel(0(1)13, nogrid) ///
        yscale(off) xscale(off) legend(off) ///
        caption("(a) production possibility sets", position(6)) ///
        plotregion(fcolor(gs15) lcolor(gs15)) aspect(1) name(pps_gr1, replace)
twoway scatteri `stairstep_coords', ///
        recast(area) lcolor(gs10) fcolor(gs10) fintensity(inten50) ///
    || scatteri `stairstep_coords', ///
            recast(line) lcolor(gs5) lwidth(medium) lpattern(solid) ///
    || scatter y x, ///
            msize(large) mcolor(gs5) msymbol(circle) mlabel(label) ///
```

```
    mlabsize(large) mlabcolor(gs5) mlabposition(11) mlabgap(tiny) ///
|| scatteri 0 0 6 3 12 6, ///
    recast(line) lcolor(gs5) lwidth(medium) lpattern(solid) ///
|| scatteri 2 2 6 3 10 7, ///
    recast(line) lcolor(gs5) lwidth(medium) lpattern(solid) ///
|| scatteri 4 2 4 2.5 4 3 4 8, ///
    recast(connected) lwidth(medium) lpattern(vshortdash) ///
    mcolor(gs5) msize(large) msymbol(circle_hollow) ///
    mlwidth(medium) ///
|| pcarrowi 11 3.5 10 5 (9) "P(CRS)" ///
        10 3.5 8  5 (9) "P(VRS)" ///
        9 3.5 6  5 (9) "P(FDH)" ///
    , mcolor(gs5) msize(2) barbsize(2) ///
    mlabsize(large) mlabcolor(gs5) lwidth(medium) msymbol(circle) ///
|| pcarrowi 0 0 0 13 (3)  "x" ///
        0 0 12 0 (12) "y", ///
    text(0 0 "0", place(sw) size(large)) headlabel ///
    mcolor(gs5) msize(2) barbsize(2) ///
    mlabsize(large) mlabcolor(gs5) lwidth(medium) msymbol(circle) ///
, ylabel(0(1)12, valuelabel noticks nogrid) xlabel(0(1)13, nogrid) ///
yscale(off) xscale(off) legend(off) ///
caption("(b) production possibility sets comparision", position(6)) ///
plotregion(fcolor(gs15) lcolor(gs15)) aspect(1) name(pps_gr2, replace)
graph combine pps_gr1 pps_gr2
graph export prod_possibility_set.eps, replace
// graph drop _all
exit
```

B1.3   Figure 2.1: do file for <Figure 3.1> Concepts of Returns to Scale and PPS

```
clear
input str2 firm y  x1    x2      x1y     x2y     var7    var8
"D"  1     2      2       2       2       4       3.95
"B"  2     2      2       1       1       2       2.95
"E" 1 2    3      2       3       1       1.95
"C"  2     2      4       1       2       0.5     0.5
"A"  3     1.5    1.5     0.5     0.5     0.5     0
end
```

twoway line var8 var7,mc(black) lc(black) mlabv(firm) ///
| | scatter x2y x1y , xlabel(0(1)5) ylabel(0(1)5) mc(black) ///
mlab(firm) mlabcolor(black) mlabpos(11) ///
|| scatteri 0 0 4 2, ms(.) recast(line) lp(dot) lc(black) lwidth(med) ///
|| scatteri 0 0 2 1, recast(line) lp(dash_dot) lc(black) ///
|| scatteri 2 1 3 2, recast(line) lp(dash_dot) lc(black) ///
|| scatteri 3 2 4 4, recast(line) lp(dash_dot) lc(black) ///
|| scatteri 1 0 1 1, recast(line) lp(dot) lc(black) ///
|| scatteri 2 1 3 2, recast(line) lp(dash_dot) lc(black) ///
|| scatteri 3 2 4 4, recast(line) lp(dash_dot) lc(black) ///
|| scatteri 0 1 2 1, recast(line) lp(dot) lc(black) ///
|| scatteri 1 0.5 "B{subscript:1}" , mlabcolor(black) mc(black) ms(Oh)
msize(medlarge) mlabpos(11) ///
|| scatteri 1 0.7 "B{subscript:2}" , mlabcolor(black) mc(black) ms(Oh)
msize(medlarge) mlabpos(5) ///
|| scatteri 1 0 "B{subscript:0}" , mlabcolor(black) mc(black) ms(Oh)
msize(medlarge) mlabpos(12) ///
|| scatteri 0.5 0.5 "VRS Frontier" , mlabcolor(black) mc(balck) ms(dot)
msize(small) mlabpos(3) ///
|| scatteri 0.2 0.5 "NDRS Frontier" , mlabcolor(black) mc(balck) msize(small)
mlabpos(3) ///
|| scatteri 4 4 "NIRS Frontier" , mlabcolor(black) mc(balck) ms(Oh)
msize(small) mlabpos(9) ///
|| scatteri 0 0.5 "A{subscript:1}" , mlabcolor(black) mc(black) ms(Oh)
msize(medlarge) mlabpos(3) ///
|| scatteri 0 1 "B{subscript:3}" , mlabcolor(black) mc(black) ms(Oh)
msize(medlarge) mlabpos(3) ///
|| scatteri 4 2 "CRS Frontier" , mlabcolor(black) mc(balck) ms(Oh) msize(small)
mlabpos(9) ///
|| scatteri 4.2 2.1 "NDRS Frontier" , mlabcolor(black) mc(balck) msize(small)
mlabpos(9) ///
|| ,legend(off) ylabel(,angle(0)) xlabel(,grid) ///
xtitle(X(input)) ///
ytitle(Y(output)) ///
graph export output10.eps,replace

exit

B1.4 Figure 4.1: do file for <Figure 4.1>

```
set more off
capture log close

clear
input str2     firm      y      x1      x2      x1y     x2y
        var7   var8
"A"  1         1.5       5      1.5     5       1.5     5
"B"  1         1         4      1       4       1       4
"G" 12         5         2      5       1       4
"C"  2         2         4      1       2       1       2
"H"  3         6         6      2       2       3       1
"D"  2         6         2      3       1       4       1
"E"  2         8         2      4       1       4       1
"F"  2         9         3      4.5     1.5     4.5     1.5

end

twoway line var8 var7,mc(black) lc(black) mlabv(firm) ///
||scatter x2y x1y , xlabel(0(1)5) ylabel(0(1)5) mc(black) ///
mlab(firm) mlabcolor(black) mlabpos(11) ///
|| scatteri 0 0 5 2, ms(.) recast(line) lp(dash) lc(black) ///
|| scatteri 0 0 2 2, ms(.) recast(line) lp(dash) lc(black) ///
|| scatteri 1.666 1.6666 "H{subscript:1}" , mlabcolor(black) mc(black) ms(Oh)
msize(medlarge) mlabpos(12) ///
|| scatteri 2.5 1 "G{subscript:1}" , mlabcolor(black) mc(black) ms(Oh)
msize(mdelarge) ///
|| ,legend(off) ylabel(,angle(0)) xlabel(,grid) ///
xtitle(X{subscript:1}/Y) ///
ytitle(X{subscript:2}/Y) ///
note("Modified from Coelli et al., (2005, p.197), Cooper et al., (2006, p.57), Ji
& Lee(2010, p.4)")
graph export output8.eps,replace
exit
```

B1.5 Figure 4.2: do file for <Figure 4.2>

```
clear
input str2    firm      y    x1    x2.  x1y  x2y    var7     var8
"D"   1       2         2    2     2    2             3.95
"B"   2       2         2    1     1    2             3.95
"E" 1 3       2         3    2     1    1.95
"C"   2       2         4    1     2    0.5     0.5
"A"   3       1.5       1.5  0.5   0.5  0.5     0
//"G" 1       3         2    2     3    1       1.95
end

twoway line var8 var7,mc(black) lc(black) mlabv(firm) ///
||scatter x2y x1y , xlabel(0(1)5) ylabel(0(1)5) mc(black) ///
mlab(firm) mlabcolor(black) mlabpos(11) ///
|| scatteri 0 0 4 2, ms(.) recast(line) lp(dot) lc(black) lwidth(med) ///
|| scatteri 0 0 2 1, recast(line) lp(dash_dot) lc(black) ///
|| scatteri 2 1 2 3, recast(line) lp(dash_dot) lc(black) ///
|| scatteri 2 1 4 2, recast(line) lp(dash_dot) lc(black) ///
|| scatteri 1 0 1 1, recast(line) lp(dot) lc(black) ///
|| scatteri 2 1 2 2, recast(line) lp(dash_dot) lc(black) ///
|| scatteri 2 2 2 3, recast(line) lp(dash_dot) lc(black) ///
|| scatteri 0 1 2 1, recast(line) lp(dot) lc(black) ///
||  scatteri 1 0.5 "B{subscript:1}" , mlabcolor(black) mc(black) ms(Oh)
msize(medlarge) mlabpos(11) ///
||  scatteri 1 0.7 "B{subscript:2}" , mlabcolor(black) mc(black) ms(Oh)
msize(medlarge) mlabpos(5) ///
||  scatteri 1 0 "B{subscript:0}" , mlabcolor(black) mc(black) ms(Oh)
msize(large) mlabpos(12) ///
||  scatteri 0.2 0.5 "VRS Frontier" , mlabcolor(black) mc(balck) ms()
msize(small) mlabpos(3) ///
||  scatteri 2 2.5 "VRS Frontier" , mlabcolor(black)`mc(balck) ms(arrow)
msize(small) mlabpos(4) ///
|| scatteri 2 3 "NIRS Frontier" , mlabcolor(black) mc(balck) ms() msize(small)
mlabpos(2) ///
||  scatteri 0 0.5 "A{subscript:1}" , mlabcolor(black) mc(black) ms(Oh)
msize(medlarge) mlabpos(3) ///
||  scatteri 0 1 "B{subscript:3}" , mlabcolor(black) mc(black) ms(Oh)
msize(medlarge) mlabpos(3) ///
|| scatteri 4 2 "CRS Frontier" , mlabcolor(black) mc(balck) ms(Oh) msize(small)
mlabpos(9) ///
||  scatteri 4 2 "NDRS Frontier" , mlabcolor(black) mc(balck) ms(Oh)
msize(small) mlabpos(4) ///
|| ,legend(off) ylabel(,angle(0)) xlabel(,grid) ///
xtitle(X(input)) ///
ytitle(Y(output)) ///
graph export output10.eps,replace

exit
```

B2.1 dea.ado

```
*! version 1.2.1  09FEB2014
capture program drop dea
program define dea, rclass byable(recall)
    version 11.0

/** HISTORY:
* --------------------------------------------------------------------------
* 2012-09-22(SAT): Add FDH(Free Disposal Hull) Model.
* 2014-01-29(THU): Separate FDH program in this file.
* 2014-02-09(SUN): Revise the sentences in syntax checking and validation.
* 2014-04-09(SUN): Add DMU(name) option in syntax.
* 2014-04-30(TUE): Allow by command.
* --------------------------------------------------------------------------*/


/** Terms Description:
* --------------------------------------------------------------------------
* RTS: Return To Scale
* CRS: Constant Return to Scale
* VRS: Variant Return to Scale
* IRS: Increasing Return to Scale
* DRS: Decreasing Retrn to Scale
* --------------------------------------------------------------------------*/


// syntax checking and validation----------------------------------------------
// rts - return to scale, ort - orientation
// input varlist = output varlist
// example:
// . sysuse auto.dta, clear
// . gen gpm = 1/mpg
// . rename make dmu
// . dea weight length displacement gpm = rep78 headroom trunk if foreign,
//   rts(crs) ort(in) toll(1e-14)
// FDH analysis can be conducted by specifing "fdh" option on dea command.
// The follwing example shows the FDH analysis using dea command.
// . dea weight length displacement gpm = rep78 headroom trunk if foreign, fdh
// --------------------------------------------------------------------
    // returns 1 if the first nonblank character of local macro `0' is a comma,
    // or if `0' is empty.
    if replay() {
        dis as err "ivars and ovars required."
        exit 198
    }

    // get and check invarnames
    gettoken word 0 : 0, parse("=,")
    while ~("`word'" == ":" | "`word'" == "=") {
        if "`word'" == "," | "`word'" == "" {
            error 198
        }
        local invarnames `invarnames' `word'
        gettoken word 0 : 0, parse("=,")
    }
    unab invarnames : `invarnames'

    #del ;
```

```
syntax varlist(min=1) [if] [in] [using/]
[,
    DMU(varname)    // indicate dmu variable name.
    RTS(string)     // ignore case sensitive,[{CRS|CCR} | {BCC|VRS} |DRS|IRS]
    ORT(string)     // ignore case sensitive,[{IN|INPUT} | {OUT|OUTPUT}]
    STAGE(integer 2) // stage 1 or 2
    FDH             // Free Disposal Hull

    TOL1(real 1e-14) // entering or leaving value tolerance
    TOL2(real 1e-8)  // B inverse tolerance: 2.22e-12
    TRACE            // Whether or not to do the log
    SAVing(string)   // log file name
    REPLACE          // Whether or not to replace the log file

    Bounded(varlist)    // bounded variables list
    ORDinal(varlist)    // order variables list
    CAtegorical(varlist) // categorical variables list
];
#del cr

local num_invar : word count `invarnames'
local i 1
while (`i'<=`num_invar') {
    local invarn : word `i' of `invarnames'
    local junk : subinstr local invarnames "`invarn'" "", ///
        word all count(local j)
    if `j' > 1 {
        di as error ///
            "cannot specify the same input variable more than once"
        error 498
    }
    local i = `i' + 1
}

// dmu variable name(default "dmu") check.
if ("`dmu'" == "") {
    local dmu = "dmu"
}

// When FDH model, option rts not allowed.
if ("`fdh'" != "") {
    if ("`rts'" != "") {
        di as error "When FDH model, option rts() not allowed."
        exit 198
    }
}

// default model - CRS(Constant Return to Scale)
// if FDH, default model is VRS.
if ("`rts'" == "") {
    if ("`fdh'" == "") local rts = "CRS"
    else local rts = "VRS"
}
else {
    local rts = upper("`rts'")
    if ("`rts'" == "CCR") local rts = "CRS"
    else if ("`rts'" == "BCC") local rts = "VRS"
    else if (~("`rts'" == "CRS" | "`rts'" == "VRS" | ///
            "`rts'" == "DRS" | "`rts'" == "IRS")) {
```

```
        di as err "option rts allow for case-insensitive " _c
        di as err "CRS (eq CCR) or VRS (eq BCC) or DRS or IRS or nothing."
        exit 198
    }
}

// default orientation - Input Oriented
if ("`ort'" == "") local ort = "IN"
else {
    local ort = upper("`ort'")
    if ("`ort'" == "I" | "`ort'" == "IN" | "`ort'" == "INPUT") {
        local ort = "IN"
    }
    else if ("`ort'" == "O" | "`ort'" == "OUT" | "`ort'" == "OUTPUT") {
        local ort = "OUT"
    }
    else {
        di as err "option ort allows for case-insensitive " _c
        di as err "(i|in|input|o|out|output) or nothing."
        exit 198
    }
}

// default stage - 1
if (~("`stage'" == "1" | "`stage'" == "2")) {
    dis as err "option stage allows 1 or 2 or nothing exclusively."
    exit 198
}

if ("`using'" != "") use "`using'", clear
if (~(`c(N)' > 0 & `c(k)' > 0)) {
    dis as err "dataset required!"
    exit 198
}
// end of syntax checking and validation -------------------------------------

    set more off
    capture log close dealog

    // to remove log header information, use "quietly" and "hline"
    di as text "{hline `c(linesize)'}"
    quietly log using "dea.log", replace text name(dealog)
    preserve

    if ("`if'" != "" | "`in'" != "") {
        qui keep `in' `if'  // filtering : keep in range [if exp]
    }

    // if variable `dmu' not found, generate variable.
    // ref: regexm("`dmu'", "^`r(varlist)'$") == 0
    capture qui novarabbrev ds `dmu'
    if (c(rc) != 0) { // maybe c(rc) is r(111)
        qui gen str `dmu' = "`dmu'" + string(_n)
    }

    if ("`bounded'" != "" | "`ordinal'" != "" | "`categorical'" != "") {
        idea, dmu(`dmu') ivars(`invarnames') ovars(`varlist') ///
            rts(`rts') ort(`ort') stage(`stage') ///
```

```
            toll(`toll') tol2(`tol2')        ///
            `trace' saving(`saving') `replace' ///
            b(`bounded') ord(`ordinal') ca(`categorical')
        }
        else if ("`fdh'" != "") {
            _dea_fdh, dmu(`dmu') ivars(`invarnames') ovars(`varlist') ///
                rts(`rts') ort(`ort') stage(`stage') ///
                toll(`toll') tol2(`tol2') ///
                `trace' saving(`saving') `replace'
        }
        else {
            deanormal, dmu(`dmu') ivars(`invarnames') ovars(`varlist') ///
                rts(`rts') ort(`ort') stage(`stage') ///
                toll(`toll') tol2(`tol2') ///
                `trace' saving(`saving') `replace'
        }
        return add
        set more on

        restore, preserve
        quietly log close dealog
        di as text "{hline `c(linesize)'}"
end

*********************************************************************
* DEA Normal - Data Envelopment Analysis Normal
*********************************************************************
program define deanormal, rclass
    #del ;
    syntax , DMU(name) IVARS(string) OVARS(string) RTS(string) ORT(string)
    [
        STAGE(integer 2) TOL1(real 1e-3) TOL2(real 1e-12)
        TRACE SAVing(string) REPLACE DMUI(integer 0)
    ];
    #del cr

    preserve
    // di _n as input ///
    //    "options: RTS(`rts') ORT(`ort') STAGE(`stage') SAVing(`saving')"
    // di as input "Input Data:"
    // list

    // -----------------------------------------------------------

    tempname dmuIn dmuOut frameMat ///
        deamainrslt dearslt vrsfrontier crslambda
    mkDmuMat `ivars', dmumat(`dmuIn') sprefix("i") dmu(`dmu')
    mkDmuMat `ovars', dmumat(`dmuOut') sprefix("o") dmu(`dmu')
    local dmuCount = colsof(`dmuIn')
    if ("`ort'" == "OUT") local minrank = 1
    else local minrank = 0

    mata: _mkframemat("`frameMat'", "`dmuIn'", "`dmuOut'", ///
        "`rts'", "`ort'")
    deamain `dmu' `dmuIn' `dmuOut' `frameMat' `rts' `ort' `stage' ///
        `toll' `tol2' `trace'
    matrix `deamainrslt' = r(deamainrslt)

    mata: _dmurank("`deamainrslt'", ///
```

```
        `=rowsof(`dmuIn')', `=rowsof(`dmuOut')', `minrank', `tol2')
matrix `dearslt' = r(rank), `deamainrslt'

// use mata function '_setup_dearslt_names' because the maximum string
// variable length needs to be kept under the 244 for all the time
mata: _setup_dearslt_names("`dearslt'", "`dmuIn'", "`dmuOut'")

if ("`rts'" == "VRS") {
    // caution : join order! (CRS -> VRS -> DRS)
    // 1. VRS TE(VRS Technical Efficiency)
    matrix `deamainrslt' = r(deamainrslt)
    matrix `vrsfrontier' = `deamainrslt'[1...,1]

    // 2. CRS TE(CRS Technical Efficiency)
    local stageForVRS = 2
    mata: _mkframemat("`frameMat'", "`dmuIn'", "`dmuOut'", ///
        "CRS", "`ort'")
    deamain `dmui' `dmuIn' `dmuOut' `frameMat' "CRS" `ort' `stageForVRS' ///
        `tol1' `tol2' `trace'
    matrix `deamainrslt' = r(deamainrslt)
    matrix `vrsfrontier' = `deamainrslt'[1...,1], `vrsfrontier'
    matrix `crslambda' = `deamainrslt'[1...,2..(`dmuCount' + 1)]

    // 3. DRS TE(DRS Technical Efficiency)
    local stageForVRS = 1
    mata: _mkframemat("`frameMat'", "`dmuIn'", "`dmuOut'", ///
        "DRS", "`ort'")
    deamain `dmui' `dmuIn' `dmuOut' `frameMat' "DRS" `ort' `stageForVRS' ///
        `tol1' `tol2' `trace'
    matrix `deamainrslt' = r(deamainrslt)
    matrix `vrsfrontier' = `vrsfrontier', `deamainrslt'[1...,1] // VRS
    mata: _roundmat("`vrsfrontier'", 1e-14) // round off

    //
    matrix `vrsfrontier' = `vrsfrontier', J(rowsof(`vrsfrontier'), 2, 0)
    matrix rownames `vrsfrontier' = : colfullnames `dmuIn"
    matrix colnames `vrsfrontier' = CRS_TE VRS_TE DRS_TE SCALE RTS

    if ("`trace'" == "trace") matrix list `crslambda'
    forvalues i = 1/`=rowsof(`vrsfrontier')' {
        matrix `vrsfrontier'[`i',4] = /*
            */ float(`vrsfrontier'[`i',1]/`vrsfrontier'[`i',2])

        /*****************************************************************
        * if CRS(CCR) == VRS(BCC) then CRS
        * else
        *     if sum of λ equals to 1, then CRS mark
        *     if sum of λ is greater than 1, then DRS mark
        *     if sum of λ is less than 1, then IRS mark
        *****************************************************************/
        // (-1:drs, 0:crs, 1:irs)
        if (`vrsfrontier'[`i',1] == `vrsfrontier'[`i',2]) {
            matrix `vrsfrontier'[`i',5] = 0
        }
        else {
            local sumlambda = 0
            forvalues j = 1/`dmuCount' {
                if (`crslambda'[`i', `j'] < .) {
                    local sumlambda = `sumlambda' + `crslambda'[`i', `j']
```

```
            }
          }
          if (`sumlambda' < 1) {
              matrix `vrsfrontier'[`i',5] = 1 // irs mark
          }
          else { // if (`sumlambda' >= 1) {
              matrix `vrsfrontier'[`i',5] = -1 // drs mark
          }
        }
      }
    }

// ----------------------------------------------------------------------
// REPORT
// ----------------------------------------------------------------------
di as result ""
di as result "options: RTS(`rts') ORT(`ort') STAGE(`stage')"
di as result "`rts'-`ort'PUT Oriented DEA Efficiency Results:"
matrix list `dearslt', noblank nohalf noheader f(%9.6g)

if ("`saving'" != "") {
    // if the saving file exists and replace option not specified,
    // make the backup file.
    if ("`replace'" == "") {
        _backup_file `saving'
    }

    if ("`rts'" != "VRS") {
        restore, preserve
        svmat `dearslt', names(eqcol)
        capture {
            renpfix _
            renpfix ref ref_
            renpfix islack is_
            renpfix oslack os_
        }
        capture save `saving', replace

        // di as result ""
        // di as result "DEA Result file:"
        // list
    }
}
return matrix dearslt = `dearslt'

if ("`rts'" == "VRS") {
    if ("`trace'" == "trace") {
        di _n(2) as result "CRS lambda(λ)"
        matrix list `crslambda' , noblank nohalf noheader f(%9.6f)
    }

    // if you don't have to verify, you can comment the following sentence.
    di _n(2) as result "VRS Frontier(-1:drs, 0:crs, 1:irs)"
    matrix list `vrsfrontier', noblank nohalf noheader f(%9.6f)

    di _n(2) as result "VRS Frontier:"
    restore, preserve
    svmat `vrsfrontier', names(col)
    rename RTS RTSNUM
```

```
      qui generate RTS = "drs" if RTSNUM == -1
      qui replace RTS = "-" if RTSNUM == 0
      qui replace RTS = "irs" if RTSNUM == 1
      drop DRS_TE RTSNUM
      format CRS_TE VRS_TE SCALE %9.6f
      list
      if ("`saving'"!="") {
         capture save `saving', replace
      }
   }
   restore, preserve
end


*******************************************************************************
* backup file.
*******************************************************************************
program define _backup_file, rclass
   args saving

   local dotpos = strpos("`saving'",".")
   if (`dotpos' > 0) {
      mata: _file_exists("`saving'")
   }
   else {
      mata: _file_exists("`saving'.dta")
   }

   if r(fileexists) {
      local curdt = subinstr("`c(current_date)'", " ", "", .) + /*
         */ subinstr("`c(current_time)'", ":", "", .)
      if (`dotpos' > 0) {
         #del ;
         local savefn = substr("`saving'", 1, `dotpos' - 1) +
               "_bak_`curdt'" +
               substr("`saving'",`dotpos', .);
         #del cr
         qui copy "`saving'" "`savefn'", replace
      }
      else {
         local savefn = "`saving'_bak_`curdt'" + ".dta"
         qui copy "`saving'.dta" "`savefn'", replace
      }
   }
end


*******************************************************************************
* DEA: FDH - Data Envelopment Analysis: Free Disposal Hull Model
*******************************************************************************
program define _dea_fdh, rclass
   #del ;
   syntax , DMU(name) IVARS(string) OVARS(string) RTS(string) ORT(string)
   [
      STAGE(integer 2) TOL1(real 1e-3) TOL2(real 1e-12)
      TRACE SAVing(string) REPLACE
   ];
   #del cr

   preserve
   // di _n as input ///
```

```
//    "options: ORT(`ort') STAGE(`stage') SAVing(`saving')"
// di as input "Input Data:"
// list

// ------------------------------------------------------------------------

tempname dmuIn dmuOut frameMat dearslt
mkDmuMat `ivars', dmumat(`dmuIn') sprefix("i") dmu(`dmu')
mkDmuMat `ovars', dmumat(`dmuOut') sprefix("o") dmu(`dmu')
local dmuCount = colsof(`dmuIn')
if ("`ort'" == "OUT") local minrank = 1
else local minrank = 0


mata: _mkframemat("`frameMat'", "`dmuIn'", "`dmuOut'", ///
    "`rts'", "`ort'")

apply_fdh `dmuIn' `dmuOut' `ort' `stage' `frameMat' `trace'
matrix `dearslt' = r(fdhrslt)

mata: _dmurank("`dearslt'", ///
    `=rowsof(`dmuIn')', `=rowsof(`dmuOut')', `minrank', `tol2')
matrix `dearslt' = r(rank), `dearslt'

// use mata function '_setup_dearslt_names' because the maximum string
// variable length needs to be kept under the 244 for all the time
mata: _setup_dearslt_names("`dearslt'", "`dmuIn'", "`dmuOut'")


// ------------------------------------------------------------------------
// REPORT
// ------------------------------------------------------------------------
di as result ""
di as result "options: ORT(`ort') STAGE(`stage')"
di as result "FDH-`ort'PUT Oriented DEA Efficiency Results:"
matrix list `dearslt', noblank nohalf noheader f(%9.6g)

if ("`saving'" != "") {
    // if the saving file exists and replace option not specified,
    // make the backup file.
    if ("`replace'" == "") {
        _backup_file `saving'
    }

    restore, preserve
    svmat `dearslt', names(eqcol)
    capture {
        renpfix _
        renpfix ref ref_
        renpfix islack is_
        renpfix oslack os_
    }
    capture save `saving', replace

    // di as result ""
    // di as result "DEA Result file:"
    // list
}

return matrix dearslt = `dearslt'
restore, preserve
```

end

```
********************************************************************************
* Imprecise DEA - Imprecise Data Envelopment Analysis
********************************************************************************
program define idea, rclass
    #del ;
    syntax , DMU(name) IVARS(string) OVARS(string) RTS(string) ORT(string)
    [
        STAGE(integer 2) TOL1(real 1e-3) TOL2(real 1e-12)
        TRACE SAVing(string) REPLACE
        Bounded(varlist) ORDinal(varlist) CAtegorical(varlist)
    ];
    #del cr

    preserve
    // ----------------------------------------------------------------------
    // di _n as input ///
    //    "options: RTS(`rts') ORT(`ort') STAGE(`stage') SAVing(`saving')"
    // di as input "Input Data:"
    // list

    // 1. decomposition variables and make base matrix
    tempname baseMat dmuIn dmuOut dea_rslt vrs_frontier crs_lambda
    mkbasemat, dmu(`dmu') ivars(`ivars') ovars(`ovars') ///
        basemat(`baseMat') b(`bounded')

    // 2. make variables for dmui
    forvalues dmui = 1/`=rowsof(`baseMat')' {
        keep `dmu'
        qui svmat `baseMat', names(col)

        if ("`bounded'" != "") {
            foreach boundedVar of var `bounded' {
                if (regexm("`ivars'", "`boundedVar'")) {
                    // when input, itself choose min value.
                    qui replace `boundedVar' = `boundedVar'_2 if _n != `dmui'
                }
                else if(regexm("`ovars'", "`boundedVar'")) {
                    // when output, itself choose max value.
                    qui replace `boundedVar' = `boundedVar'_2 if _n == `dmui'
                }
                drop `boundedVar'_2
            } // end of foreach
        } // end of first if

        if ("`ordinal'" != "") {
            foreach ordVar of var `ordinal' {
                if (regexm("`ivars'", "`ordVar'")) {
                    // when input,
                    // 1. if it's superior dmu to itself,
                    //    then replace missing value.
                    // 2. if it's not missing value, then replace the 1.
                    // 3. if it's missing value, then replace the number of dmus
                    qui {
                        replace `ordVar' = . if `ordVar' < `ordVar'[`dmui']
                        replace `ordVar' = 1 if `ordVar' != .
                        replace `ordVar' = _N if `ordVar' == .
                    }
```

127

```
                  }
                  else if(regexm("`ovars'", "`ordVar'")) {
                     // when output,
                     // 1. if it's superior dmu to itself or itself,
                     //    then replace missing value.
                     // 2. if it's not missing value, then replace the 0.
                     // 3. if it's missing value, then replace the 1.
                     qui {
                         replace `ordVar' = . if `ordVar' <= `ordVar'[`dmui']
                         replace `ordVar' = 0 if `ordVar' != .
                         replace `ordVar' = 1 if `ordVar' == .
                     }
                  }
               } // end of foreach
            } // enf of if for `ordinal'

            run_dea_for_dmui, dmu(`dmu') ///
               ivars(`ivars') ovars(`ovars') ///
               rts(`rts') ort(`ort') ///
               stage(`stage') tol1(`tol1') tol2(`tol2') ///
               `trace' saving(`saving') `replace' dmui(`dmui')

         matrix `dmuIn' = r(dmuIn)
         matrix `dmuOut' = r(dmuOut)
         matrix `dea_rslt' = nullmat(`dea_rslt') \ r(dmui_dea_rslt)

         if ("`rts'" == "VRS") {
            matrix `vrs_frontier' = nullmat(`vrs_frontier')\r(dmui_vrs_frontier)
            matrix `crs_lambda' = nullmat(`crs_lambda')\r(dmui_crs_lambda)
         }
      } // end of forvalues

      if ("`ort'" == "OUT") local minrank = 1
      else local minrank = 0
      mata: _dmurank("`dea_rslt'", ///
            `=rowsof(`dmuIn')', `=rowsof(`dmuOut')', `minrank', `tol2')
      matrix `dea_rslt' = r(rank), `dea_rslt'

      // use mata function '_setup_dearslt_names' because the maximum string
      // variable length needs to be kept under the 244 for all the time
      mata: _setup_dearslt_names("`dea_rslt'", "`dmuIn'", "`dmuOut'")
      if ("`rts'" == "VRS") {
         matrix rownames `vrs_frontier' = `: colfullnames `dmuIn'"
         matrix colnames `vrs_frontier' = CRS_TE VRS_TE DRS_TE SCALE RTS
      }

      // ----------------------------------------------------------------
      restore, preserve

      // ----------------------------------------------------------------
      // REPORT
      // ----------------------------------------------------------------
      report_dea, dearslt(`dea_rslt') ///
            crslambda(`crs_lambda') ///
            vrsfrontier(`vrs_frontier') ///
            rts(`rts') ort(`ort') ///
            stage(`stage') `trace' saving(`saving') `replace'

      // return values
```

```
    return matrix dearslt = `dea_rslt'
    restore, preserve
end

********************************************************************************
* Make base Matrix: Decomposition String Variables to Numeric Variables
********************************************************************************
program define mkbasemat, rclass
    #del ;
    syntax , DMU(name) IVARS(string) OVARS(string) BASEMAT(name)
    [
        Bounded(varlist) ORDinal(varlist) CAtegorical(varlist)
    ];
    #del cr

    // 1. decomposition variables
    if ("`bounded'" != "") {
        foreach boundedVar of var `bounded' {
            qui split `boundedVar', p(",") ///
                gen("`boundedVar'_") destring i("[]")
            order `boundedVar'_*, after(`boundedVar')
            drop `boundedVar'
            ren `boundedVar'_1 `boundedVar'
        }
    }

    // 2. make matrix
    qui ds, has(type numeric)
    mkmat `r(varlist)', matrix(`basemat') rownames(`dmu')
    matrix `basemat' = `basemat'
end

********************************************************************************
* run DEA for dmui - run Data Envelopment Analysis
********************************************************************************
program define run_dea_for_dmui, rclass
    #del ;
    syntax , DMU(name) IVARS(string) OVARS(string) RTS(string) ORT(string)
    [
        STAGE(integer 2) TOL1(real 1e-3) TOL2(real 1e-12)
        TRACE SAVing(string) REPLACE DMUI(integer 0)
    ];
    #del cr

    tempname dmuIn dmuOut frameMat deamainrslt dearslt vrsfrontier crslambda
    mkDmuMat `ivars', dmumat(`dmuIn') sprefix("i") dmu(`dmu')
    mkDmuMat `ovars', dmumat(`dmuOut') sprefix("o") dmu(`dmu')
    local dmuCount = colsof(`dmuIn')

    mata: _mkframemat("`frameMat'", "`dmuIn'", "`dmuOut'", ///
        "`rts'", "`ort'")
    deamain `dmui' `dmuIn' `dmuOut' `frameMat' `rts' `ort' `stage' ///
        `tol1' `tol2' `trace'
    matrix `deamainrslt' = r(deamainrslt)

    if ("`rts'" == "VRS") {
        // caution : join order! (CRS -> VRS -> DRS)
        // 1. VRS TE(VRS Technical Efficiency)
        matrix `deamainrslt' = r(deamainrslt)
```

A Handbook of Data Envelopment Analysis @ Stata

```
matrix `vrsfrontier' = `deamainrslt'[1...,1]

// 2. CRS TE(CRS Technical Efficiency)
local stageforVRS = 2
mata: _mkframemat("`frameMat'", "`dmuIn'", "`dmuOut'", ///
    "CRS", "`ort'")
deamain `dmui' `dmuIn' `dmuOut' `frameMat' "CRS" `ort' `stageForVRS' ///
    `tol1' `tol2' `trace'
matrix `deamainrslt' = r(deamainrslt)
matrix `vrsfrontier' = `deamainrslt'[1...,1], `vrsfrontier'
matrix `crslambda' = `deamainrslt'[1...,2..(`dmuCount' + 1)]

// 3. DRS TE(DRS Technical Efficiency)
local stageforVRS = 1
mata: _mkframemat("`frameMat'", "`dmuIn'", "`dmuOut'", ///
    "DRS", "`ort'")
deamain `dmui' `dmuIn' `dmuOut' `frameMat' "DRS" `ort' `stageForVRS' ///
    `tol1' `tol2' `trace'
matrix `deamainrslt' = r(deamainrslt)
matrix `vrsfrontier' = `vrsfrontier', `deamainrslt'[1...,1] // VRS
mata: _roundmat("`vrsfrontier'", 1e-14) // round off

//
matrix `vrsfrontier' = `vrsfrontier', J(rowsof(`vrsfrontier'), 2, 0)

if ("`trace'" == "trace") matrix list `crslambda'
forvalues i = 1/`=rowsof(`vrsfrontier')' {
    /*****************************************************************
    * if CRS(CCR) == VRS(BCC) then CRS
    * else
    *    if sum of λ equals to 1, then CRS mark
    *    if sum of λ is greater than 1, then DRS mark
    *    if sum of λ is less than 1, then IRS mark
    *****************************************************************/
    // (-1:drs, 0:crs, 1:irs)
    if (`vrsfrontier'[`i',1] == `vrsfrontier'[`i',2]) {
        matrix `vrsfrontier'[`i',5] = 0
    }
    else {
        local sumlambda = 0
        forvalues j = 1/`dmuCount' {
            if (`crslambda'[`i', `j'] < .) {
                local sumlambda = `sumlambda' + `crslambda'[`i', `j']
            }
        }
        if (`sumlambda' < 1) {
            matrix `vrsfrontier'[`i',5] = 1 // irs mark
        }
        else { // if (`sumlambda' >= 1) {
            matrix `vrsfrontier'[`i',5] = -1 // drs mark
        }
    } // end of first if~else
} // end of forvalues
} // end of vrs

// return values
return matrix dmuIn = `dmuIn'
return matrix dmuOut = `dmuOut'
return matrix dmui_dea_rslt = `deamainrslt'
```

130

```
if ("`rts'" == "VRS") {
    return matrix dmui_vrs_frontier = `vrsfrontier'
    return matrix dmui_crs_lambda = `crslambda'
}
end

*****************************************************************************
* REPORT
*****************************************************************************
program define report_dea, rclass
    #del ;
    syntax , dearslt(name) crslambda(name) vrsfrontier(name)
        RTS(string) ORT(string)
    [
        STAGE(integer 2) TRACE SAVing(string) REPLACE
    ];
    #del cr

    preserve

    di as result ""
    di as result "options: RTS(`rts') ORT(`ort') STAGE(`stage')"
    di as result "`rts'-`ort'PUT Oriented DEA Efficiency Results:"
    matrix list `dearslt', noblank nohalf noheader f(%9.6g)

    if ("`saving'" != "") {
        // if the saving file exists and replace option not specified,
        // make the backup file.
        if ("`replace'" == "") {
            _backup_file `saving'
        }

        if ("`rts'" != "VRS") {
            restore, preserve
            svmat `dearslt', names(eqcol)
            capture {
                renpfix _
                renpfix ref ref_
                renpfix islack is_
                renpfix oslack os_
            }
            capture save `saving', replace

            // di as result ""
            // di as result "DEA Result file:"
            // list
        }
    }

    if ("`rts'" == "VRS") {
        if ("`trace'" == "trace") {
            di _n(2) as result "CRS lambda(λ)"
            matrix list `crslambda' , noblank nohalf noheader f(%9.6f)
        }

        // if you don't have to verify, you can comment the following sentence.
        di _n(2) as result "VRS Frontier(-1:drs, 0:crs, 1:irs)"
        matrix list `vrsfrontier', noblank nohalf noheader f(%9.6f)
```

```
        di _n(2) as result "VRS Frontier:"
        restore, preserve
        svmat `vrsfrontier', names(col)
        rename RTS RTSNUM
        qui generate RTS = "drs" if RTSNUM == -1
        qui replace RTS = "-" if RTSNUM == 0
        qui replace RTS = "irs" if RTSNUM == 1
        drop DRS_TE RTSNUM
        format CRS_TE VRS_TE SCALE %9.6f
        list
        if ("`saving'"!="") {
            capture save `saving', replace
        }
    }

    restore, preserve
end


*****************************************************************************
* DEA Main - Data Envelopment Analysis Main
*****************************************************************************
program define deamain, rclass
    args dmui dmuIn dmuOut frameMat rts ort stage tol1 tol2 trace
    tempname efficientVec deamainrslt

    // stage step 1.
    if ("`trace'" == "trace") {
        di _n(2) as txt "RTS(`rts') ORT(`ort') 1st stage."
    }
    mata: _dealp("`frameMat'", "`dmuIn'", "`dmuOut'", "`rts'", "`ort'", ///
        1, `tol1', `tol2', "", "`efficientVec'", "`trace'", ///
        `dmui')
    matrix `deamainrslt' = r(dealprslt)

    // stage step 2.
    if ("`stage'" == "2") {
        if ("`trace'" == "trace") {
            di _n(2) as txt "RTS(`rts') ORT(`ort') 2nd stage."
        }
        matrix `efficientVec' = `deamainrslt'[1...,1]

        mata: _dealp("`frameMat'", "`dmuIn'", "`dmuOut'", "`rts'", "`ort'", ///
            2, `tol1', `tol2', "", "`efficientVec'", "`trace'", ///
            `dmui')
        matrix `deamainrslt' = r(dealprslt)
    }

    return matrix deamainrslt = `deamainrslt'
end


*****************************************************************************
* apply FDH(Free Disposal Hull) Model
*****************************************************************************
program define apply_fdh, rclass
    args dmuIn dmuOut ort stage frameMat trace
    tempname fdhrslt

    // stage step 1.
    if ("`trace'" == "trace") {
```

```
    di _n(2) as txt "FDH ORT(`ort') 1st stage."
  }
  mata: _fdh("`dmuIn'", "`dmuOut'", "`ort'", ///
    1, "`frameMat'", "`fdhrslt'", "`trace'")
  matrix `fdhrslt' = r(fdhrslt)

  // stage step 2.
  if ("`stage'" == "2") {
    if ("`trace'" == "trace") {
      di _n(2) as txt "FDH ORT(`ort') 2nd stage."
    }

    mata: _fdh("`dmuIn'", "`dmuOut'", "`ort'", ///
      2, "`frameMat'", "`fdhrslt'", "`trace'")
    matrix `fdhrslt' = r(fdhrslt)
  }

  return matrix fdhrslt = `fdhrslt'
end

// Make DMU Matrix -----------------------------------------------------------
program define mkDmuMat
  #del ;
  syntax varlist(numeric) [if] [in], DMUmat(name)
  [
    SPREfix(string)
    DMU(name)
  ];
  #del cr

  qui ds
  // variable not found error
  if ("`varlist'" == "") {
    di as err "variable not found"
    exit 111
  }

  // make matrix
  mkmat `varlist' `if' `in', matrix(`dmumat') rownames(`dmu')
  matrix roweq `dmumat' = "dmu"
  matrix coleq `dmumat' = `=lower("`sprefix'")' + "slack'"
  matrix `dmumat' = `dmumat''
end

// Start of the MATA Definition Area -----------------------------------------
version 10
mata:
mata set matastrict on

/**
 * FDH - Branch & Bounded Method
 */
function _fdh (
    string scalar dmuIn,
    string scalar dmuOut,
    string scalar ort,

    real scalar stagestep,
    string scalar frameMat,
```

```
        string scalar pre_fdhrslt,

        string scalar trace )
{
    real matrix F, DI, DO, FDHRSLT

    DI = st_matrix(dmuIn)
    DO = st_matrix(dmuOut)

    if (stagestep == 1) {
        FDHRSLT = fdh_stage1(DI, DO, ort, trace)
    }
    else { // if (stagestep == 2)
        F  = st_matrix(frameMat)
        FDHRSLT = st_matrix(pre_fdhrslt)

        FDHRSLT = fdh_stage2(DI, DO, ort, F, FDHRSLT, trace)
    }

    st_matrix("r(fdhrslt)", FDHRSLT)
}

/**
 * FDH StageI - Branch & Bounded Method
 */
real matrix function fdh_stage1 (
        real matrix DI,
        real matrix DO,
        string scalar ort,
        string scalar trace )
{
    // TM: Theta Metirx, CM: Condition Metrix
    real matrix FDHRSLT, LPRSLT, TM, CM, VM
    real scalar dmus, slackins, slackouts, slacks
    real scalar dmui, init_value, cond_value, mi, mw
    string scalar tracename

    dmus = cols(DI) // or cols(DO), because cols(DI) == cols(DO)
    slackins = rows(DI); slackouts = rows(DO)
    slacks = slackins + slackouts

    tracename = ort + "-SI"

    // define init and condition value
    init_value = 1; cond_value = dmus;

    FDHRSLT = J(0, 1 + dmus + slacks, 0)
    if (ort == "IN") {
        for (dmui=init_value; dmui<=cond_value; dmui++) {
            TM = DI:/DI[,dmui]      //; TM //
        CM = ((TM:>0):&(TM:<=1))  //; CM // 0 < theta <= 1
        CM = CM \ DO:>=DO[,dmui]   //; CM // consider output structural constraint

            VM = J(2, dmus, .) // index \ value
            LPRSLT = J(1, cols(FDHRSLT), 0)

            for(i=1; i<=dmus; i++) {
                LPRSLT[1] = .
                if (all(CM[,i])) {
```

```
            maxindex(TM[,i], 1, mi, mw)
            VM[,i] = (mi[1] \ TM[mi[1],i])
          }
      }

      minindex(VM[2,], 1, mi, mw);
      LPRSLT[1] = VM[2, mi[1]]
      for(i=1; i <= rows(mi); i++) {
         LPRSLT[1+mi[i]] = 1
      }
      FDHRSLT = FDHRSLT \ LPRSLT
   }
}
else { // if (ort == "OUT")
   for (dmui=init_value; dmui<=cond_value; dmui++) {
      TM = DO:/DO[,dmui]  //; TM //
      CM = TM:>=1         //; CM // 1 <= etha
      CM = CM \ DI:<=DI[,dmui] //; CM // consider input structural constraint

      VM = J(2, dmus, .) // index \ value
      LPRSLT = J(1, cols(FDHRSLT), 0)
      for(i=1; i<=dmus; i++) {
         LPRSLT[1] = .
         if (all(CM[,i])) {
            minindex(TM[,i], 1, mi, mw)
            VM[,i] = (mi[1] \ TM[mi[1],i])
         }
      }
      maxindex(VM[2,], 1, mi, mw)
      LPRSLT[1] = VM[2, mi[1]]
      for(i=1; i <= rows(mi); i++) {
         LPRSLT[1+mi[i]] = 1
      }
      FDHRSLT = FDHRSLT \ LPRSLT
   }
}

return(FDHRSLT)
}

/**
 * FDH StageII - Branch & Bounded Method
 */
real matrix function fdh_stage2 (
      real matrix DI,
      real matrix DO,
      string scalar ort,

      real matrix F,
      real matrix FDHRSLT,
      string scalar trace )
{
   // SVM: Slack Values Metrix
   real matrix M, SVM, SVM2, T
   real scalar dmus, slackins, slackouts, slacks, sum_of_slacks, base_lamda
   real scalar fcols, dmui, init_value, cond_value, mi, mw, base_lamda_count
   real colvector LVec // Lamda Vector
   string scalar tracename
```

```
dmus = cols(DI) // or cols(DO), because cols(DI) == cols(DO)
slackins = rows(DI); slackouts = rows(DO)
slacks = slackins + slackouts
fcols = cols(F)

tracename = ort + "-SII"

// define init and condition value
init_value = 1; cond_value = dmus;

if (ort == "IN") {
    for (dmui=init_value; dmui<=cond_value; dmui++) {
    M = F[1::1+slacks,]
    replacesubmat(M, 2, 2, DI[,dmui]*FDHRSLT[dmui, 1]) // DI*theta
    replacesubmat(M, 2+slackins, fcols, DO[,dmui])  // DO at RHS

    LVec = FDHRSLT[dmui, 2..1+dmus]
    maxindex(LVec, 1, mi, mw)
    base_lamda_count = rows(mi)
    if (base_lamda_count > 1) {
        base_lamda = mi[1]
        SVM = mksvm(M, base_lamda)
        sum_of_slacks = sum(SVM)
        for(i=2; i<=base_lamda_count; i++) {
            SVM2 = mksvm(M, mi[i])
            if (sum_of_slacks < sum(SVM2)) {
                FDHRSLT[dmui, 1+base_lamda] = 0; // set 0 at pre-lamda

                // Save current lamda
                base_lamda = mi[i]
                SVM = SVM2
                sum_of_slacks = sum(SVM)
            }
            else {
                FDHRSLT[dmui, 1+mi[i]] = 0; // set 0 at lamda
            }
        }
    }
    else {
        SVM = mksvm(M, mi[1])
    }
    replacesubmat(FDHRSLT, dmui, 2+dmus, SVM[2::1+slacks]')
    }
}
else { // if (ort == "OUT")
    for (dmui=init_value; dmui<=cond_value; dmui++) {
    M = F[1::1+slacks,]
    replacesubmat(M, 2, fcols, DI[,dmui])  // DI at RHS
    replacesubmat(M, 2+slackins, 2,
        DO[,dmui]*FDHRSLT[dmui, 1])     // DO*etha

    LVec = FDHRSLT[dmui, 2..1+dmus]
    maxindex(LVec, 1, mi, mw)
    base_lamda_count = rows(mi)
    if (base_lamda_count > 1) {
        base_lamda = mi[1]
        SVM = mksvm(M, base_lamda)
        sum_of_slacks = sum(SVM)
        for(i=2; i<=base_lamda_count; i++) {
```

```
            SVM2 = mksvm(M, mi[i])
            if (sum_of_slacks < sum(SVM2)) {
                FDHRSLT[dmui, 1+base_lamda] = 0; // set 0 at pre-lamda

                // Save current lamda
                base_lamda = mi[i]
                SVM = SVM2
                sum_of_slacks = sum(SVM)
            }
            else {
                FDHRSLT[dmui, 1+mi[i]] = 0; // set 0 at lamda
            }
          }
        }
        else {
          SVM = mksvm(M, mi[1])
        }
        // Because original formula is [etha - (sumOfLamda) + slackOut = 0]
        // but we calculated [etha - (sumOfLamda) = -slackOut]
        // so multiple minus at the results.
        replacesubmat(FDHRSLT, dmui, 2+dmus, -(SVM[2::1+slacks]'))
    }
  }

  return(FDHRSLT)
}

/**
 * Make Slace Value Matrix.
 */
real matrix function mksvm (
    real matrix M,          // Base Matrix that dmui's Theta is applied
    real scalar base_lamda )
{
  // 2: Theta, 2+base_lamda: lamda, cols(M): rhs
  return (M[,2] :+ M[,2+base_lamda] :+ (-M[,cols(M)]))
}

/**
 * FDH - Branch & Bounded Method
 */
real matrix function fdh_backup (
    real matrix F,
    real matrix DI,
    real matrix DO,
    string scalar rts,
    string scalar ort,
    real scalar stagestep,
    real scalar tol1,
    real scalar tol2,
    real colvector effvec,
    string scalar trace,
    real scalar _dmui  )
{
  real matrix M, VARS, LPRSLT, FDHRSLT, ARTIF
  real scalar dmus, slackins, slackouts, slacks, artificials, artificialrow
  real scalar frows, fcols, isin, i, dmui, mindmui, maxdmui
  real colvector l_effvec, skipdmu
  string scalar tracename
```

```
struct BoundCond matrix boundF, boundM
struct LpParamStruct scalar param




if (cols(DI) != cols(DO)) {
    _error(3200, "in and out count of dmu is not match!")
}
if (!(rts == "CRS" || rts == "VRS" || rts == "IRS" || rts == "DRS")) {
    _error(3498, "rts must be one of CRS, VRS, IRS, DRS")
}

// basic value setting for artificial variabels
isin = (ort == "IN")
frows = rows(F); fcols = cols(F)
dmus = cols(DI) // or cols(DO), because cols(DI) == cols(DO)
slackins = rows(DI); slackouts = rows(DO)

tracename = rts + "-" + ort + "-" + (stagestep == 1 ? "SI" : "SII")

// -------------------------------------------------------------------------
// define number of slacks by rts
if (rts == "CRS" || rts == "VRS") slacks = slackins + slackouts
else if (rts == "IRS" || rts == "DRS") slacks = slackins + slackouts + 1

// define number of artificials by rts, ort, stage
if (rts == "CRS" || rts == "DRS") {
    if (stagestep == 1) {
        if (isin) {
            artificials = slackins+slackouts; artificialrow = 2;
        }
        else artificials = 0
    }
    else {
        artificials = slackouts; artificialrow = 2+slackins;
    }
}
else if (rts == "VRS" || rts == "IRS") {
    if (stagestep == 1) {
        if (isin) {
            artificials = slackins+slackouts+1; artificialrow = 2;
        }
        else {
            artificials = 1; artificialrow = frows //== 2+slackins+slackouts
        }
    }
    else {
        artificials = slackouts+1; artificialrow = 2+slackins;
    }
}
if (artificials > 0) {
    ARTIF = J(1, artificials, 1) \ J(frows-1, artificials, 0)
    replacesubmat(ARTIF, artificialrow, 1, I(artificials))
    F = F[,1..fcols-1], ARTIF, F[,fcols]
    frows = rows(F); fcols = cols(F) // revise frows, fcols
```

```
}
// ------------------------------------------------------------------------

// constants value to right-hand side(rhs) and both sides multiplied by -1.
if (stagestep == 2) {
    l_effvec = effvec
    skipdmu = (effvec :== .)
    if (isin) {
        replacesubmat(F, 2, 3, -F[2..1+slackins,3::2+dmus+slackins])
    }
    else {
        replacesubmat(F, 2+slackins, 3,
            -F[2+slackins..1+slackins+slackouts,3::2+dmus+slacks])
    }
}
else skipdmu = J(1, dmus, 0)
// ------------------------------------------------------------------------
boundF = J(1, fcols, BoundCond());
// set the boundary for the efficiency variable(theta, eta):
// -INFINITE <= efficiency <= INFINITE
boundF[1,2].val = 0; boundF[1,2].lower = 0; boundF[1,2].upper = .

// set boundary for the weight variable(lamda, mu):
// 0 <= weight <= INFINITE
for (i=3; i<dmus+3; i++) {
    boundF[1,i].val = 0; boundF[1,i].lower = 0; boundF[1,i].upper = .
}

// set boundary for the non-structural variable(slack, artificial).
// 0 <= slacks and atrificials <= INFINITE
for (i=dmus+3; i<fcols; i++) {
    boundF[1,i].val = 0; boundF[1,i].lower = 0; boundF[1,i].upper = .
}
// liststruct(boundF); // for debug

// set the lp's parameters
param.rts          = rts
param.isin         = isin
param.stagestep    = stagestep
param.dmus         = dmus
param.slacks       = slacks
param.artificials  = artificials
param.tol1         = tol1
param.tol2         = tol2
param.trace        = trace
// liststruct(param); // for debug
// ------------------------------------------------------------------------
FDHRSLT = J(0, 1+ dmus + slacks, 0)

// Added by Brian(2012.06.30)
if (_dmui <= 0 || _dmui >= .) {
    mindmui = 1; maxdmui = dmus;
}
else {
    mindmui = _dmui; maxdmui = _dmui;
    if (stagestep == 2) {
        l_effvec = J(1, dmus, effvec[1])
        skipdmu = (l_effvec :== .)
    }
}
```

```
        }

        if (isin) {
            for (dmui=mindmui; dmui<=maxdmui; dmui++) {
                if (skipdmu[dmui]) {
                    LPRSLT = J(1, cols(FDHRSLT), .)
                }
                else {
                    M = F; boundM = boundF
                    if (stagestep == 1) replacesubmat(M, 2, 2, DI[,dmui])
                    else replacesubmat(M, 2, fcols, DI[,dmui]*l_effvec[dmui])
                    replacesubmat(M, 2+slackins, fcols, DO[,dmui])

                    // execute LP
                    VARS  = lp_phase1(M, boundM, dmui, tracename, param)
                    if (VARS[1,1] == .) {
                        LPRSLT = J(1, cols(FDHRSLT), .)
                    }
                    else {
                        LPRSLT = lp_phase2(M, boundM, VARS, dmui, tracename, param);
                    }
                }

                FDHRSLT = FDHRSLT \ LPRSLT
            }
        }
        else {
            for (dmui=mindmui; dmui<=maxdmui; dmui++) {
                if (skipdmu[dmui]) {
                    LPRSLT = J(1, cols(FDHRSLT), .)
                }
                else {
                    M = F; boundM = boundF
                    replacesubmat(M, 2, fcols, DI[,dmui])
                    if (stagestep == 1) {
                        if (rts == "CRS" || rts == "DRS") M[1,2] = -1
                        replacesubmat(M, 2+slackins, 2, DO[,dmui])
                    }
                    else replacesubmat(M, 2+slackins, fcols, DO[,dmui]*l_effvec[dmui])

                    // execute LP
                    if (artificials == 0) { // if artificials == 0 then skip phase 1
                        VARS  = (0, 2+dmus..1+dmus+slacks, 1..1+dmus, 0)
                        M = M[,1],
                            M[,VARS[,2::cols(VARS)-1] :+ 1],
                            M[,cols(M)]
                        boundM = boundM[,1],
                            boundM[,VARS[,2::cols(VARS)-1] :+ 1],
                            boundM[,cols(M)]
                    }
                    else {
                        VARS = lp_phase1(M, boundM, dmui, tracename, param)
                    }

                    if (VARS[1,1] == .) {
                        LPRSLT = J(1, cols(FDHRSLT), .)
                    }
                    else {
                        LPRSLT = lp_phase2(M, boundM, VARS, dmui, tracename, param);
```

```
        }
      }
        FDHRSLT = FDHRSLT \ LPRSLT
      }
    }

    // adjust efficiency
    if (stagestep == 2) {
      replacesubmat(FDHRSLT, 1, 1, effvec)
    }
    return(FDHRSLT)
  }

  end
// End of the MATA Definition Area --------------------------------------------
```

B2.2 ldea.do

```
// Start of the MATA Definition Area ------------------------------------------
version 10
mata:
mata clear
mata set matastrict on

/** HISTORY:
 * ---------------------------------------------------------------------
 * 2012-09-22(SAT): Deprecate and Remove minsubscript Option
 * -------------------------------------------------------------------------*/

/**
 * Declare the variable's boundary condition structure.
 */
struct BoundCond {
    real scalar val, lower, upper, free
}

/**
 * Declare the LP(RSM: Revised Simplex Method)'s parameter structure.
 * Substitute for the LpParamStruct in the feature.
 */
struct LpParam {
    real scalar minYn      // whether minimization or maximization

    real scalar vars       // number of variables
    real scalar slacks     // number of slacks
    real scalar artificials // number of artificials

    real scalar tol1       // tolerance 1
    real scalar tol2       // tolerance 2
    string scalar trace    // whether trace or not.
    string scalar tracename // trancename
}

/**
 * Declare the LP(for DEA)'s parameter structure.
 */
struct LpParamStruct {
    string scalar rts      // return to scale(CRS|VRS|IRS|DRS)
    real scalar isin       // if 1 then 'in', other then 'out'
    real scalar stagestep  // stage step. 1 or 2
    real scalar minYn      // whether minimization or maximization

    real scalar dmus       // number of dmus
    real scalar dmuins     // number of inputs per dmu
    real scalar dmuouts    // number of outputs per dmu
    real scalar slacks     // number of slacks
    real scalar artificials // number of artificials

    real scalar tol1       // tolerance 1
    real scalar tol2       // tolerance 2
    real scalar isminsubscript // whether min subscript or not.(Deprecated)
    string scalar trace    // whether trace or not.
}
```

142

```
/**
 * Declare the LP's result structure.
 */
struct LpResultStruct {
    real scalar xVal         // objective funtion value.
    real matrix XB                    // basic feasible solution.
    real scalar rc           // return code(zero means success)
    string scalar rmsg       // return message
}

/**
 * Declare the LP's tableau structure.
 */
struct LpTableauStruct {
    pointer(real matrix) scalar CB, CNj
    pointer(real matrix) scalar  B,  Nj, b
    pointer(real matrix) scalar Bi,CBBi, rawXB, XB
}

/**
 * make frame matrix and set matrix value at the param frameMat
 * rts - return to scale, ort - orientation
 */
function _mkframemat( string scalar frameMat,
            string scalar dmuIn,
            string scalar dmuOut,
            string scalar rts,
            string scalar ort )
{
    real matrix F, DI, DO

    DI = st_matrix(dmuIn)
    DO = st_matrix(dmuOut)

    F = mkframemat(DI, DO, rts, ort)

    // return result
    st_matrix(frameMat, F)
}

/**
 * make simplex method frame matrix
 * rts - return to scale, ort - orientation
 */
real matrix function mkframemat(
            real matrix DI,
            real matrix DO,
            string scalar rts,
            string scalar ort )
{
    real matrix F
    real scalar row, col, sig
    real scalar dmus, slackins, slackouts, slacks
    real scalar frows, fcols

    if (cols(DI) != cols(DO)) {
        _error(3200, "in and out count of dmu is not match!")
    }
```

143

```
// basic value setting for artificial variabels
sig = ((ort == "IN") ? -1 : 1)

dmus = cols(DI) // or cols(DO), because cols(DI) == cols(DO)
slackins = rows(DI); slackouts = rows(DO)
if (rts == "CRS") {
        slacks = slackins + slackouts
   // target coefficient\slackins\slackouts
   frows = 1 + slackins + slackouts
            // target coefficient,theta,dmus,slackins,slackouts,rhs
   fcols = 1 + 1 + dmus + slackins + slackouts + 1
}
else if (rts == "VRS") {
        slacks = slackins + slackouts
   // target coefficient\slackins\slackouts\sum of lamda
   frows = 1 + slackins + slackouts + 1
            // target coefficient,theta,dmus,slackins,slackouts,rhs
   fcols = 1 + 1 + dmus + slackins + slackouts + 1
}
else if (rts == "IRS") {
   slacks = slackins + slackouts + 1
   // target coefficient\slackins\slackouts\sum of lamda
   frows = 1 + slackins + slackouts + 1
            // target coefficient,theta,dmus,slackins,slackouts,sum of lamda,rhs
   fcols = 1 + 1 + dmus + slackins + slackouts + 1 + 1
}
else if (rts == "DRS") {
   slacks = slackins + slackouts + 1
   // target coefficient\slackins\slackouts\sum of lamda
   frows = 1 + slackins + slackouts + 1
            // target coefficient,theta,dmus,slackins,slackouts,sum of lamda,rhs
   fcols = 1 + 1 + dmus + slackins + slackouts + 1 + 1
}
else {
   _error(3498, "invalid rts optoin.")
}

// make frame matrix for CRS(CCR)
F = J(frows, fcols, 0)
F[1, 1] = 1
replacesubmat(F, 2, 3, sig * DI)
replacesubmat(F, 2 + slackins, 3, -sig * DO)
replacesubmat(F, 2, 3 + dmus, sig * I(slacks))

// adjustment
if (rts == "VRS") {
   replacesubmat(F, frows, 3, J(1, dmus, 1))
   F[frows,fcols] = 1
}
else if (rts == "IRS") {
   replacesubmat(F, frows, 3, J(1, dmus, 1))
   F[frows,2 + dmus + slacks] = -1
   F[frows,fcols] = 1
}
else if (rts == "DRS") {
   replacesubmat(F, frows, 3, J(1, dmus, 1))
   F[frows,2 + dmus + slacks] = 1
   F[frows,fcols] = 1
```

```
    }

    // return result
    return(F)
}

/**
 * DEA Loop - Data Envelopment Analysis Loop for DMUs
 */
function _dealp ( string scalar frameMat,
            string scalar dmuIn,
            string scalar dmuOut,
            string scalar rts,
            string scalar ort,
            real scalar stagestep,
            real scalar tol1,
            real scalar tol2,
            string scalar minsubscript, // Deprecated
            string scalar efficientVec,
            string scalar trace,
                        | real scalar dmui )
{
    real matrix F, DI, DO, DEALPRSLT
    real colvector effvec

    F  = st_matrix(frameMat)
    DI = st_matrix(dmuIn)
    DO = st_matrix(dmuOut)
    if (stagestep == 2) {
        effvec = st_matrix(efficientVec)
    }

    DEALPRSLT = dealp(F, DI, DO, rts, ort, stagestep, tol1, tol2,
                        minsubscript, effvec, trace, dmui)

    st_matrix("r(dealprslt)", DEALPRSLT)
}

/**
 * DEA Loop - Data Envelopment Analysis Loop for DMUs
 */
real matrix function dealp (
                real matrix F,
                real matrix DI,
                real matrix DO,
                string scalar rts,
                string scalar ort,
                real scalar stagestep,
                real scalar tol1,
                real scalar tol2,
                string scalar minsubscript, // Deprecated
                real colvector effvec,
                string scalar trace,
                real scalar _dmui  )
{
    real matrix M, VARS, LPRSLT, DEALPRSLT, ARTIF
    real scalar dmus, slackins, slackouts, slacks, artificials, artificialrow
    real scalar frows, fcols, isin, i, dmui, mindmui, maxdmui
    real colvector l_effvec, skipdmu
```

145

```
string scalar tracename

struct BoundCond matrix boundF, boundM
struct LpParamStruct scalar param

if (cols(DI) != cols(DO)) {
    _error(3200, "in and out count of dmu is not match!")
}
if (!(rts == "CRS" || rts == "VRS" || rts == "IRS" || rts == "DRS")) {
        _error(3498, "rts must be one of CRS, VRS, IRS, DRS")
}


// basic value setting for artificial variabels
isin = (ort == "IN")
frows = rows(F); fcols = cols(F)
dmus = cols(DI) // or cols(DO), because cols(DI) == cols(DO)
slackins = rows(DI); slackouts = rows(DO)

tracename = rts + "-" + ort + "-" + (stagestep == 1 ? "SI" : "SII")

// ------------------------------------------------------------------------
// define number of slacks by rts
if (rts == "CRS" || rts == "VRS") slacks = slackins + slackouts
else if (rts == "IRS" || rts == "DRS") slacks = slackins + slackouts + 1

// define number of artificials by rts, ort, stage
if (rts == "CRS" || rts == "DRS") {
            if (stagestep == 1) {
                if (isin) {
                        artificials = slackins+slackouts; artificialrow = 2;
                }
                else artificials = 0
            }
            else {
                artificials = slackouts; artificialrow = 2+slackins;
            }
}
else if (rts == "VRS" || rts == "IRS") {
            if (stagestep == 1) {
                if (isin) {
                        artificials = slackins+slackouts+1; artificialrow =
2;
                }
                else {
                        artificials = 1; artificialrow = frows  //==
2+slackins+slackouts
                }
            }
            else {
                artificials = slackouts+1; artificialrow = 2+slackins
            }
}
if (artificials > 0) {
            ARTIF = J(1, artificials, 1) \ J(frows-1, artificials, 0)
            replacesubmat(ARTIF, artificialrow, 1, I(artificials))
            F = F[,1..fcols-1], ARTIF, F[,fcols]
            frows = rows(F); fcols = cols(F) // revise frows, fcols
}
// ------------------------------------------------------------------------
```

```
// constants value to right-hand side(rhs) and both sides multiplied by -1.
if (stagestep == 2) {
        l_effvec = effvec
        skipdmu = (effvec :== .)
        if (isin) {
            replacesubmat(F, 2, 3, -F[2..1+slackins,3::2+dmus+slackins])
        }
        else {
            replacesubmat(F, 2+slackins, 3,
        -F[2+slackins..1+slackins+slackouts,3::2+dmus+slacks])
            }
}
else skipdmu = J(1, dmus, 0)
// -----------------------------------------------------------------------
boundF = J(1, fcols, BoundCond());
// set the boundary for the efficiency variable(theta, eta):
// -INFINITE <= efficiency <= INFINITE
boundF[1,2].val = 0; boundF[1,2].lower = 0; boundF[1,2].upper = .

// set boundary for the weight variable(lamda, mu):
// 0 <= weight <= INFINITE
for (i=3; i<dmus+3; i++) {
        boundF[1,i].val = 0; boundF[1,i].lower = 0; boundF[1,i].upper = .
}

// set boundary for the non-structural variable(slack, artificial).
// 0 <= slacks and atrificials <= INFINITE
for (i=dmus+3; i<fcols; i++) {
        boundF[1,i].val = 0; boundF[1,i].lower = 0; boundF[1,i].upper = .
}
// liststruct(boundF); // for debug

// set the lp's parameters
param.rts         = rts
param.isin                          = isin
param.stagestep   = stagestep
param.dmus        = dmus
param.slacks      = slacks
param.artificials = artificials
param.tol1        = tol1
param.tol2        = tol2
param.trace       = trace
// liststruct(param); // for debug
// -----------------------------------------------------------------------
DEALPRSLT = J(0, 1+ dmus + slacks, 0)

// Added by Brian(2012.06.30)
if (_dmui <= 0 || _dmui >= .) {
        mindmui = 1; maxdmui = dmus;
}
else {
        mindmui = _dmui; maxdmui = _dmui;
        if (stagestep == 2) {
                l_effvec = J(1, dmus, effvec[1])
                skipdmu = (l_effvec :== .)
        }
}
```

```
		if (isin) {
			for (dmui=mindmui; dmui<=maxdmui; dmui++) {
				if (skipdmu[dmui]) {
					LPRSLT = J(1, cols(DEALPRSLT), .)
				}
				else {
					M = F; boundM = boundF
					if (stagestep == 1) replacesubmat(M, 2, 2, DI[,dmui])
					else		replacesubmat(M, 2, fcols, DI[,dmui]*l_effvec[dmui])
					replacesubmat(M, 2+slackins, fcols, DO[,dmui])

					// execute LP
					VARS	= lp_phase1(M, boundM, dmui, tracename, param)
					if (VARS[1,1] == .) {
						LPRSLT = J(1, cols(DEALPRSLT), .)
					}
					else {
						LPRSLT = lp_phase2(M, boundM, VARS, dmui, tracename, param);
					}
				}

			DEALPRSLT = DEALPRSLT \ LPRSLT
			}
		}
		else {
			for (dmui=mindmui; dmui<=maxdmui; dmui++) {
				if (skipdmu[dmui]) {
					LPRSLT = J(1, cols(DEALPRSLT), .)
				}
				else {
					M = F; boundM = boundF
					replacesubmat(M, 2, fcols, DI[,dmui])
					if (stagestep == 1) {
						if (rts == "CRS" || rts == "DRS")
							replacesubmat(M, 2+slackins, 2, M[1,2] = -1  DO[,dmui])
					}
					else	replacesubmat(M, 2+slackins, fcols, DO[,dmui]*l_effvec[dmui])

					// execute LP
					if (artificials == 0) { // if artificials == 0 then skip phase 1
						VARS	= (0, 2+dmus..1+dmus+slacks, 1..1+dmus, 0)
						M = M[,1],
							M[,VARS[,2::cols(VARS)-1] :+ 1],
							M[,cols(M)]
						boundM = boundM[,1],
							boundM[,VARS[,2::cols(VARS)-1] :+ 1],
							boundM[,cols(M)]
```

```
                                                }
                                                else {
                                                        VARS  =  lp_phase1(M,  boundM,
dmui, tracename, param)
                                                }

                                                if (VARS[1,1] == .) {
                                                        LPRSLT = J(1, cols(DEALPRSLT), .)
                                                }
                                                else {
                                                        LPRSLT  =  lp_phase2(M,  boundM,
VARS, dmui, tracename, param);
                                                }
                                        }
                        DEALPRSLT = DEALPRSLT \ LPRSLT
                }
        }

        // adjust efficiency
        if (stagestep == 2) {
                replacesubmat(DEALPRSLT, 1, 1, effvec)
        }
        return(DEALPRSLT)
}

real matrix function lp_phase1 ( real matrix M,
                        struct BoundCond matrix boundM,
                        real scalar dmui,
                        string scalar aTracename,
                        struct LpParamStruct scalar param )
{
        real matrix T, VARS
        real scalar i, j, w, mrows, mcols, phase
        real vector reorderidx, bfsidx, nonbfsidx
        string scalar tracename, msg
        struct LpResultStruct scalar lpresult

        mrows = rows(M); mcols = cols(M)
        tracename = aTracename + "-PI"

        // 1st: initialize matrix.
        if (param.trace == "trace") {
                displayas("txt")
                printf("\n\n\n---------[PHASE I]----------")
                printf("\n[DMUi=%g]%s: initialize matrix.\n",
                    dmui, tracename); M
        }

        // 2nd: classify basic and nonbasic.
        VARS = (0, 1..1+param.dmus+param.slacks, -1..-param.artificials, 0)
        bfsidx = J(1, mrows-1, .); nonbfsidx = J(1, 0, .)
        for (j = 3+param.dmus; j <= mcols-1; j++) {
                /* Old Code
                T = (M[2::mrows,j] :== 1)
                if (sum(T) == 1) {
                    maxindex(T, 1, i, w); bfsidx[i] = j
                }
                else nonbfsidx = nonbfsidx, j
                */
```

```
                    // Modified by Brian(2012.08.25): because critical logic error.
                    T = M[2::mrows,j]
                    if ((sum(T :!= 0) == 1) && (sum(T) == 1)) {
                        maxindex(T, 1, i, w); bfsidx[i] = j
                    }
                    else nonbfsidx = nonbfsidx, j
                }
            reorderidx = (1, bfsidx[1,], 2..2+param.dmus, nonbfsidx[1,], mcols)
            VARS = VARS[,reorderidx];
            M = M[,reorderidx]; boundM = boundM[,reorderidx]

            if (param.trace == "trace") {
                displayas("txt")
                printf("\n[DMUi=%g]%s: classify basic and nonbasic.\n",
                    dmui, tracename); M; VARS
            }

            // 3rd: solve the linear programming(LP).
            phase = 1
            lpresult = lp(M, boundM, VARS, dmui, phase, tracename, param)

            if(lpresult.rc) VARS[1,1] = .
            return(VARS)
        }

    real matrix function lp_phase2 ( real matrix M,
                                struct BoundCond matrix boundM,
                                real matrix VARS,
                                real scalar dmui,
                                string scalar aTracename,
                                struct LpParamStruct scalar param )
    {
        real matrix T, XB, orgVARS, LPRSLT
        real scalar i, j, phase, mrows, mcols, realslacks
        real vector slackidx
        string scalar tracename, msg
        struct LpResultStruct scalar lpresult

        orgVARS = VARS
        mrows = rows(M); mcols = cols(M)

        tracename = aTracename + "-PII"

        // modify target function value:
        M[1,] = J(1,mcols,0); M[1,1] = 1
        if (param.stagestep == 1) { // X = theta
                for (j=2; j<mcols; j++) {
                        if (VARS[1,j] == 1) M[1,j] = 1 // because of theta index == 1
                }
        }
        else if (param.stagestep == 2) { // X = S1 + S2 + ... + Sn
            realslacks = (param.rts == "IRS" || param.rts == "DRS") ?
                        param.slacks-1 : param.slacks;
                slackidx = (2+param.dmus..1+param.dmus+realslacks)
                for (j=2; j<mcols; j++) {
                        for (i=1; i<=realslacks; i++) {
                                if (VARS[1,j] == slackidx[i] && !allof(M[,j], 0))
    M[1,j] = 1
```

```
                    }
                }
        }

    if (param.trace == "trace") {
        displayas("txt")
        printf("\n---------[PHASE II]----------")
        printf("\n[DMUi=%g]%s: initialize matrix.\n",
            dmui, tracename); M
        printf("\n[DMUi=%g]%s: VARS.\n", dmui, tracename); VARS
    }

    phase = 2
    lpresult = lp(M, boundM, VARS, dmui, phase, tracename, param)

    // ------------------------------------------------------------------
    // phase 2 final.
    // ------------------------------------------------------------------
    if(lpresult.rc) {
            LPRSLT = J(1, 1+param.dmus+param.slacks, .)
    }
    else {
            // lpresult = theta(1) + dmus + slacks
            LPRSLT = J(1, 1+param.dmus+param.slacks, 0)
            for (j=1; j<=rows(lpresult.XB) ; j++) {
                    if (VARS[1,j+1] > 0) LPRSLT[1, VARS[1,j+1]] =lpresult.XB[j,
1]
                    }
            if (param.stagestep == 1 && LPRSLT[1, 1] <= 0) {
                    LPRSLT[1, 1] = lpresult.xVal
                    }
    }

    if (param.trace == "trace") {
        msg = sprintf("[DMUi=%g]%s-FINAL", dmui, tracename);
        printf("\n%s: original VARS.\n", msg); orgVARS
        printf("\n%s: VARS.\n", msg); VARS
        printf("\n%s: XB.\n", msg); lpresult.XB
        printf("\n%s: LPRSLT.\n", msg); LPRSLT
    }

    return(LPRSLT)
}

/**
 * return 0: sucess
 * return 1: B inverse error
 * return 2: XB has negative value.
 */
real scalar function decompsition(real matrix M,

    struct BoundCond matrix boundM,

    real scalar mrows,

    real scalar mcols,

    real scalar slacks,
```

```
        struct LpTableauStruct scalar tbl,

        struct LpParamStruct scalar param )
    {
        real matrix CB, CNj
        real matrix B, Nj, b
        real matrix Bi,CBBi, rawXB, XB, BiNjXj
        real scalar j, Njcols, result

        // set the tableau.
        tbl.CB = &CB; tbl.CNj  = &CNj;
        tbl.B  = &B;  tbl.Nj  = &Nj;  tbl.b = &b
        tbl.Bi = &Bi; tbl.CBBi = &CBBi
        tbl.rawXB = &rawXB; tbl.XB = &XB;

        CB  = M[1,2::1+slacks];            CNj = M[1,2+slacks::mcols-1]
        B   = M[2..mrows,2::1+slacks]; Nj  = M[2..mrows,2+slacks::mcols-1]
        b   = M[2..mrows,mcols]

        Bi = lusolve(B, I(rows(B)), 1e-14)
        if (any(Bi :== .)) { // B is singular matrix.
                    return (result = 1);
                    // FIXME use??
                    // Bi = svsolve(B, I(rows(B)), 1e-14)
                    // if (any(Bi :== .)) return (result = 1);
        }

        CBBi = CB*Bi
        // BFS(basic feasible solution)
        Njcols = cols(Nj); BiNjXj = J(rows(Nj), 1, 0)
        for (j=1; j<=Njcols; j++) {
                    BiNjXj = BiNjXj :+ (Bi*Nj[.,1]*(boundM[1,1+slacks+j].val))
        }
        rawXB = Bi*b - BiNjXj
        XB = edittozerotol(rawXB, param.tol2) // BFS(basic feasible solution)
        // BFS(basic feasible solution) must be nonnegative.
        if (any(XB :< 0)) return (result = 2);

        return (result = 0); // sucess
    }

    /**
    * Refactoring Target: lp_for_dea
    *
    */
    struct LpResultStruct function lp ( real matrix M,

        struct BoundCond matrix boundM,

        real matrix VARS,

        real scalar dmui,

        real scalar phase,

        string scalar tracename,

        struct LpParamStruct scalar param )
    {
```

```
real matrix B, CB, Bi, b, XB, rawXB, BiNjXj, CBBi, Nj, CNj, Aj, alpha
real matrix T, TH1, TH2, valT, lowerT, upperT, LVi, V
real scalar i, j, w, mi, boundi, evj, lvj, Njcols, leavingCase
real scalar mrows, mcols, enteringVar, leavingVar, calci, maxiter
real scalar existArtificial, xVal, alphaVal
real scalar minYn, tcols, tempVal, minVal, maxVal
struct BoundCond matrix boundT
struct LpResultStruct scalar lpresult
// struct LpTableauStruct scalar tbl

real colvector enterings, leavings
real scalar    enteringi, leavingi

real scalar slacks, isin, tol1, tol2
string scalar trace, msg

// -------------------------------------------------------------------------
slacks = rows(M) - 1 // number of basic feasible solution
tol1 = param.tol1; tol2 = param.tol2
trace = param.trace
if (param.minYn >= .) {
        minYn = 0
        if (param.stagestep == 1) minYn = (phase == 1) ? 1 : param.isin
        else minYn = (phase == 1)
}
else {
        minYn = param.minYn
}


// -------------------------------------------------------------------------
mrows = rows(M); mcols = cols(M)
LVi = J(slacks, 1, .) // leaving variable index matrix.
// -------------------------------------------------------------------------
if (trace == "trace") {
    displayas("txt"); msg = "initial tableau in the LP."
    printf("\n[DMUi=%g]%s: %s\n", dmui, tracename, msg); M
}
    lpresult.rc = 0; lpresult.rmsg = ""
    existArtificial = (phase == 2 && any(VARS[,2::1+slacks] :< 0));
    maxiter = st_numscalar("c(maxiter)")
    for (calci=1 ; calci<=maxiter ; calci++) { // prevent infinite loop

if (trace == "trace") {
    printf("\n[DMUi=%g]%s-LOOP[%g] Start...\n", dmui, tracename, calci)
}
        B  = M[2..mrows,2::1+slacks];      CB = M[1,2::1+slacks]
        Nj = M[2..mrows,2+slacks::mcols-1]; CNj = M[1,2+slacks::mcols-1]
         b  = M[2..mrows,mcols]

        Bi = lusolve(B, I(rows(B)), 1e-14)
        if (any(Bi :== .)) { // B is singular matrix.
          Bi = svsolve(B, I(rows(B)), 1e-14)
              if (any(Bi :== .)) {
                      lpresult.rc = 3498;
                      lpresult.rmsg                              =
sprintf("%s[DMUi=%g][LOOP=%g]%s",
                             "No Solution(BFS's inverse is not
exist):",
                             dmui, calci, tracename)
```

```
                                    break;

                                    /* // TODO Confirm?
                                    display("B:");B
                                    display("rank(B) : det(B)"); rank(B), det(B)
                                    _error(3498, "No Solution(BFS's inverse is not
exist):"
                                                    +    "[DMUi="    +
strofreal(dmui) + "]"
                                                    +    "[LOOP="    +
strofreal(calci) + "]"
                                                    + tracename)
                                    */
                                }
                        }
                        CBBi = CB*Bi

                        // BFS(basic feasible solution)
                        Njcols = cols(Nj); BiNjXj = J(rows(Nj), 1, 0)
                        for (j=1; j<=Njcols; j++) {
                                BiNjXj = BiNjXj :+ (Bi*Nj[.,1]*(boundM[1,1+slacks+j].val))
                        }
                        rawXB = Bi*b - BiNjXj
                        XB = edittozerotol(rawXB, tol2) // BFS(basic feasible solution)

                        if (any(XB :== .)) {
                                    lpresult.rc = 3498;
                                    lpresult.rmsg = sprintf("%s[DMUi=%g][LOOP=%g]%s",
                                        "No Solution(XB contains missing value):",
                                        dmui, calci, tracename)
                                    break;

                                    /* // TODO Confirm?
                                    displayas("err"); msg = "If XB contains missing value, error."
                                    printf("\n[DMUi=%g]%s: %s\n", dmui, tracename, msg);
B;Bi;XB;
                                    _error(3498, "No Solution(XB have the missing value):"
                                        +    "[DMUi="    +    strofreal(dmui)    +    "]"    +
tracename);
                                    */
                        }

                        // BFS(basic feasible solution) must be nonnegative.
                /* // TODO Confirm ??
                        if (any(XB :< 0)) {
                                    displayas("err"); msg = "If XB contains negative value, error."
                                    printf("\n[DMUi=%g]%s: %s\n", dmui, tracename, msg); XB
                                    _error(3498, "No Solution(XB contains negative value):"
                                        +    "[DMUi="    +    strofreal(dmui)    +    "]"    +
tracename);
                        }
                */

                        boundT = boundM[1,2+slacks::mcols-1]
                        tcols = cols(boundT); valT = J(1,tcols,.)
                        for(j=1; j<=tcols; j++) {
                                valT[1,j] = boundT[1,j].val
                        }
                        xVal = edittozerotol((CB*rawXB + CNj*valT'), tol2) // objective funtion
```

154

value

```
        T = VARS[1,2::1+rows(XB)] // rows(XB) equal to number of slacks.

    if (trace == "trace") {
        printf("\n[DMUi=%g]%s-LOOP[%g]: CBBi * b = %g\n",
            dmui, tracename, calci, xVal);
        display("Entered index(if value is negative, that's artificial):"); T;
        display("XB = Bi*b - BiNjXj:"); rawXB;
    }


        // --------------------------------------------------------------------
        // loop terminated condition.
        // --------------------------------------------------------------------
        if (phase == 1) {
            // objective function value is zero
                if (xVal == 0 ) {
                        // if all artificals are out or remaining artificals are
at zero,
                        // stop and go phaseII
                        T = (T :< 0) // artificial remain or not?
                        if (allof(T, 0) || allof(select(XB, T'), 0)) break;

                        // If remaining artificails are not zero, No
Solution.
                        lpresult.rc = 3498
                        lpresult.rmsg                                    =
sprintf("%s[DMUi=%g][LOOP=%g]%s",
are not zero):",
                                        "No Solution(Remaining artificails
                                        dmui, calci, tracename)
                        break;

                        // TODO confirm!
                        // display("[BFS index | XB]");T;XB;
                        // _error(3498, "No Solution(Remaining
artificails are not zero):"
                        //          + "[DMUi=" + strofreal(dmui) + "]"
+ tracename)
                }
        }

        // ------------------------------------------------------------------
        // Select entering variable.
        // ------------------------------------------------------------------
        enteringVar = 0; tempVal = 0; minVal = 0; maxVal = 0; boundi = 0
        Njcols = cols(Nj); T = J(1, Njcols, .)
        for (j=1; j<=Njcols; j++) {
            tempVal = CBBi * Nj[,j] - CNj[1,j]
                if (abs(tempVal) < tol1) continue;

                boundi = 1 + slacks + j
                if (boundM[1,boundi].val == boundM[1,boundi].lower) { //
lower bound
                        T[1,j] = tempVal
                }
                else { // upper bound
                        T[1,j] = -tempVal
                }
```

```
} // end of for

        if (!minYn) { // maximization.
            T = T :/ (T :< 0)
            if (!allof(T, .)) {
                minindex(T, 1, enterings, w); enteringi = 1
                enteringVar = enterings[enteringi]
                evj = 1+slacks+enteringVar
            }
        }
        else { // minimization.
            T = T :/ (T :> 0)
            if (!allof(T, .)) {
                maxindex(T, 1, enterings, w); enteringi = 1
                enteringVar = enterings[enteringi]
                evj = 1+slacks+enteringVar
            }
        }

    // No more candidate for entering variable.
    if (enteringVar == 0) {
                if (trace == "trace") {
            printf("\n[DMUi=%g]%s-LOOP[%g]:", dmui, tracename, calci)
            printf("No more candidate for entering variable.\n:(CB*Bi*Nj)-Cj\n");T
        }
                if (phase == 1) {
                    lpresult.rc = 3498;
                    lpresult.rmsg                              =
sprintf("%s[DMUi=%g][LOOP=%g]%s",
                                                "No Solution(No more candidate for
entering variable):",
                                                dmui, calci, tracename)

                    // TODO Confirm?
                    // _error(3498, "No Solution(No more select
entering variable):"
                    //          + "[DMUi=" + strofreal(dmui) + "]"
+ tracename)
                }
            break
        }

    if (trace == "trace") {
        displayas("txt"); msg = "Select entering variable."
        printf("\n[DMUi=%g]%s-LOOP[%g]: %s(%g:%g)\n:(CB*Bi*Nj)-Cj\n",
            dmui, tracename, calci, msg, enteringVar, T[enteringVar]); T
    }

    // --------------------------------------------------------------
    // Select leaving variable.
    // --------------------------------------------------------------
    leavingVar = 0
    Aj = Nj[,enteringVar]
    alpha = edittozerotol(Bi*Aj, tol1)
    if (existArtificial) {
        T = VARS[1,2::1+slacks]; tcols = cols(T)
        for (j=1; j<=tcols; j++) {
            if (T[1,j] < 0 && alpha[j,1] != 0) {
                leavingVar = j; lvj = 1+leavingVar
```

```
                    break;
                }
            }
        }

        if (leavingVar == 0) {
            boundT = boundM[1,2::1+slacks]
            tcols = cols(boundT)
            lowerT = upperT = J(1,tcols,.)
            for(j=1; j<=tcols; j++) {
                lowerT[1,j] = boundT[1,j].lower
                upperT[1,j] = boundT[1,j].upper
            }

            // XB=Bi*b
            leavingCase = 0
            if (boundM[1,evj].val == boundM[1,evj].lower) {
                minVal = .;
                // 1. alpha's positive min value
                TH1 = boundM[1,evj].lower :+ ((rawXB :-
lowerT')
                :/ (alpha :* (alpha :> 0)))
                // TH1 = edittozerotol(TH1, tol1)
                if (any(TH1 :< minVal)) {
                    minindex(TH1, 1, mi, w)
                    leavingVar = mi[1];    lvj =
1+leavingVar
                    if (phase == 1 && w[1,2] >= 2 &&
VARS[1,lvj] > 0) {
                        // if phase 1 and same
min ratio test result,
                        // artificial variable must
leave first.
                        tcols = w[1,2]
                        for (j=2; j<=tcols; j++)
{                           if
(VARS[1,mi[j]+1] < 0) {
        leavingVar = mi[j]; lvj = 1+leavingVar
        break;
                                            }
                                        }
                                    }
                    minVal = TH1[leavingVar,1];
                    leavingCase = 1
                }
                // 2. alpha's negative min value
                TH2 = boundM[1,evj].lower :+ ((rawXB :-
upperT')
                :/ (alpha :* (alpha :< 0)))
                // TH2 = edittozerotol(TH2, tol1)
                if (any(TH2 :< minVal)) {
                    minindex(TH2, 1, mi, w)
                    leavingVar = mi[1];    lvj =
1+leavingVar
```

```
                                          minVal    =    TH1[leavingVar,1];
leavingCase = 2
                              }
                              // 3. get the enteringVar's upper value
                              if (boundM[1,evj].upper < minVal) {
                                          minVal    =    boundM[1,evj].upper;
leavingCase = 3
                              }

    if (trace == "trace") {
       displayas("txt"); msg = "Select leaving variable.[MinVal]"
       printf("\n[DMUi=%g]%s-LOOP[%g]: %s(%g:%g)\n",
          dmui, tracename, calci, msg, leavingVar, minVal)
       display("XB | alpha:(XB=Bi*b, alpha=Bi*Aj):");rawXB,alpha
       display("[MinVal]enteringVar's upper | theta1 | theta2")
       printf("\n[boundM[1,%g].upper:%g][leavingCase:%g]\n",
                          evj, boundM[1,evj].upper, leavingCase); TH1,TH2
    }

                              if (leavingCase == 1) {
                                          boundM[1,lvj].val            =
boundM[1,lvj].lower
                              }
                              else if (leavingCase == 2) {
                                          boundM[1,lvj].val            =
boundM[1,lvj].upper
                              }
                              else { // if (leavingCase == 3)
                                          boundM[1,evj].val            =
boundM[1,evj].upper; continue;
                              }
                      }
                      else { // if (boundM[1,evj].val == boundM[1,evj].upper)
                              maxVal = 0;
                              // 1. alpha's positive min value
                              TH1    =    boundM[1,evj].upper    :+    ((rawXB    :-
upperT')
                      :/ (alpha :* (alpha :> 0)))
                              // TH1 = edittozerotol(TH1, tol1)
                              if (any(TH1 :> maxVal)) {
                                          maxindex(TH1, 1, mi, w)
                                          leavingVar    =    mi[1];    lvj    =
1+leavingVar
                                          maxVal    =    TH1[leavingVar,1];
leavingCase = 1
                              }
                              // 2. alpha's negative min value
                              TH2    =    boundM[1,evj].upper    :+    ((rawXB    :-
lowerT')
                      :/ (alpha :* (alpha :< 0)))
                              // TH2 = edittozerotol(TH2, tol1)
                              if (any(TH2 :> maxVal)) {
                                          maxindex(TH2, 1, mi, w)
                                          leavingVar    =    mi[1];    lvj    =
1+leavingVar
                                          maxVal    =    TH1[leavingVar,1];
leavingCase = 2
```

158

```
                              }
                              // 3. get the enteringVar's lower value
                              if (boundM[1,evj].lower > maxVal) {
                                      maxVal   =   boundM[1,evj].lower;
leavingCase = 3
                              }

        if (trace == "trace") {
             displayas("txt"); msg = "Select leaving variable.[MaxVal]"
             printf("\n[DMUi=%g]%s-LOOP[%g]: %s(%g:%g)\n",
                 dmui, tracename, calci, msg, leavingVar, maxVal)
             display("XB | alpha:(XB=Bi*b, alpha=Bi*Aj):");XB,alpha
             display("[MaxVal]enteringVar's lower | theta1 | theta2")
             printf("\n[boundM[1,%g].lower:%g][leavingCase:%g]\n",
                              evj, boundM[1,evj].lower, leavingCase); TH1,TH2
        }

                         if (leavingCase == 1) {
                                  boundM[1,lvj].val                 =
boundM[1,lvj].upper
                         }
                         else if (leavingCase == 2) {
                                  boundM[1,lvj].val                 =
boundM[1,lvj].lower
                         }
                         else  { // if (leavingCase == 3)
                                  boundM[1,evj].val                 =
boundM[1,evj].lower; continue;
                         }
                    }
                }

        // If no leaving variable exits
        if (leavingVar == 0) {
           if (trace == "trace")
             display("Break: No more candidate for leaving variable.")

                         lpresult.rc = 3498;
                         lpresult.rmsg = sprintf("%s[DMUi=%g][LOOP=%g]%s",
                                 "No Solution(No more candidate for leaving
variable):",
                                 dmui, calci, tracename)

           break
        }
        // When theta is leaving at phase 2, break! // FIXME: is correct ?
        if (phase == 2 && VARS[,lvj] == 1) {
           if (trace == "trace") display("Break: theta(θ) is not leaving.")
           break
        }

        // -------------------------------------------------------------------
        // reply calculatation result.
        // -------------------------------------------------------------------
                    LVi[leavingVar,1] = VARS[,evj]
                    _swapcols(M, lvj, evj)
                    _swapcols(boundM, lvj, evj)
                    _swapcols(VARS, lvj, evj)
```

```
            // Clear artificial variable
            if (VARS[,evj] < 0) {
                  T = J(1, cols(VARS), 1); T[1,evj] = 0

                  VARS  = select(VARS, T)
                  M     = select(M, T)
                  boundM = select(boundM, T)
                  mcols = cols(M)

                  // if exist artificial(phase II)
                  if (existArtificial) {
                        existArtificial = any(VARS[,2::1+slacks] :< 0)
                  }
            }

if (trace == "trace") {
   printf("\n[DMUi=%g]%s-LOOP[%g]: updated tableau.[%g(%g) <--> %g(%g)]\n",
      dmui, tracename, calci, lvj, leavingVar, evj, enteringVar); M
   display("LVi: Entered variable's VARS index value."); LVi
   display("VARS: Variable's index."); VARS
}

   } //end of main for

   // return lpresult
   if (calci > maxiter) {
            lpresult.rc = 3498;
            lpresult.rmsg = sprintf("%s[DMUi=%g][LOOP=%g]%s",
                  "No Solution(LOOP greater than maxiter):",
                  dmui, calci, tracename)
   }
   if(lpresult.rc) display(lpresult.rmsg)
   lpresult.xVal = xVal
   lpresult.XB = XB
   return(lpresult)
}

/* A[.,lvj] <--> A[.,evj] */
function _swapcols( transmorphic matrix A,
                                    real scalar lvj,
                                    real scalar evj )
{
            transmorphic colvector  v

            v = A[., lvj]
            A[., lvj] = A[., evj]
            A[., evj] = v
}

function replacesubmat ( transmorphic matrix M,
            real scalar row,
            real scalar col,
            transmorphic matrix T )
{
   M[|row,col\row + rows(T) - 1, col + cols(T) - 1|] = T
}

function _setup_dearslt_names(string scalar dearsltmat,
            string scalar dmuinmat,
```

```
                        string scalar dmuoutmat )
{
    string matrix DMU_CS     // dmu in matrix column stripes
    string matrix DEARSLT_CS // dea result matrix column stripes
    string matrix DEARSLT_RS // dea result matrix row stripes
    real matrix M
    real scalar mcols, cnt, i

    M = st_matrix(dearsltmat)
    mcols = cols(M)

    // TODO replace the chars. ex) if ([a-z][A-Z][0-9][_]) is not. replace '_'
    DMU_CS = st_matrixcolstripe(dmuinmat)
    for (i = 1; i <= rows(DMU_CS); i++) {
        DMU_CS[i, 1] = "ref"
    }

    DEARSLT_CS = ("","rank"\"","theta")\DMU_CS\ // column join
        st_matrixrowstripe(dmuinmat)\st_matrixrowstripe(dmuoutmat)
    if (mcols - rows(DEARSLT_CS) > 0) {
        cnt = 0
        for (i = rows(DEARSLT_CS)+1 ; i <= mcols ; i++) {
            DEARSLT_CS = DEARSLT_CS \ ("slack", "slack_" + strofreal(++cnt))
        }
    }

    DEARSLT_RS = st_matrixcolstripe(dmuinmat)

    // name the row and column of dea result matrix
    st_matrixrowstripe(dearsltmat, DEARSLT_RS)
    st_matrixcolstripe(dearsltmat, DEARSLT_CS)
}

/**
 * deamat - dmucount x ( 1(theta) + dmu count + slcak(in, out) count)
 */
function _dmurank( string scalar deamat,
                   real scalar dmuincount,
                   real scalar dmuoutcount,
                   real scalar minrank,
                   real scalar tol )
{
    real matrix M
    real rowvector v, vv, retvec, slcaksum
    real scalar m, mm, row, i, ii, w, ww

    M = st_matrix(deamat)
    v = round(M[,1], tol)
    if (minrank) minindex(v, rows(v), i, w)
    else maxindex(v, rows(v), i, w)

    retvec = J(rows(v), 1, .)
    if (allof(w[,2], 1)) {
        retvec[i[1::rows(v)]] = (1::rows(v))
    }
    else {
        // rank correction for ties
        slcaksum = rowsum(M[| 1,cols(M) - (dmuincount + dmuoutcount - 1)\.,.|])
        for (m = 1; m <= rows(w); m++) {
```

```
            if (w[m,2] >= 2) {
                vv = i[w[m,1]::(w[m,1] + w[m,2] - 1)]
                                    minindex(slcaksum[vv], w[m,2], ii, ww)
              for (mm = 1; mm <= rows(ww); mm++) {
                  for (row = ww[mm,1]; row < ww[mm,1] + ww[mm,2]; row++) {
                      retvec[vv[ii[row]]] = w[m,1] + ww[mm,1] - 1
                  }
                }
            }
            else {
                retvec[i[w[m,1]]] = w[m,1] // row = w[m,1]
            }
          }
      }
  st_matrix("r(rank)", retvec)
}

function maxvecindex( string scalar vecname )
{
    real matrix A
    real scalar i, w

    A = st_matrix(vecname)
    maxindex(A, 1, i, w)

    st_numscalar("r(maxval)", A[i[1]])
    st_numscalar("r(maxindex)", i[1])
    st_matrix("r(maxindexes)", i)
}

function minvecindex( string scalar vecname )
{
    real matrix A
    real scalar i, w

    A = st_matrix(vecname)
    if (sum(A :< .) > 0) {
        minindex(A, 1, i, w)
        st_numscalar("r(minval)", A[i[1]])
        st_numscalar("r(minindex)", i[1])
        st_matrix("r(minindexes)", i)
    }
    // if overall missing value.
    else {
        st_numscalar("r(minval)", .)
        st_numscalar("r(minindex)", 0)
        st_matrix("r(minindexes)", 0)
    }
}

function _roundmat( string scalar matname, real scalar tol )
{
    real matrix A
    A = round(st_matrix(matname), tol)
    st_matrix(matname, A)
}

function _uniqrowmat( string scalar matname, string scalar varname )
{
```

```
    st_matrix(matname, sort(uniqrows(st_data(., varname)), 1))
}

function _file_exists( string scalar fn )
{
    st_numscalar("r(fileexists)", fileexists(fn))
}

mata mlib create ldea, dir(PERSONAL) replace
mata mlib add ldea *()
mata mlib index

end
// End of the MATA Definition Area -------------------------------------------
```

B2.3 lp.ado

```
*! version 1.0.0  30OCT2012
capture program drop lp
program define lp, rclass
    version 11.0

// syntax checking and validation----------------------------------------------
// rel - relational
// rhs - right hand side
// example:
//     lp x1 x2 x3, min
//     lp x1 x2 x3, min rel(rel_var) rhs(rhs_var)
// ----------------------------------------------------------------------------
    // returns 1 if the first nonblank character of local macro `0' is a comma,
    // or if `0' is empty.
    if replay() {
        dis as err "vars required."
        exit 198
    }

    #del ;
    syntax varlist(min=1) [if] [in] [using/]
    [,
        REL(varname)       // default is "rel", relational
        RHS(varname)       // default is "rhs"
            MIN                 // the objective is to minimize optimizaion
            MAX                 // the objective is to maximize optimization
            INTVARS(varlist)   // Integer(Mixed Integer Condition) Variables

        TOL1(real 1e-14)   // entering or leaving value tolerance
        TOL2(real 1e-8)    // B inverse tolerance: 2.22e-12
        TRACE              // Whether or not to do the log
        SAVing(string)     // result data file name
        REPLACE            // Whether or not to replace the result data file
    ];
    #del cr

    // default rel == "rel"
    if ("`rel'" == "") local rel = "rel"

    // default rhs == "rel"
    if ("`rhs'" == "") local rhs = "rhs"

    // optimization check
    local opt = "`min'`max'"
    if (!("`opt'" == "min" || "`opt'" == "max")) {
            dis as err "optimization is must min or max, and exclusively."
        exit 198
    }

    if ("`using'" != "") use "`using'", clear
    if (~(`c(N)' > 0 & `c(k)' > 0)) {
        dis as err "dataset required!"
        exit 198
    }
```

```
// end of syntax checking and validation --------------------------------------

set more off
capture log close lp_log
log using "lp.log", replace text name(lp_log)
preserve

if ("`if'" != "" | "`in'" != "") {
    qui keep `in' `if'  // filtering : keep in range [if exp]
}

// ----------------------------------------------------------------------
// LP Start
// ----------------------------------------------------------------------
if ("`intvars'" == "") {
        lpmain `varlist', rel(`rel') rhs(`rhs') opt(`opt') ///
                        tol1(`tol1') tol2(`tol2') `trace'
}
else {
        milp `varlist', rel(`rel') rhs(`rhs') opt(`opt') ///
                        intvars(`intvars') tol1(`tol1') tol2(`tol2') `trace'
}

tempname tableau lprslt temp_t
matrix `tableau' = r(tableau)
matrix `lprslt' = r(lprslt)
local nvars = r(nvars)
local nslacks = r(nslacks)
local nartificials = r(nartificials)

// setup lprslt colnames and rownames
matrix `temp_t' = `tableau'[1...,1..`=colsof(`lprslt')']
matrix colnames `lprslt' = `: colnames `temp_t''
matrix rownames `lprslt' = "opt_val"

// ----------------------------------------------------------------------
// REPORT
// ----------------------------------------------------------------------
di as result _n(2) "Input Values:"
matrix list `tableau', noblank nohalf noheader f(%9.6g)

di as result _n(2) "LP Results: options(`opt')"
matrix list `lprslt', noblank nohalf noheader f(%9.6g)

di as text _n(2) ""

return matrix tableau = `tableau'
return matrix lprslt = `lprslt'
return local nvars = `nvars'
return local nslacks = `nslacks'
return local narticials = `nartificials'

set more on
restore, preserve
log close lp_log

end
```

```
*******************************************************************************
* MILP - Mixed Integer Linear Programming
*******************************************************************************
program define milp, rclass
    #del ;
    syntax varlist, rel(varname) rhs(varname) opt(string) intvars(varlist)
    [
        cnt(integer 0) tol1(real 1e-14) tol2(real 1e-8) trace
    ];
    #del cr

    tempname tableau lprslt baseval

    // #L0
    lpmain `varlist', rel(`rel') rhs(`rhs') opt(`opt') ///
                                          tol1(`tol1') tol2(`tol2') `trace'
    matrix `tableau' = r(tableau)
    matrix `lprslt' = r(lprslt)

    // for debug
    di as result _n(2) "MILP L`cnt' Input Values:"
    list
    matrix list `tableau', noblank nohalf noheader f(%9.6g)

    di as result _n(2) "MILP L`cnt' Results: options(`opt')"
    matrix list `lprslt', noblank nohalf noheader f(%9.6g)
    di as text _n "------------------------------------------------"
    di as text _n

    // infeasible
    if (`lprslt'[1,1] >= .) {
            return add // all results of lpmain
    }
    else {
            // check that all variables is an integer
            local max_varname = ""
            local max_mantissa = 0
            foreach varname of varlist `intvars' {
                    // because tableau and lprslt are same order
                    local varvalue = ///
                            round(`lprslt'[1, colnumb(`tableau',"`varname'")],
`tol1')

                    local mantissa = `varvalue' - floor(`varvalue')
                    if (`mantissa' > `max_mantissa') {
                            local max_mantissa = `mantissa'
                            local max_varname = "`varname'"
                            local `baseval' = `varvalue'
                    }
            }

            // if all variables is an integer
            if ("`max_varname'" == "") {
                    return add // all results of lpmain
            }
            // some variables is not an integer
            else {
                    // #L1
                    preserve
                    qui {
```

```
set obs `=c(N)+1'
replace `max_varname' = 1 in `c(N)'
replace `rel' = ">=" in `c(N)'
replace `rhs' = ceil(``baseval'') in `c(N)'
foreach varname of varlist `varlist' {
        if ("`max_varname'" != "`varname'")
{
                                replace `varname' = 0 in
`c(N)'
        }
}
}

// recursive call
milp `varlist', rel(`rel') rhs(`rhs') opt(`opt') cnt(`=`cnt'+1') ///
        intvars(`intvars') tol1(`tol1') tol2(`tol2') `trace'

matrix `tableau' = r(tableau)
matrix `lprslt' = r(lprslt)
local nvars = r(nvars)
local nslacks = r(nslacks)
local nartificials = r(nartificials)

// #L2
restore, preserve
qui {
        set obs `=c(N)+1'
        replace `max_varname' = 1 in `c(N)'
        replace `rel' = "<=" in `c(N)'
        replace `rhs' = floor(``baseval'') in `c(N)'
        foreach varname of varlist `varlist' {
                if ("`max_varname'" != "`varname'")
{
                                replace `varname' = 0 in
`c(N)'
                }
        }
}

// recursive call
milp `varlist', rel(`rel') rhs(`rhs') opt(`opt') cnt(`=`cnt'+2') ///
        intvars(`intvars') tol1(`tol1') tol2(`tol2') `trace'

// #L1 and #L2 are infeasible or feasible
// if #L1 is infeasible or #L2 > #L1 then select #L2
tempname L2
matrix `L2' = r(lprslt)

if ("`opt'" == "max") {
        if (`lprslt'[1,1] >= . | `L2'[1,1] > `lprslt'[1,1]) {
                matrix `tableau' = r(tableau)
                matrix `lprslt' = r(lprslt)
                local nvars = r(nvars)
                local nslacks = r(nslacks)
                local nartificials = r(nartificials)
        }
}
else { // else if ("`opt'" == "min") {
```

167

A Handbook of Data Envelopment Analysis @ Stata

```
                                        if (`lprslt'[1,1] >= . | `L2'[1,1] < `lprslt'[1,1]) {
                                            matrix `tableau' = r(tableau)
                                            matrix `lprslt' = r(lprslt)
                                            local nvars = r(nvars)
                                            local nslacks = r(nslacks)
                                            local nartificials = r(nartificials)
                                        }
                                    }

                                restore

                                // return the final results
                                return matrix tableau = `tableau'
                                return matrix lprslt = `lprslt'
                                return local nvars = `nvars'
                                return local nslacks = `nslacks'
                                return local narticials = `nartificials'
                            }
                    }

        end


*******************************************************************************
* LP Main - Linear Programming Main
*******************************************************************************
program define lpmain, rclass
    #del ;
    syntax varlist, rel(varname) rhs(varname) opt(string)
    [
        tol1(real 1e-14) tol2(real 1e-8) trace
    ];
    #del cr

    tempname tableau

    // make tableau
    mktableau `varlist' `rhs', opt(`opt') rel(`rel') tableau(`tableau')
    local nvars : list sizeof varlist    // number of variables
    local nslacks = r(nslacks)           // number of slacks
    local nartificials = r(nartificials) // number of artificials

    // run lp phase I and II
    mata: _lp_phase("`tableau'", "`opt'", ///
                                        `nvars', `nslacks', `nartificials', ///
                                        `tol1', `tol2', "`trace'")

    // return results for lp
    return local nvars = `nvars'
    return local nslacks = `nslacks'
    return local narticials = `nartificials'
    return matrix tableau = `tableau'
    return add // r(lprslt)
end


*******************************************************************************
* LP Main - Linear Programming Main
*******************************************************************************
```

168

```
program define lpmain_1, rclass
    #del ;
    syntax varlist, rel(varname) rhs(varname) opt(string) lprslt(name)
                                    tableau(name)  vars(real)  slacks(real)
artificials(real)
    [
        intvars(varlist) tol1(real 1e-14) tol2(real 1e-8) trace
    ];
    #del cr

    mata: _lp_phase("`tableau'", "`opt'", ///
                                        `vars', `slacks', `artificials', ///
                                        `tol1', `tol2', "`trace'")

    tempname c_lprslt // current lprslt
    matrix `c_lprslt' = r(lprslt)
    matrix colnames `c_lprslt' = `: colnames(`lprslt')'
    matrix rownames `c_lprslt' = `: rownames(`lprslt')'

    // FIXME
    // di as result _n "lprslt:"
    // matrix list `lprslt', noblank nohalf noheader f(%9.6g)
    // di as result _n "c_lprslt:"
    // matrix list `c_lprslt', noblank nohalf noheader f(%9.6g)

    if ("`intvars'" != "" && `c_lprslt'[1,1] < .) { // if MILP then,
            local max_varname = ""
            local max_mantissa = 0
            foreach varname of varlist `intvars' {
                    local varvalue = ///
                                    round(`c_lprslt'[1,
colnumb(`c_lprslt',"`varname'")], `tol1')
                    local varvalue = `varvalue' - floor(`varvalue')
                    if (`varvalue' > `max_mantissa') {
                            local max_mantissa = `varvalue'
                            local max_varname = "`varname'"
                    }
            }

            if ("`max_varname'" != "") { // variables is not at all integer
                    tempname t_tableau t_obj t_vars t_slacks t_artificials t_rhs
t_st
                    tempname r1_lprslt r2_lprslt temp_t

                    local           varvalue        =           `c_lprslt'[1,
colnumb(`c_lprslt',"`max_varname'")]

                    preserve
                    qui {
                            set obs `=c(N)+1'
                            replace `max_varname' = 1 in `c(N)'
                            replace `rel' = ">=" in `c(N)'
                            replace `rhs' = ceil(`varvalue') in `c(N)'
                            foreach varname of varlist `varlist' {
                                    if ("`max_varname'" != "`varname'")
{
                                            replace `varname' = 0 in
`c(N)'
                                    }
```

```
                              }
                          }

    // make tableau
    mktableau `varlist' `rhs', opt(`opt') rel(`rel') tableau(`t_tableau')
    local r1_vars = `vars'
    local r1_slacks = r(nslacks)
    local r1_artificials = r(nartificials)

    // make lprslt and setup lprslt colnames and rownames
    matrix `r1_lprslt' = J(1, `=(1 + `vars' + `r1_slacks')', .)
    matrix `temp_t' = `t_tableau'[1...,1..`=colsof(`r1_lprslt')']
    matrix colnames `r1_lprslt' = `: colnames `temp_t"
    matrix rownames `r1_lprslt' = "opt_val"

    // call the lp main function
    lpmain `varlist', rel(`rel') rhs(`rhs') opt(`opt') ///
                      lprslt(`r1_lprslt') tableau(`t_tableau') ///
                      vars(`vars') slacks(`r1_slacks') artificials(`r1_artificials') ///
                      intvars(`intvars') tol1(`tol1') tol2(`tol2') `trace'

    // setup result of lprslt
    matrix `r1_lprslt' = r(lprslt)
/*
    if (`r1_lprslt'[1,1] >= .) {
            break
    }
*/                               restore, preserve

            }
            else { // select lprslt because all variables are integer
                    if (`lprslt'[1,1] >= .) {
                            matrix `lprslt' = `c_lprslt'
                    }
                    else if ("`opt'" == "max") {
                            if (`c_lprslt'[1,1] > `lprslt'[1,1]) {
                                    matrix `lprslt' = `c_lprslt'
                            }
                    }
                    else { // else if ("`opt'" == "min") {
                            if (`c_lprslt'[1,1] < `lprslt'[1,1]) {
                                    matrix `lprslt' = `c_lprslt'
                            }
                    }
            }
    }
    else if (`c_lprslt'[1,1] < .) {
            matrix `lprslt' = `c_lprslt'
    }

    // FIXME
    di as result _n "final lprslt:"
    matrix list `lprslt', noblank nohalf noheader f(%9.6g)

        return matrix lprslt = `lprslt'
    end

    // Make Tableau Matrix ------------------------------------------------------
    program define mktableau, rclass
```

```
syntax varlist(numeric) [if] [in], opt(string) rel(varname) tableau(name)

// make matrix
mkmat `varlist' `if' `in', matrix(`tableau') rownames(`rel')

// r_vec: row vector, s_mat: slacks matrix, a_mat: artificials matrix
tempname r_vec s_mat a_mat

local s_names = ""
local a_names = ""
local rel_values : rownames `tableau'
forvalues i = 2/`=rowsof(`tableau')' {
        matrix `r_vec' = J(rowsof(`tableau'), 1, 0)
        local rel_value = word("`rel_values'", `i')

        if ("`rel_value'" == "<" || "`rel_value'" == "<=" ) {
                // slack
                matrix `r_vec'[`i', 1] = 1
                matrix `s_mat' = nullmat(`s_mat'), `r_vec'
                local s_names = "`s_names' s`=colsof(`s_mat')'"
        }
        else if ("`rel_value'" == ">" || "`rel_value'" == ">=") {
                // slcak
                matrix `r_vec'[`i', 1] = -1
                matrix `s_mat' = nullmat(`s_mat'), `r_vec'
                local s_names = "`s_names' s`=colsof(`s_mat')'"

                // artificial
                matrix `r_vec'[1, 1] = 1 // coefficients of aritificial
                matrix `r_vec'[`i', 1] = 1
                matrix `a_mat' = nullmat(`a_mat'), `r_vec'
                local a_names = "`a_names' a`=colsof(`a_mat')'"
        }
        else if ("`rel_value'" == "=") {
                // artificial
                matrix `r_vec'[1, 1] = 1 // coefficients of aritificial
                matrix `r_vec'[`i', 1] = 1
                matrix `a_mat' = nullmat(`a_mat'), `r_vec'
                local a_names = "`a_names' a`=colsof(`a_mat')'"
        }
        else {
                di as err "not allowed value of relational. :[`rel_value'] "
        exit 198 // TODO error code confirm
        }
} // end of forvalues statements

// make return values
tempname ret_tableau

// #01. init objective and variables
matrix `r_vec' = J(rowsof(`tableau'), 1, 0)
matrix `r_vec'[1,1] = 1
matrix colnames `r_vec' = "z" // Objective name

matrix `ret_tableau' = `r_vec', `tableau'[1...,1..(colsof(`tableau')-1)]

// #02. append slacks
if ("`s_names'" != "") {
        matrix colnames `s_mat' = `s_names'
```

```
                matrix `ret_tableau' = `ret_tableau', `s_mat'
                return local nslacks = colsof(`s_mat') // number of slacks
        }
        else return local nslacks = 0

        // #03. append artificials
        if ("`a_names'" != "") {
                matrix colnames `a_mat' = `a_names'
                matrix `ret_tableau' = `ret_tableau', `a_mat'
                return local nartificials = colsof(`a_mat') // number of artificials
        }
        else return local nartificials = 0

        // #04. append rhs
        matrix `ret_tableau' = `ret_tableau', `tableau'[1...,colsof(`tableau')]

        // #05. return results
        matrix `tableau' = `ret_tableau'
end

// Start of the MATA Definition Area ---------------------------------------
version 10
mata:
mata set matastrict on

void function _lp_phase (
                string scalar tableau,
                string scalar opt,
                real scalar vars,
                real scalar slacks,
                real scalar artificials,
                real scalar tol1,
                real scalar tol2,
                string scalar trace )
{
        real matrix M, VARS
        real fcols

        struct BoundCond matrix boundM
        struct LpParam scalar param
        struct LpResultStruct scalar lpresult

        // 1st. load matrix and variable indexes
        M = st_matrix(tableau)
        VARS = (0, 1..vars+slacks, -1..-artificials, 0)

        // 2rd. make boundary matrix
        // 0 <= weight, slacks, atrificials <= INFINITE
        boundM = J(1, cols(M), BoundCond());
        for (i=1; i<cols(M); i++) {
                boundM[1,i].val = 0; boundM[1,i].lower = 0; boundM[1,i].upper = .
        }

        // 3th. set the lp's parameters
        param.minYn         = (opt == "min"); // 0: max, 1: min

        param.vars      = vars
        param.slacks    = slacks
        param.artificials = artificials
```

```
param.tol1        = tol1
param.tol2        = tol2
param.trace       = trace
param.tracename   = "LP for RSM"

lpresult = lp_phase(M, boundM, VARS, param)

// -------------------------------------------------------------------
// final.
// -------------------------------------------------------------------
if(lpresult.rc) {
        LPRSLT = J(1, 1+param.vars+param.slacks, .)
}
else {
        // lpresult = theta(1) + vars + slacks
        LPRSLT = J(1, param.vars+param.slacks, 0)
        for (j=1; j<=rows(lpresult.XB) ; j++) {
                if (VARS[1,j+1] > 0) LPRSLT[1, VARS[1,j+1]] = lpresult.XB[j,
1]
        }
        LPRSLT = lpresult.xVal, LPRSLT
}

if (param.trace == "trace") {
    msg = sprintf("%s-FINAL", param.tracename);
    // printf("\n%s: original VARS.\n", msg); orgVARS
    printf("\n%s: VARS.\n", msg); VARS
    printf("\n%s: XB.\n", msg); lpresult.XB
    printf("\n%s: LPRSLT.\n", msg); LPRSLT
}

st_matrix("r(lprslt)", LPRSLT)
}

/**
 * @param VARS          - Variable Index Matrix
 *                        [z, B, N, b]'s index in the original Tableau
 * @param M  - Tableau: [z, A, S, Af, b] --> [z, B, N, b]
 * @param phase - if have artificials, then phase 1 and 2,
 *                                      otherwise only phase 2
 * @param param - parameter struct for Lp RSM
 *
 * @return result of LP
 */
struct LpResultStruct function lp_phase (
    real matrix M,
    struct BoundCond matrix boundM,
    real matrix VARS,
    struct LpParam scalar param )
{
    real scalar phase, mrows, mcols, j, idx
    string scalar tracename
    real vector reorderidx, bfsidx, nonbfsidx
    real vector coef_of // coefficient of objective function
    struct LpParamStruct scalar lpParam
    struct LpResultStruct scalar lpResult

    // validation checking.
    if (param.minYn >= .) { //
```

```
                displayas("err");
                _error(3351, "You have to set the minimization(1) or maximization(0) "
                        + "at the LpParam.minYn")
        }

        coef_of = M[1, 2..1+param.vars] // keep the objective function
        replacesubmat(M, 1, 2, J(1, param.vars, 0))

// initialize matrix.
if (param.trace == "trace") {
        displayas("txt")
        printf("\n\n%s: initialize matrix.\n", param.tracename); M
}

        mrows = rows(M); mcols = cols(M)

        // classify basic and nonbasic.
        bfsidx = J(1, mrows-1, .); nonbfsidx = J(1, 0, .)
        for (j = 2+param.vars; j <= mcols-1; j++) {
                T = M[2::mrows,j]
                if ((sum(T :!= 0) == 1) && (sum(T) == 1)) {
                        maxindex(T, 1, i, w); bfsidx[i] = j
                }
                else nonbfsidx = nonbfsidx, j
        }
        reorderidx = (1, bfsidx[1,], 2..1+param.vars, nonbfsidx[1,], mcols)
        VARS = VARS[,reorderidx];
        M = M[,reorderidx]; boundM = boundM[,reorderidx]

        if (param.trace == "trace") {
                displayas("txt")
                printf("\n%s: classify basic and nonbasic.\n", tracename); M; VARS
        }

        // set the lp's parameters
        lpParam.dmus           = param.vars
        lpParam.slacks         = param.slacks
        lpParam.artificials = param.artificials
        lpParam.tol1           = param.tol1
        lpParam.tol2           = param.tol2
        lpParam.trace          = param.trace

        // solve the linear programming(LP): phase I
        if (param.artificials > 0) {
                phase = 1
                lpParam.minYn = 1; // min because of phase 1
                tracename = param.tracename + "-PI"
                lpResult = lp(M, boundM, VARS, 0, phase, tracename, lpParam)

                if (lpResult.rc) return(lpResult)
        }

        // solve the linear programming(LP): phase II
        phase = 2
        lpParam.minYn = param.minYn // according to the optimization.
        tracename = param.tracename + "-PII"

        // set the objective function.
        mcols = cols(M)
```

```
    for (j=2; j<mcols; j++) {
            idx = VARS[1,j]
            if (0 < idx && idx <= param.vars) {
                    M[1,j] = coef_of[idx] // according to variable's index
            }
    }
    lpResult = lp(M, boundM, VARS, 0, phase, tracename, lpParam)

    // return result.
    return(lpResult)
}

end
// End of the MATA Definition Area --------------------------------------------
```

B2.4 dea_sbm.ado

```
*! version 1.0.0  21JUL2012
capture program drop dea_sbm
program define dea_sbm, rclass
    version 10.0

/** Terms Description:
 * -------------------------------------------------------------------------
 * RTS: Return To Scale
 * CRS: Constant Return to Scale
 * VRS: Variant Return to Scale
 * -------------------------------------------------------------------------
 */

// syntax checking and validation------------------------------------
// rts - return to scale, ort - orientation
// input varlist = output varlist
// example:
//    dea_sbm Employee Area = Sales Profits, rts(CRS) ort(IN) tol1(1e-14)
//    dea_sbm Employee Area = Sales Profits, sav
// -------------------------------------------------------------------
    // returns 1 if the first nonblank character of local macro `0' is a comma,
    // or if `0' is empty.
    if replay() {
        dis as err "ivars and ovars required."
        exit 198
    }

    // get and check invarnames
    gettoken word 0 : 0, parse("=,")
    while ~("`word'" == ":" | "`word'" == "=") {
        if "`word'" == "," | "`word'" == "" {
            error 198
        }
        local invarnames `invarnames' `word'
        gettoken word 0 : 0, parse("=,")
    }
    unab invarnames : `invarnames'

    #del ;
    syntax varlist(min=1) [if] [in] [using/]
    [,
        RTS(string)      // ignore case sensitive,[{CRS|CCR}|{BCC|VRS}]
            ORT(string)      // ignore case sensitive,
                                                                    //
[{I/IN|INPUT}|{O/OUT|OUTPUT}|{IO|INOUT|INOUTPUT}]
        TOL1(real 1e-14)    // entering or leaving value tolerance
        TOL2(real 1e-8)     // B inverse tolerance: 2.22e-12
        TRACE           // Whether or not to do the log
        SAVing(string)      // log file name
        REPLACE          // Whether or not to replace the log file
    ];
    #del cr

    local num_invar : word count `invarnames'
    local i 1
```

176

```
while (`i'<=`num_invar') {
    local invarn : word `i' of `invarnames'
    local junk : subinstr local invarnames "`invarn'" "", ///
        word all count(local j)
    if `j' > 1 {
        di as error ///
            "cannot specify the same input variable more than once"
        error 498
    }
    local i = `i' + 1
}

// default model - CRS(Constant Return to Scale)
if ("`rts'" == "") local rts = "CRS"
else {
    local rts = upper("`rts'")
    if ("`rts'" == "CCR") local rts = "CRS"
    else if ("`rts'" == "BCC") local rts = "VRS"
    else if (~("`rts'" == "CRS" | "`rts'" == "VRS")) {
        di as err "option rts allow for case-insensitive " _c
        di as err "CRS (eq CCR) or VRS (eq BCC) or nothing."
        exit 198
    }
}

// default orientation - Input Oriented
if ("`ort'" != "") {
    local ort = upper("`ort'")
    if ("`ort'" == "I" | "`ort'" == "IN" | "`ort'" == "INPUT") {
        local ort = "IN"
    }
    else if ("`ort'" == "O" | "`ort'" == "OUT" | "`ort'" == "OUTPUT") {
        local ort = "OUT"
    }
    else if ("`ort'" == "IO" | "`ort'" == "INOUT" | "`ort'" ==
"INOUTPUT") {
        local ort = "INOUT"
    }
    else {
        di as err "option ort allows for case-insensitive " _c
        di as err "(i|in|input|o|out|output|io|inout|inoutput) or nothing."
        exit 198
    }
}
else {
        local ort = "IN"
}

if ("`using'" != "") use "`using'", clear
if (~(`c(N)' > 0 & `c(k)' > 0)) {
    dis as err "dataset required!"
    exit 198
}

// end of syntax checking and validation -------------------------------------

set more off
capture log close dea_sbm_log
log using "dea_sbm.log", replace text name(dea_sbm_log)
```

```
preserve

if ("`if'" != "" | "`in'" != "") {
    qui keep `in' `if'  // filtering : keep in range [if exp]
}


_dea_sbm, ivars(`invarnames') ovars(`varlist') rts(`rts') ort(`ort') ///
            tol1(`tol1') tol2(`tol2') `trace' saving(`saving') `replace'
return add

restore, preserve
log close dea_sbm_log
end
```

```
*********************************************************************************
* DEA SBM - Data Envelopment Analysis Slack Based Model
*********************************************************************************
program define _dea_sbm, rclass
    #del ;
    syntax , IVARS(string) OVARS(string) RTS(string)
    [
            ORT(string) TOL1(real 1e-14) TOL2(real 1e-8)
            TRACE SAVing(string) REPLACE
    ];
    #del cr

    preserve

    // -----------------------------------------------------------------------

    tempname dmuIn dmuOut frameMat deamainrslt dearslt vrsfrontier crslambda
    mkDmuMat `ivars', dmumat(`dmuIn') sprefix("i")
    mkDmuMat `ovars', dmumat(`dmuOut') sprefix("o")
    local dmuCount = colsof(`dmuIn')
    local minrank = 0

    mata: _l_mkframemat("`frameMat'", "`dmuIn'", "`dmuOut'", "`rts'", "`ort'")
    mata: _l_dealp ("`frameMat'", "`dmuIn'", "`dmuOut'", "`rts'", "`ort'", ///
            `tol1', `tol2', "`trace'")
    matrix `deamainrslt' = r(dealprslt)

    // -----------------------------------------------------------------------
    mata: _dmurank("`deamainrslt'", ///
            `=rowsof(`dmuIn')', `=rowsof(`dmuOut')', `minrank', `tol2')
    matrix `dearslt' = r(rank), `deamainrslt'
    // -----------------------------------------------------------------------

    // use mata function '_setup_dearslt_names' because the maximum string
    // variable length needs to be kept under the 244 for all the time
    mata: _setup_dearslt_names("`dearslt'", "`dmuIn'", "`dmuOut'")

    // -----------------------------------------------------------------------
    restore, preserve

    // REPORT
    report_dea_sbm, dearslt(`dearslt') rts(`rts') ort(`ort') ///
                    `trace' saving(`saving') `replace'

    return matrix dearslt = `dearslt'
```

```
    restore, preserve
end

********************************************************************************
* REPORT
********************************************************************************
program define report_dea_sbm, rclass
    #del ;
    syntax , dearslt(name) RTS(string)
    [
        ORT(string) TRACE SAVing(string) REPLACE
    ];
    #del cr

    preserve
    // ------------------------------------------------------------------------
    di as result ""
    di as input "options: RTS(`rts') ORT(`ort')"
    di as result "`rts' DEA-SBM Efficiency Results:"
    matrix list `dearslt', noblank nohalf noheader f(%9.6g)

    if ("`saving'" != "") {
        // if the saving file exists and replace option not specified,
        // make the backup file.
        if ("`replace'" == "") {
            local dotpos = strpos("`saving'",".")
            if (`dotpos' > 0) {
                mata: _file_exists("`saving'")
            }
            else {
                mata: _file_exists("`saving'.dta")
            }
            if r(fileexists) {
                local curdt = subinstr("`c(current_date)'", " ", "", .) + /*
                    */ subinstr("`c(current_time)'", ":", "", .)
                if (`dotpos' > 0) {
                    #del ;
                    local savefn = substr("`saving'", 1, `dotpos' - 1) +
                        "_bak_`curdt'" +
                        substr("`saving'",`dotpos', .);
                    #del cr
                    qui copy "`saving'" "`savefn'", replace
                }
                else {
                    local savefn = "`saving'_bak_`curdt'" + ".dta"
                    qui copy "`saving'.dta" "`savefn'", replace
                }
            }
        }
    }

    restore, preserve
            svmat `dearslt', names(eqcol)
            capture {
                    renpfix _
                    renpfix ref ref_
                    renpfix islack is_
                    renpfix oslack os_
            }
            capture save `saving', replace
```

```
    }
    // ------------------------------------------------------------------
    restore, preserve
end

********************************************************************************
* Data Import and Conversion
********************************************************************************

// Make DMU Matrix ------------------------------------------------------
program define mkDmuMat
    #del ;
    syntax varlist(numeric) [if] [in], DMUmat(name)
    [
        SPREfix(string)
    ];
    #del cr

    qui ds
    // variable not found error
    if ("`varlist'" == "") {
        di as err "variable not found"
        exit 111
    }

    // make matrix
    mkmat `varlist' `if' `in', matrix(`dmumat') rownames(dmu)
    matrix roweq `dmumat' = "dmu"
    matrix coleq `dmumat' = `=lower("`sprefix'")' + "slack'"
    matrix `dmumat' = `dmumat"
end

// Start of the MATA Definition Area ----------------------------------
version 10
mata:
mata set matastrict on

/**
 * make frame matrix and set matrix value at the param frameMat
 * rts - return to scale, ort - orientation
 */
function _l_mkframemat(
                string scalar frameMat,
                string scalar dmuIn,
                string scalar dmuOut,
                string scalar rts,
                string scalar ort )
{
    real matrix F, DI, DO
    real scalar dmus, slackins, slackouts, exist_param_t
    real scalar frows, fcols

    DI = st_matrix(dmuIn)
    DO = st_matrix(dmuOut)
    if (cols(DI) != cols(DO)) {
        _error(3200, "in and out count of dmu is not match!")
    }

    exist_param_t = (ort == "INOUT")
```

```
dmus = cols(DI) // or cols(DO), because cols(DI) == cols(DO)
slackins = rows(DI); slackouts = rows(DO)
if (rts == "CRS") {
    // target coefficient\slackins\slackouts\{param_t}
    frows = 1 + slackins + slackouts + exist_param_t
                // target coefficient,param_t,dmus,slackins,slackouts,rhs
    fcols = 1 + 1 + dmus + slackins + slackouts + 1
}
else if (rts == "VRS") {
                // target coefficient\slackins\slackouts\{param_t}\sum of lamda
    frows = 1 + slackins + slackouts + exist_param_t + 1
                // target coefficient,param_t,dmus,slackins,slackouts,rhs
    fcols = 1 + 1 + dmus + slackins + slackouts + 1
}
else {
    _error(3498, "invalid rts optoin.")
}

// make frame matrix for CRS(CCR)
F = J(frows, fcols, 0)
F[1, 1] = 1
if (ort == "INOUT") {
                replacesubmat(F, 2, 3, DI)
                replacesubmat(F, 2 + slackins, 3, -DO)
                replacesubmat(F, 2, 3 + dmus, I(slackins))
                replacesubmat(F, 2 + slackins, 3 + dmus + slackins, I(slackouts))
                replacesubmat(F, 2 + slackins + slackouts, 2, 1) // param_t
                replacesubmat(F, 2 + slackins + slackouts, fcols, 1) // param_t's rhs
}
else { // ort == "IN" or "OUT"
                replacesubmat(F, 2, 3, DI)
                replacesubmat(F, 2 + slackins, 3, DO)
                replacesubmat(F, 2, 3 + dmus, I(slackins))
                replacesubmat(F, 2 + slackins, 3 + dmus + slackins, -I(slackouts))
}

// adjustment
if (rts == "VRS") {
    replacesubmat(F, frows, 3, J(1, dmus, 1))
    F[frows,fcols] = 1
}

// return result
st_matrix(frameMat, F)
}

/**
 * DEA Loop - Data Envelopment Analysis Loop for DMUs
 */
function _l_dealp (
                string scalar frameMat,
                string scalar dmuIn,
                string scalar dmuOut,
                string scalar rts,
                string scalar ort,
                real scalar tol1,
                real scalar tol2,
                string scalar trace )
{
```

181

```
real matrix F, DI, DO, M, VARS, LPRSLT, DEALPRSLT, ARTIF
real scalar dmus, slackins, slackouts, slacks, artificials, artificialrow
real scalar frows, fcols, i, dmui, exist_param_t
real colvector effvec, slackidx, param_t_row, param_t_col
string scalar tracename

struct BoundCond matrix boundF, boundM
struct LpParamStruct scalar param

F  = st_matrix(frameMat)
DI = st_matrix(dmuIn)
DO = st_matrix(dmuOut)
if (cols(DI) != cols(DO)) {
    _error(3200, "in and out count of dmu is not match!")
}
if (!(rts == "CRS" || rts == "VRS")) {
        _error(3498, "rts must be one of CRS, VRS")
}

// basic value setting for artificial variabels
frows = rows(F); fcols = cols(F)
dmus = cols(DI) // or cols(DO), because cols(DI) == cols(DO)
slackins = rows(DI); slackouts = rows(DO)

tracename = rts + "-" + ort

// -----------------------------------------------------------------------
// define number of slacks by rts
slacks = slackins + slackouts

// define number of artificials by rts, ort, stage
exist_param_t = (ort == "INOUT")
if (rts == "CRS") {
        artificials = slackouts+exist_param_t; artificialrow = 2+slackins;
}
else if (rts == "VRS") {
        artificials = slackouts+exist_param_t+1; artificialrow = 2+slackins
}
if (artificials > 0) {
        ARTIF = J(1, artificials, 1) \ J(frows-1, artificials, 0)
        replacesubmat(ARTIF, artificialrow, 1, I(artificials))
        F = F[,1..fcols-1], ARTIF, F[,fcols]
        frows = rows(F); fcols = cols(F) // revise frows, fcols
}

// -----------------------------------------------------------------------
boundF = J(1, fcols, BoundCond());
// set the boundary for the efficiency variable(theta, eta):
// -INFINITE <= efficiency <= INFINITE
boundF[1,2].val = 0; boundF[1,2].lower = 0; boundF[1,2].upper = .

// set boundary for the weight variable(lamda, mu):
// 0 <= weight <= INFINITE
for (i=3; i<dmus+3; i++) {
        boundF[1,i].val = 0; boundF[1,i].lower = 0; boundF[1,i].upper = .
}

// set boundary for the non-structural variable(slack, artificial).
// 0 <= slacks and atrificials <= INFINITE
```

```
for (i=dmus+3; i<fcols; i++) {
        boundF[1,i].val = 0; boundF[1,i].lower = 0; boundF[1,i].upper = .
}
// liststruct(boundF); // for debug

// set the lp's parameters
param.rts        = rts
param.isin       = 0 // don't care
param.minYn       = 1 // min
param.stagestep    = 2 // 2 step
param.dmus        = dmus
param.dmuins      = slackins
param.dmuouts      = slackouts
param.slacks      = slacks
param.artificials  = artificials
param.tol1        = tol1
param.tol2        = tol2
param.isminsubscript = 0 // false
param.trace       = trace
// liststruct(param); // for debug
// -------------------------------------------------------------------------
DEALPRSLT = J(0, 1+ dmus + slacks, 0)
if (ort == "INOUT") {
        param_t_row = 2+slacks; param_t_col = fcols-artificials-slackouts
        for (dmui=1; dmui<=dmus; dmui++) {
                M = F; boundM = boundF
                replacesubmat(M, 2, 2, -DI[,dmui])
                replacesubmat(M, 2+slackins, 2, DO[,dmui])
                replacesubmat(M, param_t_row, param_t_col,

((1:/DO[,dmui]):*(1/slackouts))');

                        // execute LP
                        VARS  = lp_phase1(M, boundM, dmui, tracename, param)
                        if (VARS[1,1] == .) {
                                LPRSLT = J(1, cols(DEALPRSLT), .)
                        }
                        else {
                                LPRSLT = l_lp_phase2(DI, DO, ort, M, boundM,
VARS, dmui,

                                                tracename, param);
                        }
                        DEALPRSLT = DEALPRSLT \ LPRSLT
                }
        }
        else {
                for (dmui=1; dmui<=dmus; dmui++) {
                        M = F; boundM = boundF
                        replacesubmat(M, 2, fcols, DI[,dmui])
                        replacesubmat(M, 2+slacks, fcols, DO[,dmui])

                        // execute LP
                        VARS  = lp_phase1(M, boundM, dmui, tracename, param)
                        if (VARS[1,1] == .) {
                                LPRSLT = J(1, cols(DEALPRSLT), .)
                        }
                        else {
                                if (ort == "OUT") param.minYn = 0 // max
                                LPRSLT = l_lp_phase2(DI, DO, ort, M, boundM,
```

```
VARS, dmui,
                                                    tracename, param);
                            if (ort == "OUT") param.minYn = 1 // min
                        }
                        DEALPRSLT = DEALPRSLT \ LPRSLT
                }
        }

        st_matrix("r(dealprslt)", DEALPRSLT)
}

        real matrix function l_lp_phase2 (
                real matrix DI,
                real matrix DO,
                string scalar ort,

                real matrix M,
                struct BoundCond matrix boundM,
                real matrix VARS,
                real scalar dmui,
                string scalar aTracename,
                struct LpParamStruct scalar param )
{
        real matrix T, XB, orgVARS, LPRSLT
        real scalar i, j, phase, mrows, mcols
        real vector slackidx
        string scalar tracename, msg
        struct LpResultStruct scalar lpresult

        orgVARS = VARS
        mrows = rows(M); mcols = cols(M)

        tracename = aTracename + "-PII"

        // modify target function value:
        if (ort == "INOUT") {
                // X = t - 1/iC * (iS1/iV1 + iS2/iV2 + ... + iSn/iVn)
                slackidx = (2+param.dmus..1+param.dmus+param.dmuins)
                for (j=2; j<mcols; j++) {
                        if (VARS[1,j] == 1 && !allof(M[,j], 0)) M[1,j] = 1 // if t
                        else {
                                for (i=1; i<=param.dmuins; i++) {
                                        if    (VARS[1,j]    ==    slackidx[i]
&& !allof(M[,j], 0)) {
                                                M[1,j]        =        -
((1/param.dmuins)* (1/DI[i,dmui]))
                                        }
                                }
                        }
                }
        }
        else if (ort == "IN") {
                // Z = 1 - 1/iC * (iS1/iV1 + iS2/iV2 + ... + iSn/iVn)
                // -Z + 1 - 1/iC * (iS1/iV1 + iS2/iV2 + ... + iSn/iVn) = 0
                // if -X = -Z + 1, then
                // -X - 1/iC * (iS1/iV1 + iS2/iV2 + ... + iSn/iVn) = 0
                slackidx = (2+param.dmus..1+param.dmus+param.dmuins)
                for (j=2; j<mcols; j++) {
                        for (i=1; i<=param.dmuins; i++) {
```

```
                                    if (VARS[1,j] == slackidx[i] && !allof(M[,j], 0)) {
                                        M[1,j]    =    -((1/param.dmuins)*
(1/DI[i,dmui]))
                                    }
                                }
                            }
                        }
        else if (ort == "OUT") {
                // Z = 1 + 1/oC * (oS1/oV1 + oS2/oV2 + ... + oSn/oVn)
                // -Z + 1 + 1/oC * (oS1/oV1 + oS2/oV2 + ... + oSn/oVn) = 0
                // if -X = -Z + 1, then
                // -X + 1/oC * (oS1/oV1 + oS2/oV2 + ... + oSn/oVn) = 0
                slackidx = (2+param.dmus+param.dmuins..

        1+param.dmus+param.dmuins+param.dmuouts)
                for (j=2; j<mcols; j++) {
                        for (i=1; i<=param.dmuouts; i++) {
                                if (VARS[1,j] == slackidx[i] && !allof(M[,j], 0)) {
                                        M[1,j]    =    (1/param.dmuouts)*
(1/DO[i,dmui])
                                }
                            }
                        }
        else {
                displayas("err")
                printf("\n[DMUi=%g]%s: input parma error[ort=%s].\n",
                        dmui, tracename, ort)
                exit(198)
        }

        if (param.trace == "trace") {
            displayas("txt")
            printf("\n----------[PHASE II]----------")
            printf("\n[DMUi=%g]%s: initialize matrix.\n",
                dmui, tracename); M
            printf("\n[DMUi=%g]%s: VARS.\n", dmui, tracename); VARS
        }

        phase = 2
        lpresult = lp(M, boundM, VARS, dmui, phase, tracename, param)

        // -----------------------------------------------------------------------
        // phase 2 final.
        // -----------------------------------------------------------------------
        if(lpresult.rc) {
                LPRSLT = J(1, 1+param.dmus+param.slacks, .)
        }
        else {
                // lpresult = theta(1) + dmus + slacks
                LPRSLT = J(1, 1+param.dmus+param.slacks, 0)

                for (j=1; j<=rows(lpresult.XB) ; j++) {
                        if (VARS[1,j+1] > 0) LPRSLT[1, VARS[1,j+1]] =lpresult.XB[j,
1]
                }

                if (ort == "INOUT") {
                        LPRSLT = LPRSLT :/ LPRSLT[1, 1] // slack value = slack /
```

```
t
                                LPRSLT[1, 1] = lpresult.xVal // theta = target function value.
                         }
                         else { // ort == "IN" or "OUT"
                                // -X = -Z + 1 -> Z = X + 1 (theta = target function value +
1)
                                LPRSLT[1, 1] = lpresult.xVal + 1
                         }
                }

           if (param.trace == "trace") {
              msg = sprintf("[DMUi=%g]%s-FINAL", dmui, tracename);
              printf("\n%s: original VARS.\n", msg); orgVARS
              printf("\n%s: VARS.\n", msg); VARS
              printf("\n%s: XB.\n", msg); lpresult.XB
              printf("\n%s: LPRSLT.\n", msg); LPRSLT
           }

           return(LPRSLT)
        }

     end
     // End of the MATA Definition Area ---------------------------------------------
```

B2.5 dea_supereff.ado

```
*! version 1.0.0  02JUN2012
capture program drop dea_supereff
program define dea_supereff, rclass
    version 10.0

/** Terms Description:
 * ------------------------------------------------------------------------
 * RTS: Return To Scale
 * CRS: Constant Return to Scale
 * VRS: Variant Return to Scale
 * IRS: Increasing Return to Scale
 * DRS: Decreasing Retrn to Scale
 *
 * ser: super efficiency radial
 * ------------------------------------------------------------------------
 */

// syntax checking and validation---------------------------------------
// rts - return to scale, ort - orientation
// input varlist = output varlist
// example:
//    dea_supereff Employee Area = Sales Profits, rts(CRS) ort(IN) tol1(1e-14)
//    dea_supereff Employee Area = Sales Profits, sav
// ------------------------------------------------------------------------
    // returns 1 if the first nonblank character of local macro `0' is a comma,
    // or if `0' is empty.
    if replay() {
        dis as err "ivars and ovars required."
        exit 198
    }

    // get and check invarnames
    gettoken word 0 : 0, parse("=,")
    while ~("`word'" == ":" | "`word'" == "=") {
        if "`word'" == "," | "`word'" == "" {
            error 198
        }
        local invarnames `invarnames' `word'
        gettoken word 0 : 0, parse("=,")
    }
    unab invarnames : `invarnames'

    #del ;
    syntax varlist(min=1) [if] [in] [using/]
    [,
        RTS(string)       // ignore case sensitive,[{CRS|CCR} | {BCC|VRS}|DRS|IRS]
        ORT(string)       // ignore case sensitive,[{IN|INPUT} | {OUT|OUTPUT}]
        STAGE(integer 2)  // stage 1 or 2
        TOL1(real 1e-14)  // entering or leaving value tolerance
        TOL2(real 1e-8)   // B inverse tolerance: 2.22e-12
        MINSUBScript      // minimal subscript pivot
        TRACE             // Whether or not to do the log
        SAVing(string)    // log file name
        REPLACE           // Whether or not to replace the log file
    ];
```

```
#del cr

local num_invar : word count `invarnames'
local i 1
while (`i'<=`num_invar') {
    local invarn : word `i' of `invarnames'
    local junk : subinstr local invarnames "`invarn'" "", ///
        word all count(local j)
    if `j' > 1 {
        di as error ///
            "cannot specify the same input variable more than once"
        error 498
    }
    local i = `i' + 1
}

// default model - CRS(Constant Return to Scale)
if ("`rts'" == "") local rts = "CRS"
else {
    local rts = upper("`rts'")
    if ("`rts'" == "CCR") local rts = "CRS"
    else if ("`rts'" == "BCC") local rts = "VRS"
    else if (~("`rts'" == "CRS" | "`rts'" == "VRS" | ///
            "`rts'" == "DRS" | "`rts'" == "IRS")) {
        di as err "option rts allow for case-insensitive " _c
        di as err "CRS (eq CCR) or VRS (eq BCC) or DRS or IRS or nothing."
        exit 198
    }
}

// default orientation - Input Oriented
if ("`ort'" == "") local ort = "IN"
else {
    local ort = upper("`ort'")
    if ("`ort'" == "I" | "`ort'" == "IN" | "`ort'" == "INPUT") {
        local ort = "IN"
    }
    else if ("`ort'" == "O" | "`ort'" == "OUT" | "`ort'" == "OUTPUT") {
        local ort = "OUT"
    }
    else {
        di as err "option ort allows for case-insensitive " _c
        di as err "(i|in|input|o|out|output) or nothing."
        exit 198
    }
}

// default stage - 1
if (~("`stage'" == "1" | "`stage'" == "2")) {
    dis as err "option stage allows 1 or 2 or nothing exclusively."
    exit 198
}

if ("`using'" != "") use "`using'", clear
if (~(`c(N)' > 0 & `c(k)' > 0)) {
    dis as err "dataset required!"
    exit 198
}
```

```
// end of syntax checking and validation ------------------------------------

set more off
capture log close dea_supereff_log
log using "dea_supereff.log", replace text name(dea_supereff_log)
preserve

if ("`if'" != "" | "`in'" != "") {
    qui keep `in' `if'  // filtering : keep in range [if exp]
}

deanormal, ivars(`invarnames') ovars(`varlist') ///
        rts(`rts') ort(`ort') stage(`stage') ///
        tol1(`tol1') tol2(`tol2') `minsubscript' ///
        `trace' saving(`saving') `replace'
return add

restore, preserve
log close dea_supereff_log
end

*******************************************************************************
* DEA Normal - Data Envelopment Analysis Normal
*******************************************************************************
program define deanormal, rclass
    #del ;
    syntax , IVARS(string) OVARS(string) RTS(string) ORT(string)
    [
        STAGE(integer 2) TOL1(real 1e-3) TOL2(real 1e-12) MINSUBScript
        TRACE SAVing(string) REPLACE
    ];
    #del cr

    preserve
    // di _n as input ///
    //     "options: RTS(`rts') ORT(`ort') STAGE(`stage') SAVing(`saving')"
    // di as input "Input Data:"
    // list

    // -----------------------------------------------------------------------

    tempname dmuIn dmuOut frameMat deamainrslt dearslt vrsfrontier crslambda
    mkDmuMat `ivars', dmumat(`dmuIn') sprefix("i")
    mkDmuMat `ovars', dmumat(`dmuOut') sprefix("o")
    local dmuCount = colsof(`dmuIn')
    if ("`minsubscript'" == "") local minsubscript = "nominsubscript"
    if ("`ort'" == "OUT") local minrank = 1
    else local minrank = 0

    mata: _mkframemat("`frameMat'", "`dmuIn'", "`dmuOut'", ///
        "`rts'", "`ort'")
    deamain `dmuIn' `dmuOut' `frameMat' `rts' `ort' `stage' ///
        `tol1' `tol2' `minsubscript' `trace'
    matrix `deamainrslt' = r(deamainrslt)

    mata: _dmurank("`deamainrslt'", ///
        `=rowsof(`dmuIn')', `=rowsof(`dmuOut')', `minrank', `tol2')
    matrix `dearslt' = r(rank), `deamainrslt'
```

```
// use mata function '_setup_dearslt_names' because the maximum string
// variable length needs to be kept under the 244 for all the time
mata: _setup_dearslt_names("`dearslt'", "`dmuIn'", "`dmuOut'")

if ("`rts'" == "VRS") {
    // caution : join order! (CRS -> VRS -> DRS)
    // 1. VRS TE(VRS Technical Efficiency)
    matrix `deamainrslt' = r(deamainrslt)
    matrix `vrsfrontier' = `deamainrslt'[1...,1]

    // 2. CRS TE(CRS Technical Efficiency)
    local stageForVRS = 2
    mata: _mkframemat("`frameMat'", "`dmuIn'", "`dmuOut'", ///
        "CRS", "`ort'")
    deamain `dmuIn' `dmuOut' `frameMat' "CRS" `ort' `stageForVRS' ///
        `tol1' `tol2' `minsubscript' `trace'
    matrix `deamainrslt' = r(deamainrslt)
    matrix `vrsfrontier' = `deamainrslt'[1...,1], `vrsfrontier'
    matrix `crslambda' = `deamainrslt'[1...,2..(`dmuCount' + 1)]

    // 3. DRS TE(DRS Technical Efficiency)
    local stageForVRS = 1
    mata: _mkframemat("`frameMat'", "`dmuIn'", "`dmuOut'", ///
        "DRS", "`ort'")
    deamain `dmuIn' `dmuOut' `frameMat' "DRS" `ort' `stageForVRS' ///
        `tol1' `tol2' `minsubscript' `trace'
    matrix `deamainrslt' = r(deamainrslt)
    matrix `vrsfrontier' = `vrsfrontier', `deamainrslt'[1...,1] // VRS
    mata: _roundmat("`vrsfrontier'", 1e-14) // round off

    //
    matrix `vrsfrontier' = `vrsfrontier', J(rowsof(`vrsfrontier'), 2, 0)
    matrix rownames `vrsfrontier' = : colfullnames `dmuIn'"
    matrix colnames `vrsfrontier' = CRS_TE VRS_TE DRS_TE SCALE RTS

    if ("`trace'" == "trace") matrix list `crslambda'
    forvalues i = 1/`=rowsof(`vrsfrontier')' {
        matrix `vrsfrontier'[`i',4] = /*
            */ float(`vrsfrontier'[`i',1]/`vrsfrontier'[`i',2])

        /***************************************************************
        * if CRS(CCR) == VRS(BCC) then CRS
        * else
        *     if sum of λ equals to 1, then CRS mark
        *     if sum of λ is greater than 1, then DRS mark
        *     if sum of λ is less than 1, then IRS mark
        ****************************************************************/
        // (-1:drs, 0:crs, 1:irs)
        if (`vrsfrontier'[`i',1] == `vrsfrontier'[`i',2]) {
            matrix `vrsfrontier'[`i',5] = 0
        }
        else {
            local sumlambda = 0
            forvalues j = 1/`dmuCount' {
                if (`crslambda'[`i', `j'] < .) {
                    local sumlambda = `sumlambda' + `crslambda'[`i', `j']
                }
            }
            if (`sumlambda' < 1) {
```

```
            matrix `vrsfrontier'[`i',5] = 1 // irs mark
        }
        else { // if (`sumlambda' >= 1) {
            matrix `vrsfrontier'[`i',5] = -1 // drs mark
        }
    }
  }
}

// --------------------------------------------------------------------
// REPORT
// --------------------------------------------------------------------
di as result ""
di as input "options: RTS(`rts') ORT(`ort') STAGE(`stage')"
di as result "`rts'-`ort'PUT Oriented DEA Efficiency Results:"
matrix list `dearslt', noblank nohalf noheader f(%9.6g)

if ("`saving'" != "") {
    // if the saving file exists and replace option not specified,
    // make the backup file.
    if ("`replace'" == "") {
        local dotpos = strpos("`saving'",".")
        if (`dotpos' > 0) {
            mata: _file_exists("`saving'")
        }
        else {
            mata: _file_exists("`saving'.dta")
        }
        if r(fileexists) {
            local curdt = subinstr("`c(current_date)'", " ", "", .) + /*
                */ subinstr("`c(current_time)'", ":", "", .)
            if (`dotpos' > 0) {
                #del ;
                local savefn = substr("`saving'", 1, `dotpos' - 1) +
                    "_bak_`curdt'" +
                    substr("`saving'",`dotpos', .);
                #del cr
                qui copy "`saving'" "`savefn'", replace
            }
            else {
                local savefn = "`saving'_bak_`curdt'" + ".dta"
                qui copy "`saving'.dta" "`savefn'", replace
            }
        }
    }

    if ("`rts'" != "VRS") {
        restore, preserve
        svmat `dearslt', names(eqcol)
        capture {
            renpfix _
            renpfix ref ref_
            renpfix islack is_
            renpfix oslack os_
        }
        capture save `saving', replace

        // di as result ""
        // di as result "DEA Result file:"
```

```
        // list
    }
}
return matrix dearslt = `dearslt'

if ("`rts'" == "VRS") {
    if ("`trace'" == "trace") {
        di _n(2) as result "CRS lambda(λ)"
        matrix list `crslambda' , noblank nohalf noheader f(%9.6f)
    }

    // if you don't have to verify, you can comment the following sentence.
    di _n(2) as result "VRS Frontier(-1:drs, 0:crs, 1:irs)"
    matrix list `vrsfrontier', noblank nohalf noheader f(%9.6f)

    di _n(2) as result "VRS Frontier:"
    restore, preserve
    svmat `vrsfrontier', names(col)
    rename RTS RTSNUM
    qui generate RTS = "drs" if RTSNUM == -1
    qui replace RTS = "-" if RTSNUM == 0
    qui replace RTS = "irs" if RTSNUM == 1
    drop DRS_TE RTSNUM
    format CRS_TE VRS_TE SCALE %9.6f
    list
    if ("`saving'"!="") {
        capture save `saving', replace
    }
}
restore, preserve
end

**********************************************************************
* DEA Main - Data Envelopment Analysis Main
**********************************************************************
program define deamain, rclass
    args dmuIn dmuOut frameMat rts ort stage tol1 tol2 minsubscript trace

    tempname efficientVec deamainrslt

    // stage step 1.
    if ("`trace'" == "trace") {
        di _n(2) as txt "RTS(`rts') ORT(`ort') 1st stage."
    }
    mata: _dealp_for_supereff("`frameMat'", "`dmuIn'", "`dmuOut'", ///
        "`rts'", "`ort'", 1, ///
        `tol1', `tol2', "`minsubscript'", "`efficientVec'", "`trace'")
    matrix `deamainrslt' = r(dealprslt)

    // stage step 2.
    if ("`stage'" == "2") {
        if ("`trace'" == "trace") {
            di _n(2) as txt "RTS(`rts') ORT(`ort') 2nd stage."
        }
        matrix `efficientVec' = `deamainrslt'[1...,1]

        mata: _dealp_for_supereff("`frameMat'", "`dmuIn'", "`dmuOut'", ///
                "`rts'", "`ort'", 2, ///
            `tol1', `tol2', "`minsubscript'", "`efficientVec'", "`trace'")
```

```
        matrix `deamainrslt' = r(dealprslt)
    }

    return matrix deamainrslt = `deamainrslt'
end

********************************************************************************
* Data Import and Conversion
********************************************************************************

// Make DMU Matrix -------------------------------------------------------
program define mkDmuMat
    #del ;
    syntax varlist(numeric) [if] [in], DMUmat(name)
    [
        SPREfix(string)
    ];
    #del cr

    qui ds
    // variable not found error
    if ("`varlist'" == "") {
        di as err "variable not found"
        exit 111
    }

    // make matrix
    mkmat `varlist' `if' `in', matrix(`dmumat') rownames(dmu)
    matrix roweq `dmumat' = "dmu"
    matrix coleq `dmumat' = `=lower("`sprefix'")' + "slack'"
    matrix `dmumat' = `dmumat''
end

// Start of the MATA Definition Area ------------------------------------
version 10
mata:
mata clear
mata set matastrict on

/**
 * DEA Loop - Data Envelopment Analysis Loop for DMUs
 */
function _dealp_for_supereff (
        string scalar frameMat,
                string scalar dmuIn,
                string scalar dmuOut,
                string scalar rts,
                string scalar ort,
                real scalar stagestep,
                real scalar tol1,
                real scalar tol2,
                string scalar minsubscript,
                string scalar efficientVec,
                string scalar trace )
{
    real matrix F, DI, DO, DEALPRSLT
    real colvector effvec

    F  = st_matrix(frameMat)
```

193

```
            DI = st_matrix(dmuIn)
            DO = st_matrix(dmuOut)
            if (stagestep == 2) {
                effvec = st_matrix(efficientVec)
            }

            DEALPRSLT = dealp_for_supereff(F, DI, DO, rts, ort, stagestep, tol1, tol2,
                            minsubscript, effvec, trace)

            st_matrix("r(dealprslt)", DEALPRSLT)
        }


        /**
         * DEA Loop - Data Envelopment Analysis Loop for DMUs
         */
        real matrix function dealp_for_supereff (
                        real matrix F,
                        real matrix DI,
                        real matrix DO,
                        string scalar rts,
                        string scalar ort,
                        real scalar stagestep,
                        real scalar tol1,
                        real scalar tol2,
                        string scalar minsubscript,
                        real colvector effvec,
                        string scalar trace)
        {
            real matrix M, VARS, LPRSLT, DEALPRSLT, ARTIF
            real scalar dmus, slackins, slackouts, slacks, artificials, artificialrow
            real scalar frows, fcols, isin, isminsubscript, i, dmui
            real colvector slackidx, skipdmu
            string scalar tracename

            struct BoundCond matrix boundF, boundM
            struct LpParamStruct scalar param

            if (cols(DI) != cols(DO)) {
                _error(3200, "in and out count of dmu is not match!")
            }
            if (!(rts == "CRS" || rts == "VRS" || rts == "IRS" || rts == "DRS")) {
                _error(3498, "rts must be one of CRS, VRS, IRS, DRS")
            }

            // basic value setting for artificial variabels
            isin = (ort == "IN")
            isminsubscript = (minsubscript != "nominsubscript")
            frows = rows(F); fcols = cols(F)
            dmus = cols(DI) // or cols(DO), because cols(DI) == cols(DO)
            slackins = rows(DI); slackouts = rows(DO)

            tracename = rts + "-" + ort + "-" + (stagestep == 1 ? "SI" : "SII")

            // -----------------------------------------------------------------------
            // define number of slacks by rts
            if (rts == "CRS" || rts == "VRS") slacks = slackins + slackouts
            else if (rts == "IRS" || rts == "DRS") slacks = slackins + slackouts + 1

            // define number of artificials by rts, ort, stage
```

```
if (rts == "CRS" || rts == "DRS") {
        if (stagestep == 1) {
                if (isin) {
                        artificials = slackins+slackouts; artificialrow = 2;
                }
                else artificials = 0
        }
        else {
                artificials = slackouts; artificialrow = 2+slackins;
        }
}
else if (rts == "VRS" || rts == "IRS") {
        if (stagestep == 1) {
                if (isin) {
                        artificials = slackins+slackouts+1; artificialrow =
2;
                }
                else {
                        artificials = 1; artificialrow = frows //==
2+slackins+slackouts
                }
        }
        else {
                artificials = slackouts+1; artificialrow = 2+slackins
        }
}
if (artificials > 0) {
        ARTIF = J(1, artificials, 1) \ J(frows-1, artificials, 0)
        replacesubmat(ARTIF, artificialrow, 1, I(artificials))
        F = F[,1..fcols-1], ARTIF, F[,fcols]
        frows = rows(F); fcols = cols(F) // revise frows, fcols
}
// --------------------------------------------------------------------

// constants value to right-hand side(rhs) and both sides multiplied by -1.
if (stagestep == 2) {
        skipdmu = (effvec :== .)
        if (isin) {
                replacesubmat(F, 2, 3, -F[2..1+slackins,3::2+dmus+slackins])
        }
        else {
                replacesubmat(F, 2+slackins, 3,
        -F[2+slackins..1+slackins+slackouts,3::2+dmus+slacks])
        }
}
else skipdmu = J(1, dmus, 0)
// --------------------------------------------------------------------
boundF = J(1, fcols, BoundCond());
// set the boundary for the efficiency variable(theta, eta):
// -INFINITE <= efficiency <= INFINITE
boundF[1,2].val = 0; boundF[1,2].lower = 0; boundF[1,2].upper = .

// set boundary for the weight variable(lamda, mu):
// 0 <= weight <= INFINITE
for (i=3; i<dmus+3; i++) {
        boundF[1,i].val = 0; boundF[1,i].lower = 0; boundF[1,i].upper = .
}

// set boundary for the non-structural variable(slack, artificial).
```

```
// 0 <= slacks and atrificials <= INFINITE
for (i=dmus+3; i<fcols; i++) {
        boundF[1,i].val = 0; boundF[1,i].lower = 0; boundF[1,i].upper = .
}
// liststruct(boundF); // for debug

// set the lp's parameters
param.rts          = rts
param.isin                          = isin
param.stagestep    = stagestep
param.dmus         = dmus
param.slacks       = slacks
param.artificials  = artificials
param.tol1         = tol1
param.tol2         = tol2
param.isminsubscript = isminsubscript
param.trace        = trace
// liststruct(param); // for debug
// --------------------------------------------------------------------
DEALPRSLT = J(0, 1+ dmus + slacks, 0)
if (isin) {
    for (dmui=1; dmui<=dmus; dmui++) {
            if (skipdmu[dmui]) {
                    LPRSLT = J(1, cols(DEALPRSLT), .)
            }
            else {
                    M = F; boundM = boundF
                    if (stagestep == 1) replacesubmat(M, 2, 2,
DI[,dmui])
                    else        replacesubmat(M,    2,    fcols,
DI[,dmui]*effvec[dmui])
                    replacesubmat(M, 2+slackins, fcols, DO[,dmui])
                    replacesubmat(M, 2, 2+dmui, M[2..frows, 1]) //
super efficiency

                    // execute LP
                    VARS   = lp_phase1(M, boundM, dmui,
tracename, param)
                    if (VARS[1,1] == .) {
                            LPRSLT = J(1, cols(DEALPRSLT), .)
                    }
                    else {
                            LPRSLT = lp_phase2(M, boundM,
VARS, dmui, tracename, param);
                    }
            }
            DEALPRSLT = DEALPRSLT \ LPRSLT
    }
}
else {
    for (dmui=1; dmui<=dmus; dmui++) {
            if (skipdmu[dmui]) {
                    LPRSLT = J(1, cols(DEALPRSLT), .)
            }
            else {
                    M = F; boundM = boundF
                    replacesubmat(M, 2, fcols, DI[,dmui])
                    if (stagestep == 1) {
                            if (rts == "CRS" || rts == "DRS")
```

196

```
M[1,2] = -1
DO[,dmui])

DO[,dmui]*effvec[dmui])
super efficiency

phase 1
2+dmus..1+dmus+slacks, 1..1+dmus, 0)

M[,VARS[,2::cols(VARS)-1] :+ 1],

boundM[,VARS[,2::cols(VARS)-1] :+ 1],

boundM[,cols(M)]

dmui, tracename, param)

VARS, dmui, tracename, param);
                }
            DEALPRSLT = DEALPRSLT \ LPRSLT
        }
    }

    // adjust efficiency
    if (stagestep == 2) {
        replacesubmat(DEALPRSLT, 1, 1, effvec)
    }
    return(DEALPRSLT)
}

    end
// End of the MATA Definition Area -------------------------------------------
```

```
            replacesubmat(M,    2+slackins,    2,

}
else    replacesubmat(M,    2+slackins,    fcols,
replacesubmat(M, 2, 2+dmui, M[2..frows, 1]) //

// execute LP
if (artificials == 0) { // if artificials == 0 then skip
VARS                            =           (0,
M = M[,1],
                            M[,cols(M)]
boundM = boundM[,1],

}
else {
            VARS    =    lp_phase1(M,    boundM,
}

if (VARS[1,1] == .) {
            LPRSLT = J(1, cols(DEALPRSLT), .)
}
else {
            LPRSLT    =    lp_phase2(M,    boundM,
}
```

B2.6 dea_supersbm.ado

```
*! version 1.0.0  25AUG2012
capture program drop dea_supersbm
program define dea_supersbm, rclass
    version 10.0

/** Terms Description:
* -------------------------------------------------------------------------
* RTS: Return To Scale
* CRS: Constant Return to Scale
* VRS: Variant Return to Scale
*
* ser: super efficiency radial
* -------------------------------------------------------------------------
*/

// syntax checking and validation-----------------------------------
// rts - return to scale, ort - orientation
// input varlist = output varlist
// example:
//    dea_supersbm Employee Area = Sales Profits, rts(CRS) ort(IN) tol1(1e-14)
//    dea_supersbm Employee Area = Sales Profits, sav
// -------------------------------------------------------------------------
    // returns 1 if the first nonblank character of local macro `0' is a comma,
    // or if `0' is empty.
    if replay() {
        dis as err "ivars and ovars required."
        exit 198
    }

    // get and check invarnames
    gettoken word 0 : 0, parse("=,")
    while ~("`word'" == ":" | "`word'" == "=") {
        if "`word'" == "," | "`word'" == "" {
            error 198
        }
        local invarnames `invarnames' `word'
        gettoken word 0 : 0, parse("=,")
    }
    unab invarnames : `invarnames'

    #del ;
    syntax varlist(min=1) [if] [in] [using/]
    [,
        RTS(string)      // ignore case sensitive,[{CRS|CCR} | {BCC|VRS}]
            ORT(string)       // ignore case sensitive,
                                                                    //
[{{I/IN|INPUT} | {O/OUT|OUTPUT} | {IO|INOUT|INOUTPUT}}]
        TOL1(real 1e-14)   // entering or leaving value tolerance
        TOL2(real 1e-8)      // B inverse tolerance: 2.22e-12
        TRACE            // Whether or not to do the log
        SAVing(string)    // log file name
        REPLACE          // Whether or not to replace the log file
    ];
    #del cr
```

```
local num_invar : word count `invarnames'
local i 1
while (`i'<=`num_invar') {
   local invarn : word `i' of `invarnames'
   local junk : subinstr local invarnames "`invarn'" "", /// 
       word all count(local j)
   if `j' > 1 {
       di as error /// 
           "cannot specify the same input variable more than once"
       error 498
   }
   local i = `i' + 1
}

// default model - CRS(Constant Return to Scale)
if ("`rts'" == "") local rts = "CRS"
else {
   local rts = upper("`rts'")
   if ("`rts'" == "CCR") local rts = "CRS"
   else if ("`rts'" == "BCC") local rts = "VRS"
   else if (~("`rts'" == "CRS" | "`rts'" == "VRS")) {
       di as err "option rts allow for case-insensitive " _c
       di as err "CRS (eq CCR) or VRS (eq BCC) or nothing."
       exit 198
   }
}

// default orientation - Input Oriented
if ("`ort'" != "") {
   local ort = upper("`ort'")
   if ("`ort'" == "I" | "`ort'" == "IN" | "`ort'" == "INPUT") {
       local ort = "IN"
   }
   else if ("`ort'" == "O" | "`ort'" == "OUT" | "`ort'" == "OUTPUT") {
       local ort = "OUT"
   }
           else if ("`ort'" == "IO" | "`ort'" == "INOUT" | "`ort'" ==
"INOUTPUT") {
           local ort = "INOUT"
   }
   else {
       di as err "option ort allows for case-insensitive " _c
       di as err "(i|in|input|o|out|output|io|inout|inoutput) or nothing."
       exit 198
   }
}
else {
       local ort = "IN"
}

if ("`using'" != "") use "`using'", clear
if (~(`c(N)' > 0 & `c(k)' > 0)) {
   dis as err "dataset required!"
   exit 198
}

// end of syntax checking and validation ---------------------------------------

set more off
```

```
capture log close dea_supersbm_log
log using "dea_supersbm.log", replace text name(dea_supersbm_log)
preserve

if ("`if'" != "" | "`in'" != "") {
    qui keep `in' `if'  // filtering : keep in range [if exp]
}

_dea_supersbm, ivars(`invarnames') ovars(`varlist') rts(`rts') ort(`ort') ///
        tol1(`tol1') tol2(`tol2') `trace' saving(`saving') `replace'
return add

restore, preserve
log close dea_supersbm_log
end
```

```
********************************************************************************
* DEA Super SBM - Data Envelopment Analysis Slack Based Model
********************************************************************************
program define _dea_supersbm, rclass
    #del ;
    syntax , IVARS(string) OVARS(string) RTS(string) ORT(string)
    [
            TOL1(real 1e-14) TOL2(real 1e-8) TRACE SAVing(string) REPLACE
    ];
    #del cr

    preserve

    // ----------------------------------------------------------------------

    tempname dmuIn dmuOut frameMat deamainrslt dearslt vrsfrontier crslambda
    mkDmuMat `ivars', dmumat(`dmuIn') sprefix("i")
    mkDmuMat `ovars', dmumat(`dmuOut') sprefix("o")
    local dmuCount = colsof(`dmuIn')
    // local minrank = 1

    mata: _mkfmat_4supersbm ("`frameMat'", "`dmuIn'", "`dmuOut'", ///
            "`rts'", "`ort'")
    mata: _dealp_4supersbm ("`frameMat'", "`dmuIn'", "`dmuOut'", ///
            "`rts'", "`ort'", `tol1', `tol2', "`trace'")
    matrix `deamainrslt' = r(dealprslt)
    matrix `dearslt' = J(`dmuCount', 1, .), `deamainrslt' // rank column

    // TODO if you need rank, substitution above a line.
    // ----------------------------------------------------------------------
    // mata: _dmurank("`deamainrslt'", ///
    //     `=rowsof(`dmuIn')', `=rowsof(`dmuOut')', `minrank', `tol2')
    // matrix `dearslt' = r(rank), `deamainrslt'
    // ----------------------------------------------------------------------

    // use mata function '_setup_dearslt_names' because the maximum string
    // variable length needs to be kept under the 244 for all the time
    mata: _setup_dearslt_names("`dearslt'", "`dmuIn'", "`dmuOut'")

    // rank column delete
    matrix `dearslt' = `dearslt'[1...,2...]

    // ----------------------------------------------------------------------
```

```
    restore, preserve

    // REPORT
    report_4supersbm, dearslt(`dearslt') rts(`rts') ort(`ort') ///
                        `trace' saving(`saving') `replace'

    return matrix dearslt = `dearslt'
    restore, preserve
end

*******************************************************************************
* REPORT
*******************************************************************************
program define report_4supersbm, rclass
    #del ;
    syntax , dearslt(name) RTS(string)
    [
        ORT(string) TRACE SAVing(string) REPLACE
    ];
    #del cr

    preserve
    // ----------------------------------------------------------------------
    di as result ""
    di as input "options: RTS(`rts') ORT(`ort')"
    di as result "`rts' DEA-SUPER-SBM Efficiency Results:"
    matrix list `dearslt', noblank nohalf noheader f(%9.6g)

    if ("`saving'" != "") {
        // if the saving file exists and replace option not specified,
        // make the backup file.
        if ("`replace'" == "") {
            local dotpos = strpos("`saving'",".")
            if (`dotpos' > 0) {
                mata: _file_exists("`saving'")
            }
            else {
                mata: _file_exists("`saving'.dta")
            }
            if r(fileexists) {
                local curdt = subinstr("`c(current_date)'", " ", "", .) + /*
                    */ subinstr("`c(current_time)'", ":", "", .)
                if (`dotpos' > 0) {
                    #del ;
                    local savefn = substr("`saving'", 1, `dotpos' - 1) +
                            "_bak_`curdt'" +
                            substr("`saving'",`dotpos', .);
                    #del cr
                    qui copy "`saving'" "`savefn'", replace
                }
                else {
                    local savefn = "`saving'_bak_`curdt'" + ".dta"
                    qui copy "`saving'.dta" "`savefn'", replace
                }
            }
        }
    }

    restore, preserve
            svmat `dearslt', names(eqcol)
```

```
                capture {
                        renpfix _
                        renpfix ref ref_
                        renpfix islack is_
                        renpfix oslack os_
                }
                capture save `saving', replace
        }
        // -----------------------------------------------------------------------
        restore, preserve
end


*****************************************************************************
* Data Import and Conversion
*****************************************************************************

// Make DMU Matrix ---------------------------------------------------------
program define mkDmuMat
    #del ;
    syntax varlist(numeric) [if] [in], DMUmat(name)
    [
        SPREfix(string)
    ];
    #del cr

    qui ds
    // variable not found error
    if ("`varlist'" == "") {
        di as err "variable not found"
        exit 111
    }

    // make matrix
    mkmat `varlist' `if' `in', matrix(`dmumat') rownames(dmu)
    matrix roweq `dmumat' = "dmu"
    matrix coleq `dmumat' = `=lower("`sprefix'")' + "slack"'
    matrix `dmumat' = `dmumat''
end

// Start of the MATA Definition Area --------------------------------------
version 10
mata:
mata clear
mata set matastrict on

/**
 * make frame matrix and set matrix value at the param frameMat
 * rts - return to scale, ort - orientation
 */
function _mkfmat_4supersbm (
                string scalar frameMat,
                string scalar dmuIn,
                string scalar dmuOut,
                string scalar rts,
                string scalar ort )
{
    real matrix F, DI, DO
    real scalar dmus, slackins, slackouts, exist_param_t
    real scalar frows, fcols
```

```
DI = st_matrix(dmuIn)
DO = st_matrix(dmuOut)
if (cols(DI) != cols(DO)) {
    _error(3200, "in and out count of dmu is not match!")
}

exist_param_t = (ort == "INOUT")
dmus = cols(DI) // or cols(DO), because cols(DI) == cols(DO)
slackins = rows(DI); slackouts = rows(DO)
if (rts == "CRS") {
    // target coefficient\slackins\slackouts\{param_t}
    frows = 1 + slackins + slackouts + exist_param_t
            // target coefficient,param_t,dmus,slackins,slackouts,rhs
    fcols = 1 + 1 + dmus + slackins + slackouts + 1
}
else if (rts == "VRS") {
            // target coefficient\slackins\slackouts\{param_t}\sum of lamda
    frows = 1 + slackins + slackouts + exist_param_t + 1
            // target coefficient,param_t,dmus,slackins,slackouts,rhs
    fcols = 1 + 1 + dmus + slackins + slackouts + 1
}
else {
    _error(3498, "invalid rts optoin.")
}

// make frame matrix for CRS(CCR)
F = J(frows, fcols, 0)
F[1, 1] = 1
if (ort == "INOUT") {
            replacesubmat(F, 2, 3, DI)
            replacesubmat(F, 2 + slackins, 3, DO)
            replacesubmat(F, 2, 3 + dmus, I(slackins))
            replacesubmat(F, 2 + slackins, 3 + dmus + slackins, -I(slackouts))
            replacesubmat(F, 2 + slackins + slackouts, 2, 1) // param_t
            replacesubmat(F, 2 + slackins + slackouts, fcols, 1) // param_t's rhs
}
else { // ort == "IN" or "OUT"
            replacesubmat(F, 2, 3, DI)
            replacesubmat(F, 2 + slackins, 3, DO)
            replacesubmat(F, 2, 3 + dmus, I(slackins))
            replacesubmat(F, 2 + slackins, 3 + dmus + slackins, -I(slackouts))
}

// adjustment
if (rts == "VRS") {
    replacesubmat(F, frows, 3, J(1, dmus, 1))
    F[frows,fcols] = 1
}

// return result
st_matrix(frameMat, F)
}

/**
* DEA Loop - Data Envelopment Analysis Loop for DMUs
*/
function _dealp_4supersbm (
            string scalar frameMat,
```

```
                    string scalar dmuIn,
                    string scalar dmuOut,
                    string scalar rts,
                    string scalar ort,
                    real scalar tol1,
                    real scalar tol2,
                    string scalar trace )
{
     real matrix F, DI, DO, M, VARS, LPRSLT, DEALPRSLT, ARTIF, S
     real scalar dmus, slackins, slackouts, slacks, artificials, artificialrow
     real scalar frows, fcols, i, dmui, exist_param_t, param_t_row, param_t_col
     real scalar s_ratios, sr_col
     real colvector effvec
     string scalar tracename

     struct BoundCond matrix boundF, boundM
     struct LpParamStruct scalar param

     F  = st_matrix(frameMat)
     DI = st_matrix(dmuIn)
     DO = st_matrix(dmuOut)
     if (cols(DI) != cols(DO)) {
         _error(3200, "in and out count of dmu is not match!")
     }
     if (!(rts == "CRS" || rts == "VRS")) {
             _error(3498, "rts must be one of CRS, VRS")
     }

     // basic value setting for artificial variabels
     frows = rows(F); fcols = cols(F)
     dmus = cols(DI) // or cols(DO), because cols(DI) == cols(DO)
     slackins = rows(DI); slackouts = rows(DO)

     tracename = rts + "-" + ort

     // ------------------------------------------------------------------
     // define number of slacks by rts
     slacks = slackins + slackouts

     // define number of slack's ratio and slack ratio start column.
     if (ort == "INOUT") s_ratios = slacks
     else if (ort == "IN") s_ratios = slackins
     else if (ort == "OUT") s_ratios = slackouts
     sr_col = 3 + dmus + slacks

     // define number of artificials by rts, ort, stage
     exist_param_t = (ort == "INOUT")
     if (rts == "CRS") {
             artificials = slackouts+exist_param_t; artificialrow = 2+slackins;
     }
     else if (rts == "VRS") {
             artificials = slackouts+exist_param_t+1; artificialrow = 2+slackins
     }

     // remake frame matrix
     if (artificials > 0) {
             ARTIF = J(1, artificials, 1) \ J(frows-1, artificials, 0)
             replacesubmat(ARTIF, artificialrow, 1, I(artificials))
             F = F[,1..fcols-1], J(frows, s_ratios, 0), ARTIF, F[,fcols]
```

```
        frows = rows(F); fcols = cols(F) // revise frows, fcols
}


// ------------------------------------------------------------------------
boundF = J(1, fcols, BoundCond());
// set the boundary for the efficiency variable(theta, eta):
// -INFINITE <= efficiency <= INFINITE
boundF[1,2].val = 0; boundF[1,2].lower = 0; boundF[1,2].upper = .

// set boundary for the weight variable(lamda, mu):
// 0 <= weight <= INFINITE
for (i=3; i<dmus+3; i++) {
        boundF[1,i].val = 0; boundF[1,i].lower = 0; boundF[1,i].upper = .
}

// set boundary for the non-structural variable(slack, artificial).
// 0 <= slacks and atrificials <= INFINITE
for (i=dmus+3; i<fcols; i++) {
        boundF[1,i].val = 0; boundF[1,i].lower = 0; boundF[1,i].upper = .
}
// liststruct(boundF); // for debug

// set the lp's parameters
param.rts          = rts
param.isin         = 0 // don't care
param.minYn        = 1 // min
param.stagestep    = 2 // 2 step
param.dmus         = dmus
param.dmuins       = slackins
param.dmuouts      = slackouts
param.slacks       = slacks
param.artificials  = artificials
param.tol1         = tol1
param.tol2         = tol2
param.isminsubscript = 0 // false
param.trace        = trace
// liststruct(param); // for debug
// ------------------------------------------------------------------------
DEALPRSLT = J(0, 1+ dmus + slacks, 0)
if (ort == "INOUT") {
        param_t_row = 2+slacks; param_t_col = fcols-artificials-slackouts
        S = J(1, slackouts, 1)
        for (dmui=1; dmui<=dmus; dmui++) {
                M = F; boundM = boundF
                replacesubmat(M, 2, 2, -DI[,dmui])
                replacesubmat(M, 2+slackins, 2, -DO[,dmui])
                replacesubmat(M, 2, 2+dmui, M[2..frows, 1]) // fill zero value
                replacesubmat(M,   param_t_row,   param_t_col,   -
S:*(1/slackouts))
                for(i = 0; i < slackins ; i++ ) {
                        M[i+2, i+sr_col] = -DI[i+1,dmui]
                }
                for(i = 0; i < slackouts ; i++ ) {
                        M[i+2+slackins,   i+sr_col+slackins]   =
DO[i+1,dmui]
                }

                // execute LP
                VARS                                           =
```

205

```
lp_phase1_4supersbm(M,boundM,dmui,tracename,param,s_ratios)
                    if (VARS[1,1] == .) {
                            LPRSLT = J(1, cols(DEALPRSLT), .)
                    }
                    else {
                            LPRSLT = lp_phase2_4supersbm(DI, DO, ort,
M, boundM,
                                    VARS, dmui, tracename, param);
                    }
                    DEALPRSLT = DEALPRSLT \ LPRSLT
            }
    }
    else {
            for (dmui=1; dmui<=dmus; dmui++) {
                    M = F; boundM = boundF
                    replacesubmat(M, 2, fcols, DI[,dmui])
                    replacesubmat(M, 2+slackins, fcols, DO[,dmui])
                    replacesubmat(M, 2, 2+dmui, M[2..frows, 1]) // fill zero value
                    if (ort == "IN") {
                            for(i = 0; i < slackins ; i++ ) {
                                    M[i+2, i+sr_col] = -DI[i+1,dmui]
                            }
                    }
                    else {
                            for(i = 0; i < slackouts ; i++ ) {
                                    M[i+2+slackins,     i+sr_col]     =
DO[i+1,dmui]
                            }
                    }

                    // execute LP
                    VARS                                            =
lp_phase1_4supersbm(M,boundM,dmui,tracename,param,s_ratios)
                    if (VARS[1,1] == .) {
                            LPRSLT = J(1, cols(DEALPRSLT), .)
                    }
                    else {
                            if (ort == "OUT") param.minYn = 0 // max
                            LPRSLT = lp_phase2_4supersbm(DI, DO, ort,
M, boundM,
                                    VARS, dmui, tracename, param);
                            if (ort == "OUT") param.minYn = 1 // min
                    }
                    DEALPRSLT = DEALPRSLT \ LPRSLT
            }
    }

    st_matrix("r(dealprslt)", DEALPRSLT)
}

real matrix function lp_phase1_4supersbm (
            real matrix M,
            struct BoundCond matrix boundM,
            real scalar dmui,
            string scalar aTracename,
            struct LpParamStruct scalar param,
            real scalar s_ratios )
{
    real matrix T, VARS
```

```
real scalar i, j, w, mrows, mcols, phase
real vector reorderidx, bfsidx, nonbfsidx, sr_idxs
string scalar tracename, msg
struct LpResultStruct scalar lpresult

mrows = rows(M); mcols = cols(M)
tracename = aTracename + "-PI"

// 1st: initialize matrix.
if (param.trace == "trace") {
    displayas("txt")
    printf("\n\n\n----------[PHASE I]----------")
    printf("\n[DMUi=%g]%s: initialize matrix.\n",
        dmui, tracename); M
}


// 2nd: classify basic and nonbasic.
// i = 3+param.dmus+param.slacks; sr_idxs = (i..i+s_ratios-1) // org code
i = mcols - param.artificials - s_ratios; sr_idxs = (i..i+s_ratios-1)
VARS = (0, 1..1+param.dmus+param.slacks+s_ratios, -1..-param.artificials, 0)
bfsidx = J(1, mrows-1, .); nonbfsidx = J(1, 0, .)
for (j = 3+param.dmus; j <= mcols-1; j++) {
            // Orinal Code
            /*
            T = (M[2::mrows,j] :== 1)
            if (sum(T) == 1) {
                maxindex(T, 1, i, w); bfsidx[i] = j
            }
            else nonbfsidx = nonbfsidx, j
            */

            // Modified by Brian(2012.08.25): because critical logic error.
            T = M[2::mrows,j] // Only for Super SBM: !any(sr_idxs :== j)
            if (!any(sr_idxs :== j) && (sum(T :!= 0) == 1) && (sum(T) == 1)) {
                maxindex(T, 1, i, w); bfsidx[i] = j
            }
            else nonbfsidx = nonbfsidx, j
}
reorderidx = (1, bfsidx[1,], 2..2+param.dmus, nonbfsidx[1,], mcols)
VARS = VARS[,reorderidx]
M = M[,reorderidx]; boundM = boundM[,reorderidx]

if (param.trace == "trace") {
    displayas("txt")
    printf("\n[DMUi=%g]%s: classify basic and nonbasic.\n",
        dmui, tracename); M; VARS
}

// 3rd: solve the linear programming(LP).
phase = 1
lpresult = lp(M, boundM, VARS, dmui, phase, tracename, param)

if(lpresult.rc) VARS[1,1] = .
return(VARS)
}

real matrix function lp_phase2_4supersbm (
            real matrix DI,
            real matrix DO,
```

```
                        string scalar ort,

                            real matrix M,
                    struct BoundCond matrix boundM,
                    real matrix VARS,
                    real scalar dmui,
                    string scalar aTracename,
                    struct LpParamStruct scalar param )
            {
                real matrix T, XB, orgVARS, LPRSLT
                real scalar i, j, phase, mrows, mcols, rslt_cols, bcols // base column
                real s_ratios, sr_val               // slack ratio value
                real colvector sr_idxs               // slack ratio indexes
                string scalar tracename, msg
                struct LpResultStruct scalar lpresult

                orgVARS = VARS
                mrows = rows(M); mcols = cols(M)

                tracename = aTracename + "-PII"

                // modify target function value:
                if (ort == "INOUT") {
                        s_ratios = param.slacks
                        sr_idxs = (2 + param.dmus + param.slacks..
                                    1  +  param.dmus  +  param.slacks  +
        param.dmuins)
                        sr_val = 1/param.dmuins
                        for (j=2; j<mcols; j++) {
                                if (VARS[1,j] == 1 && !allof(M[,j], 0)) M[1,j] = 1 // if t
                                else {
                                        for (i=1; i<=param.dmuins; i++) {
                                                if   (VARS[1,j]   ==   sr_idxs[i]
        && !allof(M[,j], 0)) {
                                                        M[1,j] = sr_val
                                                }
                                        }
                                }
                        }
                }
                else if (ort == "IN") {
                        s_ratios = param.dmuins
                        sr_idxs = (2 + param.dmus + param.slacks..
                                    1  +  param.dmus  +  param.slacks  +
        param.dmuins)
                        sr_val = 1/param.dmuins
                        for (j=2; j<mcols; j++) {
                                for (i=1; i<=param.dmuins; i++) {
                                        if (VARS[1,j] == sr_idxs[i] && !allof(M[,j], 0)) {
                                                M[1,j] = sr_val
                                        }
                                }
                        }
                }
                else if (ort == "OUT") {
                        s_ratios = param.dmuouts
                        sr_idxs = (2 + param.dmus + param.slacks..
                                    1  +  param.dmus  +  param.slacks  +
        param.dmuouts)
```

Appendix B2.6 dea_supersbm.ado

```
                sr_val = -(1/param.dmuouts)
                for (j=2; j<mcols; j++) {
                        for (i=1; i<=param.dmuouts; i++) {
                                if (VARS[1,j] == sr_idxs[i] && !allof(M[,j], 0)) {
                                        M[1,j] = sr_val
                                }
                        }
                }
        }
        else {
                displayas("err")
                printf("\n[DMUi=%g]%s: input parma error[ort=%s].\n",
                        dmui, tracename, ort)
                exit(198)
        }

        if (param.trace == "trace") {
                displayas("txt")
                printf("\n----------[PHASE II]----------")
                printf("\n[DMUi=%g]%s: initialize matrix.\n",
                        dmui, tracename); M
                printf("\n[DMUi=%g]%s: VARS.\n", dmui, tracename); VARS
        }

        phase = 2
        lpresult = lp(M, boundM, VARS, dmui, phase, tracename, param)

        // -----------------------------------------------------------------------
        // phase 2 final.
        // -----------------------------------------------------------------------
        if(lpresult.rc) {
                LPRSLT = J(1, 1+param.dmus+param.slacks, .)
        }
        else {
                // lpresult = theta(1) + dmus + slacks + s_ratios
                LPRSLT = J(1, 1+param.dmus+param.slacks+s_ratios, 0)
                for (j=1; j<=rows(lpresult.XB); j++) {
                        if (VARS[1,j+1] > 0) LPRSLT[1, VARS[1,j+1]] =lpresult.XB[j,
1]
                }

                rslt_cols = cols(LPRSLT)
                if (ort == "INOUT") {
                        // remove virtual slack
                        LPRSLT = LPRSLT[1,1..1+param.dmus],
                                LPRSLT[1,rslt_cols-
s_ratios+1..rslt_cols]

                        LPRSLT = LPRSLT :/ LPRSLT[1, 1] // slack value = slack /
t
                        LPRSLT[1, 1] = lpresult.xVal // theta = target function value.
                        // input slack
                        bcols = 2+param.dmus
                        T = LPRSLT[1, bcols..bcols+param.dmuins-1]:*(DI[,dmui]')
                        replacesubmat(LPRSLT, 1, bcols, T)
                        // output slack
                        bcols = 2+param.dmus+param.dmuins
                        T = LPRSLT[1, bcols..bcols+param.dmuouts-1]:*(DO[,dmui]')
                        replacesubmat(LPRSLT, 1, bcols, T)
```

```
                              }
                              else { // ort == "IN" or "OUT"
                                     // Z = 1 - 1/oC * (oS1 + oS2 + ... + oSn)
                                     if (ort == "IN") {
                                            LPRSLT[1, 1] = 1 + lpresult.xVal
                                            LPRSLT = LPRSLT[1,1..1+param.dmus],
                                                                LPRSLT[1,rslt_cols-
s_ratios+1..rslt_cols]:*(DI[,dmui]'),
                                                                J(1, param.dmuouts, 0)
                                            }
                                            else {
                                                   LPRSLT[1, 1] = 1 / (1 + lpresult.xVal)
                                                   LPRSLT = LPRSLT[1,1..1+param.dmus],
                                                                J(1, param.dmuins, 0),
                                                                LPRSLT[1,rslt_cols-
s_ratios+1..rslt_cols]:*(DO[,dmui]')
                                                   }
                                            }
                              }

                 if (param.trace == "trace") {
                       msg = sprintf("[DMUi=%g]%s-FINAL", dmui, tracename);
                       printf("\n%s: original VARS.\n", msg); orgVARS
                       printf("\n%s: VARS.\n", msg); VARS
                       printf("\n%s: XB.\n", msg); lpresult.XB
                       printf("\n%s: LPRSLT.\n", msg); LPRSLT
                       }

                 return(LPRSLT)
                 }

           end
           // End of the MATA Definition Area ---------------------------------------------
```

B2.7 dea_vprice.ado

```
*! version 1.0.0  09JUN2012
capture program drop dea_vprice
program define dea_vprice, rclass
   version 10.0

/** Terms Description:
 * --------------------------------------------------------------------------
 * vprice: virtual price, multiplier(cooper)
 * --------------------------------------------------------------------------
 */

// syntax checking and validation----------------------------------------------
// rts - return to scale, ort - orientation
// input varlist = output varlist
// example:
//    dea_vprice Employee Area = Sales Profits, ort(IN) tol1(1e-14)
//    dea_vprice Employee Area = Sales Profits, sav
// ----------------------------------------------------------------------------
   // returns 1 if the first nonblank character of local macro `0' is a comma,
   // or if `0' is empty.
   if replay() {
      dis as err "ivars and ovars required."
      exit 198
   }

   // get and check invarnames
   gettoken word 0 : 0, parse("=,")
   while ~("`word'" == ":" | "`word'" == "=") {
      if "`word'" == "," | "`word'" == "" {
         error 198
      }
      local invarnames `invarnames' `word'
      gettoken word 0 : 0, parse("=,")
   }
   unab invarnames : `invarnames'

   #del ;
   syntax varlist(min=1) [if] [in] [using/]
   [,
      ORT(string)       // ignore case sensitive,[{IN|INPUT}|{OUT|OUTPUT}]
      TOL1(real 1e-14)  // entering or leaving value tolerance
      TOL2(real 1e-8)   // B inverse tolerance: 2.22e-12
      TRACE             // Whether or not to do the log
      SAVing(string)    // log file name
      REPLACE           // Whether or not to replace the log file
   ];
   #del cr

   local num_invar : word count `invarnames'
   local i 1
   while (`i'<=`num_invar') {
      local invarn : word `i' of `invarnames'
      local junk : subinstr local invarnames "`invarn'" "", ///
         word all count(local j)
```

211

```
    if `j' > 1 {
        di as error ///
            "cannot specify the same input variable more than once"
        error 498
    }
    local i = `i' + 1
}

// default orientation - Input Oriented
if ("`ort'" == "") local ort = "IN"
else {
    local ort = upper("`ort'")
    if ("`ort'" == "I" | "`ort'" == "IN" | "`ort'" == "INPUT") {
        local ort = "IN"
    }
    else if ("`ort'" == "O" | "`ort'" == "OUT" | "`ort'" == "OUTPUT") {
        local ort = "OUT"
    }
    else {
        di as err "option ort allows for case-insensitive " _c
        di as err "(i|in|input|o|out|output) or nothing."
        exit 198
    }
}

if ("`using'" != "") use "`using'", clear
if (~(`c(N)' > 0 & `c(k)' > 0)) {
    dis as err "dataset required!"
    exit 198
}
```

`// end of syntax checking and validation -------------------------------------`

```
    set more off
    capture log close dea_vpricelog
    log using "dea_vprice.log", replace text name(dea_vpricelog)
    preserve

    if ("`if'" != "" | "`in'" != "") {
        qui keep `in' `if'  // filtering : keep in range [if exp]
    }

    _dea_vprice, ivars(`invarnames') ovars(`varlist') ort(`ort') ///
            tol1(`tol1') tol2(`tol2') `trace' saving(`saving') `replace'
    return add

    restore, preserve
    log close dea_vpricelog
end
```

```
*********************************************************************************
* DEA Virtual Price - Data Envelopment Analysis Virtual Price Model
*********************************************************************************
program define _dea_vprice, rclass
    #del ;
    syntax , IVARS(string) OVARS(string) ORT(string)
    [
        TOL1(real 1e-14) TOL2(real 1e-8)
                TRACE SAVing(string) REPLACE
```

```
];
#del cr

preserve

// -------------------------------------------------------------------------

tempname dmuIn dmuOut frameMat deamainrslt dearslt vrsfrontier crslambda
mkDmuMat `ivars', dmumat(`dmuIn') sprefix("i")
mkDmuMat `ovars', dmumat(`dmuOut') sprefix("o")
local dmuCount = colsof(`dmuIn')
local minrank = 1

mata: _l_mkframemat("`frameMat'", "`dmuIn'", "`dmuOut'", "`ort'")
mata: _l_dealp ("`frameMat'", "`dmuIn'", "`dmuOut'", "`ort'", ///
         `tol1', `tol2', "`trace'")
matrix `deamainrslt' = r(dealprslt)
matrix `dearslt' = `deamainrslt'

// use mata function '_l_setup_dearslt_names' because the maximum string
// variable length needs to be kept under the 244 for all the time
mata: _l_setup_dearslt_names("`ort'", "`dearslt'", "`dmuIn'", "`dmuOut'")

// -------------------------------------------------------------------------
// REPORT
// -------------------------------------------------------------------------
di as result ""
di as input "options: ORT(`ort')"
di as result "`rts' DEA-Virtual Price Efficiency Results:"
matrix list `dearslt', noblank nohalf noheader f(%9.6g)

if ("`saving'" != "") {
    // if the saving file exists and replace option not specified,
    // make the backup file.
    if ("`replace'" == "") {
        local dotpos = strpos("`saving'",".")
        if (`dotpos' > 0) {
            mata: _file_exists("`saving'")
        }
        else {
            mata: _file_exists("`saving'.dta")
        }
        if r(fileexists) {
            local curdt = subinstr("`c(current_date)'", " ", "", .) + /*
                */ subinstr("`c(current_time)'", ":", "", .)
            if (`dotpos' > 0) {
                #del ;
                local savefn = substr("`saving'", 1, `dotpos' - 1) +
                        "_bak_`curdt'" +
                        substr("`saving'",`dotpos', .);
                #del cr
                qui copy "`saving'" "`savefn'", replace
            }
            else {
                local savefn = "`saving'_bak_`curdt'" + ".dta"
                qui copy "`saving'.dta" "`savefn'", replace
            }
        }
    }
}
```

```
        restore, preserve
                svmat `dearslt', names(eqcol)
                capture {
                        renpfix _
                        renpfix iweight iw_
                        renpfix oweight ow_
                }
                capture save `saving', replace
        }
        return matrix dearslt = `dearslt'
        restore, preserve
end


*******************************************************************************
* Data Import and Conversion
*******************************************************************************

// Make DMU Matrix -------------------------------------------------
program define mkDmuMat
    #del ;
    syntax varlist(numeric) [if] [in], DMUmat(name)
    [
        SPREfix(string)
    ];
    #del cr

    qui ds
    // variable not found error
    if ("`varlist'" == "") {
        di as err "variable not found"
        exit 111
    }

    // make matrix
    mkmat `varlist' `if' `in', matrix(`dmumat') rownames(dmu)
    matrix roweq `dmumat' = "dmu"
    matrix coleq `dmumat' = `=lower("`sprefix'")' + "weight"'
    matrix `dmumat' = `dmumat''
end

// Start of the MATA Definition Area ------------------------------------
version 10
mata:
mata set matastrict on

/**
 * make frame matrix and set matrix value at the param frameMat
 * ort - orientation
 */
function _l_mkframemat(
                string scalar frameMat,
                string scalar dmuIn,
                string scalar dmuOut,
                string scalar ort )
{
    real matrix F, DI, DO
    real scalar dmus, dmuins, dmuouts, slacks
    real scalar frows, fcols
```

```
DI = st_matrix(dmuIn)
DO = st_matrix(dmuOut)
if (cols(DI) != cols(DO)) {
    _error(3200, "in and out count of dmu is not match!")
}

dmus = cols(DI) // or cols(DO), because cols(DI) == cols(DO)
dmuins = rows(DI); dmuouts = rows(DO); slacks = dmus
if (ort == "IN") {
    // target dmus\vprice
    frows = 1 + dmus + 1
            // target dmuouts,dmuins,slacks,artificials,rhs
    fcols = 1 + dmuouts + dmuins + slacks + 1 + 1
}
else if (ort == "OUT") {
            // target dmus\vprice
    frows = 1 + dmus + 1
            // target dmuins,dmuouts,slacks,artificials,rhs
    fcols = 1 + dmuouts + dmuins + slacks + 1 + 1
}
else {
    _error(3498, "invalid ort optoin.")
}

// make frame matrix
F = J(frows, fcols, 0)
F[1, 1] = 1
F[1, fcols - 1] = 1
F[frows, fcols - 1] = 1
F[frows, fcols] = 1
replacesubmat(F, 2, 2, DO')
replacesubmat(F, 2, 2 + dmuouts, -DI')
replacesubmat(F, 2, 2 + dmuins + dmuouts, I(dmus))

// return result
st_matrix(frameMat, F)
}

/**
* DEA Loop - Data Envelopment Analysis Loop for DMUs
*/
function _l_dealp (
                string scalar frameMat,
                string scalar dmuIn,
                string scalar dmuOut,
                string scalar ort,
                real scalar tol1,
                real scalar tol2,
                string scalar trace )
{
    real matrix F, DI, DO, M, VARS, LPRSLT, DEALPRSLT
    real scalar dmus, dmuins, dmuouts, slacks
    real scalar frows, fcols, i, dmui, isin
    string scalar tracename

    struct BoundCond matrix boundF, boundM
    struct LpParamStruct scalar param
```

```
F  = st_matrix(frameMat)
DI = st_matrix(dmuIn)
DO = st_matrix(dmuOut)
if (cols(DI) != cols(DO)) {
    _error(3200, "in and out count of dmu is not match!")
}

// basic value setting for artificial variabels
isin = (ort == "IN")
frows = rows(F); fcols = cols(F)
dmus = cols(DI) // or cols(DO), because cols(DI) == cols(DO)
dmuins = rows(DI); dmuouts = rows(DO)
slacks = dmus

tracename = ort + "-SI"


// -----------------------------------------------------------------
boundF = J(1, fcols, BoundCond());
// set boundary for the weight variable:
// 0 <= weight <= INFINITE
for (i=2; i<2+dmuins+dmuouts; i++) {
        boundF[1,i].val = 0; boundF[1,i].lower = 0; boundF[1,i].upper = .
}

// set boundary for the non-structural variable(slack, artificial).
// 0 <= slacks and atrificials <= INFINITE
for (i=2+dmuins+dmuouts; i<fcols; i++) {
        boundF[1,i].val = 0; boundF[1,i].lower = 0; boundF[1,i].upper = .
}
//liststruct(boundF); // for debug

// set the lp's parameters
param.rts        = "" // not used at this model
param.isin       = isin
param.stagestep  = 1 // 1 step
param.dmus       = dmus
param.dmuins     = dmuins
param.dmuouts    = dmuouts
param.slacks     = slacks
param.artificials = 1 // fix
param.tol1       = tol1
param.tol2       = tol2
param.isminsubscript = 0 // false
param.trace      = trace
//liststruct(param); // for debug
// -----------------------------------------------------------------
DEALPRSLT = J(0, dmuins + dmuouts, 0)
for (dmui=1; dmui<=dmus; dmui++) {
        M = F; boundM = boundF
        if (isin) replacesubmat(M, frows, 2+dmuouts, DI[,dmui]')
        else replacesubmat(M, frows, 2, DO[,dmui]')

        // execute LP
        param.minYn = 1
        VARS = l_lp_phase1(M, boundM, dmui, tracename, param)
        if (VARS[1,1] == .) {
                LPRSLT = J(1, cols(DEALPRSLT), .)
        }
        else {
```

```
                        param.minYn = !isin
                        LPRSLT = l_lp_phase2(M, boundM, VARS, dmui, tracename,
param);
                    }
                    DEALPRSLT = DEALPRSLT \ LPRSLT
            }

        st_matrix("r(dealprslt)", DEALPRSLT)
    }

    real matrix function l_lp_phase1 (
            real matrix M,
            struct BoundCond matrix boundM,
            real scalar dmui,
            string scalar aTracename,
            struct LpParamStruct scalar param )
    {
        real matrix T, VARS
        real scalar i, j, w, mrows, mcols, phase, dmuinouts
        real vector reorderidx, bfsidx, nonbfsidx
        string scalar tracename, msg
        struct LpResultStruct scalar lpresult

        mrows = rows(M); mcols = cols(M)
        dmuinouts = param.dmuins + param.dmuouts
        tracename = aTracename + "-PI"

        // 1st: initialize matrix.
        if (param.trace == "trace") {
            displayas("txt")
            printf("\n\n\n----------[PHASE I]----------")
            printf("\n[DMUi=%g]%s: initialize matrix.\n",
                dmui, tracename); M
        }

        // 2nd: classify basic and nonbasic.
        VARS = (0, 1..mcols-3, -1..-param.artificials, 0)
        bfsidx = J(1, mrows-1, .); nonbfsidx = J(1, 0, .)
        for (j = 2+dmuinouts; j < mcols; j++) {
                T = (M[2::mrows,j] :== 1)
                if (any(T)) {
                    maxindex(T, 1, i, w); bfsidx[i] = j
                }
                else nonbfsidx = nonbfsidx, j
        }
        // target,bfs,inout,nonbfs,rhs
        reorderidx = (1, bfsidx[1,], 2..dmuinouts+1, nonbfsidx[1,], mcols)
        VARS = VARS[,reorderidx];
        M = M[,reorderidx]; boundM = boundM[,reorderidx]
        if (param.trace == "trace") {
            displayas("txt")
            printf("\n[DMUi=%g]%s: classify basic and nonbasic.\n",
                dmui, tracename); M; VARS
        }

        // 3rd: solve the linear programming(LP).
        phase = 1
        lpresult = lp(M, boundM, VARS, dmui, phase, tracename, param)
```

```
        if(lpresult.rc) VARS[1,1] = .
        return(VARS)
}

real matrix function l_lp_phase2 (
        real matrix M,
        struct BoundCond matrix boundM,
        real matrix VARS,
        real scalar dmui,
        string scalar aTracename,
        struct LpParamStruct scalar param )
{

    real matrix T, XB, orgVARS, LPRSLT
    real scalar i, j, phase, mrows, mcols, dmuinouts, idx, loopcount
    real vector idxs
    string scalar tracename, msg
    struct LpResultStruct scalar lpresult

    orgVARS = VARS
    mrows = rows(M); mcols = cols(M)
    dmuinouts = param.dmuins+param.dmuouts

    tracename = aTracename + "-PII"

    // modify target function value:
    //M[1,] = J(1,mcols,0); M[1,1] = 1
    if (param.isin) { // note: when ort is "IN"
            idxs = (1..param.dmuouts)
            for (j=2; j<mcols; j++) {
                // because of output index per dmu is less than param.dmuouts
                    // and set the dmu's output value
                    if (any(idxs :== VARS[1,j])) M[1,j] = abs(M[1+dmui,j])
            }
    }
    else { // note: when ort is "OUT"
            idxs = (1+param.dmuouts..param.dmuins+param.dmuouts)
            for (j=2; j<mcols; j++) {
                // because of input index per dmu is less than param.dmuins
                    // and set the dmu's input value
                    if (any(idxs :== VARS[1,j])) M[1,j] = abs(M[1+dmui,j])
            }
    }

    if (param.trace == "trace") {
        displayas("txt")
        printf("\n----------[PHASE II]----------")
        printf("\n[DMUi=%g]%s: initialize matrix.\n",
            dmui, tracename); M
        printf("\n[DMUi=%g]%s: VARS.\n", dmui, tracename); VARS
    }

    phase = 2
    lpresult = lp(M, boundM, VARS, dmui, phase, tracename, param)

    // ------------------------------------------------------------------------
    // phase 2 final.
    // ------------------------------------------------------------------------
    if(lpresult.rc) {
```

```
                    LPRSLT = J(1, dmuinouts, .)
          }
          else {
                    LPRSLT = J(1, dmuinouts, 0); loopcount = rows(lpresult.XB)
                    for (j=1; j<=loopcount; j++) {
                              idx = VARS[1,j+1]
                              if (idx > 0 && idx <= dmuinouts) LPRSLT[1, idx]
=lpresult.XB[j, 1]
                    }
          }

     if (param.trace == "trace") {
        msg = sprintf("[DMUi=%g]%s-FINAL", dmui, tracename);
        printf("\n%s: original VARS.\n", msg); orgVARS
        printf("\n%s: VARS.\n", msg); VARS
        printf("\n%s: XB.\n", msg); lpresult.XB
        printf("\n%s: LPRSLT.\n", msg); LPRSLT
     }

     return(LPRSLT)
}

function _l_setup_dearslt_names (
                    string scalar ort,
                    string scalar dearsltmat,
          string scalar dmuinmat,
          string scalar dmuoutmat )
{
     string matrix DEARSLT_CS // dea result matrix column stripes
     string matrix DEARSLT_RS // dea result matrix row stripes

     DEARSLT_CS = st_matrixrowstripe(dmuoutmat)\st_matrixrowstripe(dmuinmat)
     DEARSLT_RS = st_matrixcolstripe(dmuinmat)

     // name the row and column of dea result matrix
     st_matrixrowstripe(dearsltmat, DEARSLT_RS)
     st_matrixcolstripe(dearsltmat, DEARSLT_CS)
}
end
// End of the MATA Definition Area --------------------------------------------
```

B2.8 malmq.ado

```
*! version 1.2.0  18JUN2011
capture program drop malmq
program define malmq, rclass
   version 10.0

// syntax checking and validation----------------------------------------------
// rts - return to scale, ort - orientation
// input varlist = output varlist
// ---------------------------------------------------------------------
   // returns 1 if the first nonblank character of local macro `0' is a comma,
   // or if `0' is empty.
   if replay() {
      dis as err "ivars and ovars must be inputed."
      exit 198
   }

   // get and check invarnames
   gettoken word 0 : 0, parse(" =:,")
   while `"`word'"' != ":" & `"`word'"' != "=" {
      if `"`word'"' == "," | `"`word'"'=="" {
         error 198
      }
      local invarnames `invarnames' `word'
      gettoken word 0 : 0, parse(" :,")
   }
   unab invarnames : `invarnames'

   #del ;
   syntax varlist(min=1) [if] [in] [using/]
   [,
      Period(name)
            Gml        // global Malmquist-Luenberger
            RTS(string)    // ignore case sensitive,[{CRS|CCR} | {VRS|BCC}]
      ORT(string)      // ignore case sensitive,[{IN|INPUT} | {OUT|OUTPUT}]
      TOL1(real 1e-14)  // entering or leaving value tolerance
      TOL2(real 1e-8)   // B inverse tolerance: 2.22e-12
      TRACE         // Whether or not to do the log
      SAVing(string)   // log file name
      REPLACE        // Whether or not to replace the log file
   ];
   #del cr

   local num_invar : word count `invarnames'
   local i 1
   while (`i'<=`num_invar') {
      local invarn : word `i' of `invarnames'
      local junk : subinstr local invarnames "`invarn'" "", ///
         word all count(local j)
      if `j' > 1 {
         di as error ///
            "cannot specify the same input variable more than once"
         error 498
      }
      local i = `i' + 1
```

220

```
}

// default model - CRS(Constant Return to Scale)
if ("`rts'" == "") local rts = "CRS"
else {
    local rts = upper("`rts'")
    if ("`rts'" == "CCR") local rts = "CRS"
    else if ("`rts'" == "BCC") local rts = "VRS"
    else if (~("`rts'" == "CRS" | "`rts'" == "VRS") {
        di as err "option rts allow for case-insensitive " _c
        di as err "CRS (eq CCR) or VRS (eq BCC) or nothing."
        exit 198
    }
}

// default orientation - Input Oriented
if ("`ort'" == "") local ort = "IN"
else {
    local ort = upper("`ort'")
    if ("`ort'" == "I" | "`ort'" == "IN" | "`ort'" == "INPUT") {
        local ort = "IN"
    }
    else if ("`ort'" == "O" | "`ort'" == "OUT" | "`ort'" == "OUTPUT") {
        local ort = "OUT"
    }
    else {
        di as err "option ort allow for case-insensitive " _c
        di as err "(i|in|input|o|out|output) or nothing."
        exit 198
    }
}

if ("`using'" != "") use "`using'", clear
if (~(`c(N)' > 0 & `c(k)' > 0)) {
    dis as err "dataset is not ready!"
    exit 198
}

if ("`period'" == "") {
    di as err "you must specify period (varname)"
    exit 198
}

// end of syntax checking and validation -------------------------------------

set more off
capture log close malmquistlog
log using "malmquist.log", replace text name(malmquistlog)
preserve

if ("`if'" != "" | "`in'" != "") {
    qui keep `in' `if'  // filtering : keep in range [if exp]
}

if ("`gml'" == "") {
        malmquist `period', ivars(`invarnames') ovars(`varlist') ///
                                    ort(`ort') tol1(`tol1') tol2(`tol2') ///
                                    `trace' saving(`saving') `replace'
}
```

221

```
            else {
                    g_malmquist `period', ivars(`invarnames') ovars(`varlist') ///
                                            rts(`rts')      ort(`ort')      tol1(`tol1')
tol2(`tol2') ///
                                            `trace' saving(`saving') `replace'
            }
            return add

            restore, preserve
            log close malmquistlog
        end

        *******************************************************************************
        * Malmquist
        *******************************************************************************
        program define malmquist, rclass
            #del ;
            syntax varname(numeric), IVARS(string) OVARS(string) ORT(string)
                [
                    TOL1(real 1e-3) TOL2(real 1e-12)
                    TRACE SAVing(string) REPLACE
                ];
            #del cr
            preserve

            // di _n(2) as input "options: ts(`varlist') ORT(`ort')"
            // di as input "Input Data:"
            // list

            tempname tsvec
            local tsn = "`varlist'"
            mata: _uniqrowmat("`tsvec'", "`tsn'") // sorted unique row matrix
            if (rowsof(`tsvec') < 2) {
                di as err "time series `tsn' observations must be ge 2"
                exit 451 // invalid values for time variable
            }

            // tfpch: Total Factor Productivity CHange
            // effch: EFFiciency CHange
            // techch: TECHnical efficiency CHange
            // pech: Pure Efficiency CHange
            // sech: Scale Efficiency CHange
            // crs{i|o|f|r}: crs {input|output|frame|result}
            // t, t1: t+1, c: cross --> crsi_ct1: crsi cross t+1,
            tempname crsi_t crso_t crsf_t crsr_t crsi_t1 crso_t1 crsf_t1 crsr_t1
            tempname crsr_ct crsr_ct1
            tempname vrsi_t vrso_t vrsf_t vrsr_t vrsi_t1 vrso_t1 vrsf_t1 vrsr_t1
            tempname crossrslt effr_t1 effrslt prodidxr_t prodidxrslt
            tempname tfpch effch techch pech sech
            local stage = 1
            forvalues t = 1/`=rowsof(`tsvec') - 1' {
                local tsval_t = `tsvec'[`t',1]
                local tsval_t1 = `tsvec'[`t'+1,1]

                // CRS-DEA t
                local rts = "CRS"
                if (`t' == 1) {
                    if ("`trace'" != "") di _newline "CRS-DEA ts[`tsval_t']:"
                    mkDmuMat `ivars' if `tsn'==`tsval_t', dmumat(`crsi_t') sprefix("i")
```

```
  mkDmuMat `ovars' if `tsn'==`tsval_t', dmumat(`crso_t') sprefix("o")
  mata: _mkframemat("`crsf_t'", "`crsi_t'", "`crso_t'", ///
       "`rts'", "`ort'")
  deamain `crsi_t' `crso_t' `crsf_t' `rts' `ort' `stage' ///
       `tol1' `tol2' `trace'
  matrix `crsr_t' = r(deamainrslt)
}
else {
  matrix `crsi_t' = `crsi_t1'
  matrix `crso_t' = `crso_t1'
  matrix `crsf_t' = `crsf_t1'
  matrix `crsr_t' = `crsr_t1'
}
// CRS-DEA t+1
if ("`trace'" != "") di _newline "CRS-DEA ts[`tsval_t1']:"
mkDmuMat `ivars' if `tsn'==`tsval_t1', dmumat(`crsi_t1') sprefix("i")
mkDmuMat `ovars' if `tsn'==`tsval_t1', dmumat(`crso_t1') sprefix("o")
mata: _mkframemat("`crsf_t1'", "`crsi_t1'", "`crso_t1'", ///
       "`rts'", "`ort'")
deamain `crsi_t1' `crso_t1' `crsf_t1' `rts' `ort' `stage' ///
       `tol1' `tol2' `trace'
matrix `crsr_t1' = r(deamainrslt)

// Cross CRS-DEA t
if ("`trace'" != "") di _newline "Cross CRS-DEA t[`tsval_t']:"
deamain `crsi_t1' `crso_t1' `crsf_t' `rts' `ort' `stage' ///
       `tol1' `tol2' `trace'
matrix `crsr_ct' = r(deamainrslt)
// Cross CRS-DEA t+1
if ("`trace'" != "") di _newline "Cross CRS-DEA t+1[`tsval_t1']:"
deamain `crsi_t' `crso_t' `crsf_t1' `rts' `ort' `stage' ///
       `tol1' `tol2' `trace'
matrix `crsr_ct1' = r(deamainrslt)

// VRS-DEA t
local rts = "VRS"
if (`t' == 1) {
  if ("`trace'" != "") di _newline "VRS-DEA ts[`tsval_t']:"
  mkDmuMat `ivars' if `tsn'==`tsval_t', dmumat(`vrsi_t') sprefix("i")
  mkDmuMat `ovars' if `tsn'==`tsval_t', dmumat(`vrso_t') sprefix("o")
  mata: _mkframemat("`vrsf_t'", "`vrsi_t'", "`vrso_t'", ///
       "`rts'", "`ort'")
  deamain `vrsi_t' `vrso_t' `vrsf_t' `rts' `ort' `stage' ///
       `tol1' `tol2' `trace'
  matrix `vrsr_t' = r(deamainrslt)
}
else {
  matrix `vrsi_t' = `vrsi_t1'
  matrix `vrso_t' = `vrso_t1'
  matrix `vrsf_t' = `vrsf_t1'
  matrix `vrsr_t' = `vrsr_t1'
}
// VRS-DEA t+1
if ("`trace'" != "") di _newline "VRS-DEA ts[`tsval_t1']:"
mkDmuMat `ivars' if `tsn'==`tsval_t1', dmumat(`vrsi_t1') sprefix("i")
mkDmuMat `ovars' if `tsn'==`tsval_t1', dmumat(`vrso_t1') sprefix("o")
mata: _mkframemat("`vrsf_t1'", "`vrsi_t1'", "`vrso_t1'", ///
       "`rts'", "`ort'")
deamain `vrsi_t1' `vrso_t1' `vrsf_t1' `rts' `ort' `stage' ///
```

```stata
        `tol1' `tol2' `trace'
matrix `vrsr_t1' = r(deamainrslt)

// ------------
// make Malmquist efficiency DEA Results
if (`t' == 1) {
    local dmuCount = colsof(`crsi_t')
    local rnames : colfullnames `crsi_t'
    local cnames = "`tsn' CRS_eff VRS_eff"


    matrix `effrslt' = J(`dmuCount', 1, `tsval_t')
    matrix `effrslt' = `effrslt', `crsr_t'[1...,1], `vrsr_t'[1...,1]
    matrix rownames `effrslt' = `rnames'
    matrix colnames `effrslt' = `cnames'
}
matrix `effr_t1' = J(`dmuCount', 1, `tsval_t1')
matrix `effr_t1' = `effr_t1', `crsr_t1'[1...,1], `vrsr_t1'[1...,1]
matrix rownames `effr_t1' = `rnames'

matrix `effrslt' = `effrslt' \ `effr_t1'

// make Malmquist productivity index DEA Results
// tfpch: total factor productivity change
// effch: techinical efficiency change
// techch: technological change
// pech: pure techinical efficiency change
// sech: scale efficiency change
matrix `prodidxr_t' = J(`dmuCount', 1, `tsval_t')
matrix `prodidxr_t' = `prodidxr_t', J(`dmuCount', 1, `tsval_t1')
matrix `prodidxr_t' = `prodidxr_t', J(`dmuCount', 5, 0)
forvalues dmui = 1/`dmuCount' {
    scalar `tfpch' = sqrt((`crsr_ct'[`dmui',1] ///
                / `crsr_t'[`dmui',1]) ///
                * (`crsr_t1'[`dmui',1] ///
                / `crsr_ct1'[`dmui',1]))
    scalar `effch' = `crsr_t1'[`dmui',1]/`crsr_t'[`dmui',1]
    scalar `techch' = sqrt((`crsr_ct'[`dmui',1] ///
                / `crsr_t1'[`dmui',1]) ///
                * (`crsr_t'[`dmui',1] ///
                / `crsr_ct1'[`dmui',1]))
    scalar `pech' = `vrsr_t1'[`dmui',1]/`vrsr_t'[`dmui',1]
    scalar `sech' = `effch'/`pech'
    matrix `prodidxr_t'[`dmui', 3] = ///
        (`tfpch', `effch', `techch', `pech', `sech')
}
matrix rownames `prodidxr_t' = `rnames'
if (`t' == 1) matrix colnames ///
    `prodidxr_t' = from thru tfpch effch techch pech sech

matrix `prodidxrslt' = nullmat(`prodidxrslt') \ `prodidxr_t'

matrix `crossrslt' = nullmat(`crossrslt') \ ///
    (`prodidxr_t'[1...,1..2], `crsr_ct'[1...,1], `crsr_ct1'[1...,1])
}

// -----------------------------------------------------------------------
// REPORT
// -----------------------------------------------------------------------
di _n(2) as txt "Cross CRS-DEA Result:"
```

```
matrix colnames `crossrslt' = from thru t t1
matrix rownames `crossrslt' = `: rowfullnames `prodidxrslt"
matrix list `crossrslt', noblank nohalf noheader f(%9.6g)

di _n "Malmquist efficiency `ort'PUT Oriented DEA Results:"
// matrix list `effrslt', noblank nohalf noheader f(%9.6g)
qui {
        drop _all
        svmat `effrslt', names(col)
        // generate dmu
        gen str dmu = ""
        // order dmu, after(`tsn') // options not allowed. why?
        order dmu
        order `tsn'
        local matrownames: rownames(`effrslt')
        forvalues i = 1/`: word count `matrownames" {
                replace dmu = `"`: word `i' of `matrownames'"'" in `i'
        }
    format CRS_eff VRS_eff %9.6g
}
list
return matrix effrslt = `effrslt'

di _n "Malmquist productivity index `ort'PUT Oriented DEA Results:"
// matrix list `prodidxrslt', noblank nohalf noheader f(%9.6g)
restore, preserve
qui {
        drop _all
        svmat `prodidxrslt', names(col)
        // generate dmu
        gen str dmu = ""
        order dmu
        local matrownames: rownames(`prodidxrslt')
        forvalues i = 1/`: word count `matrownames" {
                replace dmu = `"`: word `i' of `matrownames'"'" in `i'
        }
        // generate period
        gen str period = ""
        order period
        replace period = string(from) + "~" + string(thru)
    drop from thru
        format tfpch effch techch pech sech %9.6g
}
list
return matrix prodidxrslt = `prodidxrslt'

    savedata, saving(`saving') `replace'
    restore, preserve
end

*******************************************************************************
* Global Malmquist
*******************************************************************************
program define g_malmquist, rclass
    #del ;
    syntax varname(numeric), IVARS(string) OVARS(string) RTS(string) ORT(string)
        [
        TOL1(real 1e-3) TOL2(real 1e-12)
        TRACE SAVing(string) REPLACE
```

```
    ];
#del cr
preserve

// di _n(2) as input "options: ts(`varlist') ORT(`ort')"
// di as input "Input Data:"
// list

tempname tsvec
local tsn = "`varlist'"
mata: _uniqrowmat("`tsvec'", "`tsn'") // sorted unique row matrix
if (rowsof(`tsvec') < 2) {
    di as err "time series `tsn' observations must be ge 2"
    exit 451 // invalid values for time variable
}

// tfpch: Total Factor Productivity CHange
// effch: EFFiciency CHange
// techch: TECHnical efficiency CHange
// pech: Pure Efficiency CHange
// sech: Scale Efficiency CHange
// g[i|o|f|r|e]: global[input|output|frame|result|efficiency]
// t, t1: t+1
tempname i_t o_t f_t r_t
tempname i_t1 o_t1 f_t1 r_t1
tempname gi go gf grslt ge_t ge_t1

tempname effr_t1 effrslt prodidxr_t prodidxrslt
tempname tfpch effch techch

local stage = 1
forvalues t = 1/`=rowsof(`tsvec') - 1' {
    local tsval_t = `tsvec'[`t',1]
    local tsval_t1 = `tsvec'[`t'+1,1]

    // t
    if (`t' == 1) {
        if ("`trace'" != "") di _newline "`rts'-DEA ts[`tsval_t']:"
        mkDmuMat `ivars' if `tsn'==`tsval_t', dmumat(`i_t') sprefix("i")
        mkDmuMat `ovars' if `tsn'==`tsval_t', dmumat(`o_t') sprefix("o")
        mata: _mkframemat("`f_t'", "`i_t'", "`o_t'", ///
            "`rts'", "`ort'")
        deamain `i_t' `o_t' `f_t' `rts' `ort' `stage' ///
            `tol1' `tol2' `trace'
        matrix `r_t' = r(deamainrslt)

    }
    else {
        matrix `i_t' = `i_t1'
        matrix `o_t' = `o_t1'
        matrix `f_t' = `f_t1'
        matrix `r_t' = `r_t1'
                        matrix `ge_t' = `ge_t1'
    }

    // t+1
    if ("`trace'" != "") di _newline "`rts'-DEA ts[`tsval_t1']:"
    mkDmuMat `ivars' if `tsn'==`tsval_t1', dmumat(`i_t1') sprefix("i")
    mkDmuMat `ovars' if `tsn'==`tsval_t1', dmumat(`o_t1') sprefix("o")
```

```
mata: _mkframemat("`f_t1'", "`i_t1'", "`o_t1'", ///
     "`rts'", "`ort'")
deamain `i_t1' `o_t1' `f_t1' `rts' `ort' `stage' ///
     `tol1' `tol2' `trace'
matrix `r_t1' = r(deamainrslt)

     // global t
if (`t' == 1) {
                    local tsval = `tsvec'[rowsof(`tsvec'),1]
                    mkDmuMat `ivars' if `tsn'<=`tsval', dmumat(`gi') sprefix("i")
                    mkDmuMat `ovars' if `tsn'<=`tsval', dmumat(`go') sprefix("o")
                    mata: _mkframemat("`gf'", "`gi'", "`go'", "`rts'", "`ort'")
                    deamain `gi' `go' `gf' `rts' `ort' `stage' `tol1' `tol2' `trace'
                    matrix `grslt' = r(deamainrslt)

                    if  ("`trace'"  !=  "")  di  _newline  "Global  `rts'-DEA
ts[`tsval_t1']:"
          matrix `ge_t' = `grslt'[1..colsof(`i_t'),1]
}
else {
                    matrix `ge_t' = `ge_t1'
}

// global t+1
if ("`trace'" != "") di _newline "Global `rts'-DEA ts[`tsval_t1']:"
          qui count if `tsn'<=`tsval_t'
          local s_idx = r(N)
          qui count if `tsn'<=`tsval_t1'
          local e_idx = r(N)
          matrix `ge_t1' = `grslt'[`s_idx'+1..`e_idx',1]

// -----------
// make Global Malmquist efficiency DEA Results
if (`t' == 1) {
     matrix `effrslt' = J(colsof(`i_t'), 1, `tsval_t'), `r_t'[1...,1]
     matrix rownames `effrslt' = `: colfullnames `i_t''
     matrix colnames `effrslt' = `tsn' "`rts'_eff"
}
matrix `effr_t1' = J(colsof(`i_t1'), 1, `tsval_t1'), `r_t1'[1...,1]
matrix rownames `effr_t1' = `: colfullnames `i_t1''
matrix `effrslt' = `effrslt' \ `effr_t1'

// make Malmquist productivity index DEA Results
// tfpch: total factor productivity change
// effch: techinical efficiency change
// techch: technological change
          local dmuCount = rowsof(`r_t')
matrix `prodidxr_t' = J(`dmuCount', 1, `tsval_t')
matrix `prodidxr_t' = `prodidxr_t', J(`dmuCount', 1, `tsval_t1')
matrix `prodidxr_t' = `prodidxr_t', J(`dmuCount', 3, 0)
forvalues dmui = 1/`dmuCount' {
     scalar `effch' = `r_t1'[`dmui',1]/`r_t'[`dmui',1]
     scalar `techch' = (`ge_t1'[`dmui',1] / `r_t1'[`dmui',1]) ///
               / (`ge_t'[`dmui',1] / `r_t'[`dmui',1])
                    scalar `tfpch' = `effch' * `techch'
     matrix `prodidxr_t'[`dmui', 3] = (`tfpch', `effch', `techch')
}
matrix rownames `prodidxr_t' = `:colfullnames `i_t''
if (`t' == 1) {
```

```
                                        matrix colnames `prodidxr_t' = from thru tfpch effch techch
                        }

        matrix `prodidxrslt' = nullmat(`prodidxrslt') \ `prodidxr_t'
}

// --------------------------------------------------------------------
// REPORT
// --------------------------------------------------------------------
di _n "Global Malmquist efficiency `rts' `ort'PUT Oriented DEA Results:"
// matrix list `effrslt', noblank nohalf noheader f(%9.6g)
qui {
                drop _all
                svmat `effrslt', names(col)
                // generate dmu
                gen str dmu = ""
                // order dmu, after(`tsn') // options not allowed. why?
                order dmu
                order `tsn'
                local matrownames: rownames(`effrslt')
                forvalues i = 1/`: word count `matrownames" {
                                replace dmu = `"`: word `i' of `matrownames'"'" in `i'
                }
        format `rts'_eff %9.6g
}
list
return matrix effrslt = `effrslt'

di as result _n "Global Malmquist productivity index " ///
                "`rts' `ort'PUT Oriented DEA Results:"
// matrix list `prodidxrslt', noblank nohalf noheader f(%9.6g)
restore, preserve

qui {
                drop _all
                svmat `prodidxrslt', names(col)
                // generate dmu
                gen str dmu = ""
                order dmu
                local matrownames: rownames(`prodidxrslt')
                forvalues i = 1/`: word count `matrownames" {
                                replace dmu = `"`: word `i' of `matrownames'"'" in `i'
                }
                // generate period
                gen str period = ""
                order period
                replace period = string(from) + "~" + string(thru)
        drop from thru
                format tfpch effch techch %9.6g
}
list
return matrix prodidxrslt = `prodidxrslt'

savedata, saving(`saving') `replace'
restore, preserve
end

*****************************************************************************
* Global Malmquist
```

```
*******************************************************************************
program define g_malmquist_backup, rclass
    #del ;
    syntax varname(numeric), IVARS(string) OVARS(string) RTS(string) ORT(string)
        [
            TOL1(real 1e-3) TOL2(real 1e-12)
            TRACE SAVing(string) REPLACE
        ];
    #del cr
    preserve

    // di _n(2) as input "options: ts(`varlist') ORT(`ort')"
    // di as input "Input Data:"
    // list

    tempname tsvec
    local tsn = "`varlist'"
    mata: _uniqrowmat("`tsvec'", "`tsn'") // sorted unique row matrix
    if (rowsof(`tsvec') < 2) {
        di as err "time series `tsn' observations must be ge 2"
        exit 451 // invalid values for time variable
    }

    // tfpch: Total Factor Productivity CHange
    // effch: EFFiciency CHange
    // techch: TECHnical efficiency CHange
    // pech: Pure Efficiency CHange
    // sech: Scale Efficiency CHange
    // g[i|o|f|r|e]: global[input|output|frame|result|efficiency]
    // t, t1: t+1
    tempname i_t o_t f_t r_t e_t
    tempname i_t1 o_t1 f_t1 r_t1 e_t1
    tempname gi_t go_t gf_t gr_t ge_t
    tempname gi_t1 go_t1 gf_t1 gr_t1 ge_t1

    tempname crossrslt effr_t1 effrslt prodidxr_t prodidxrslt
    tempname tfpch effch techch pech sech

    local stage = 1
    forvalues t = 1/`=rowsof(`tsvec') - 1' {
        local tsval_t = `tsvec'[`t',1]
        local tsval_t1 = `tsvec'[`t'+1,1]

        // t
        if (`t' == 1) {
            if ("`trace'" != "") di _newline "`rts'-DEA ts[`tsval_t']:"
            mkDmuMat `ivars' if `tsn'==`tsval_t', dmumat(`i_t') sprefix("i")
            mkDmuMat `ovars' if `tsn'==`tsval_t', dmumat(`o_t') sprefix("o")
            mata: _mkframemat("`f_t'", "`i_t'", "`o_t'", ///
                "`rts'", "`ort'")
            deamain `i_t' `o_t' `f_t' `rts' `ort' `stage' ///
                `tol1' `tol2' `trace'
            matrix `r_t' = r(deamainrslt)
                                    matrix `e_t' = `r_t'[1...,1]
        }
        else {
            matrix `i_t' = `i_t1'
            matrix `o_t' = `o_t1'
            matrix `f_t' = `f_t1'
```

```
            matrix `r_t' = `r_t1'
                    matrix `e_t' = `e_t1'
}


// t+1
if ("`trace'" != "") di _newline "'`rts'-DEA ts[`tsval_t1']:"
mkDmuMat `ivars' if `tsn'==`tsval_t1', dmumat(`i_t1') sprefix("i")
mkDmuMat `ovars' if `tsn'==`tsval_t1', dmumat(`o_t1') sprefix("o")
mata: _mkframemat("`f_t1'", "`i_t1'", "`o_t1'", ///
        "`rts'", "`ort'")
deamain `i_t1' `o_t1' `f_t1' `rts' `ort' `stage' ///
        `tol1' `tol2' `trace'
matrix `r_t1' = r(deamainrslt)
        matrix `e_t1' = `r_t1'[1...,1]


        // global t
if (`t' == 1) {
    if ("`trace'" != "") di _newline "Global `rts'-DEA ts[`tsval_t']:"
    mkDmuMat `ivars' if `tsn'<=`tsval_t', dmumat(`gi_t') sprefix("i")
    mkDmuMat `ovars' if `tsn'<=`tsval_t', dmumat(`go_t') sprefix("o")
    mata: _mkframemat("`gf_t'", "`gi_t'", "`go_t'", ///
            "`rts'", "`ort'")
    deamain `gi_t' `go_t' `gf_t' `rts' `ort' `stage' ///
            `tol1' `tol2' `trace'
    matrix `gr_t' = r(deamainrslt)
            matrix `ge_t' = `gr_t'[1...,1]
}
else {
    matrix `gi_t' = `gi_t1'
    matrix `go_t' = `go_t1'
    matrix `gf_t' = `gf_t1'
    matrix `gr_t' = `gr_t1'
            matrix `ge_t' = `ge_t1'
}


// global t+1
if ("`trace'" != "") di _newline "Global `rts'-DEA ts[`tsval_t1']:"
mkDmuMat `ivars' if `tsn'<=`tsval_t1', dmumat(`gi_t1') sprefix("i")
mkDmuMat `ovars' if `tsn'<=`tsval_t1', dmumat(`go_t1') sprefix("o")
mata: _mkframemat("`gf_t1'", "`gi_t1'", "`go_t1'", ///
        "`rts'", "`ort'")
deamain `gi_t1' `go_t1' `gf_t1' `rts' `ort' `stage' ///
        `tol1' `tol2' `trace'
matrix `gr_t1' = r(deamainrslt)
        matrix `ge_t1' = `gr_t1'[rowsof(`gr_t')+1...,1]


// ------------
// make Global Malmquist efficiency DEA Results
if (`t' == 1) {
    matrix `effrslt' = J(colsof(`i_t'), 1, `tsval_t'), `e_t'[1...,1]
    matrix rownames `effrslt' = `: colfullnames `i_t'"
    matrix colnames `effrslt' = `tsn' "`rts'_eff"
}
matrix `effr_t1' = J(colsof(`i_t1'), 1, `tsval_t1'), `e_t1'[1...,1]
matrix rownames `effr_t1' = `: colfullnames `i_t1'"
matrix `effrslt' = `effrslt' \ `effr_t1'

matrix list `effrslt'
```

```
/*
    // make Malmquist productivity index DEA Results
    // tfpch: total factor productivity change
    // effch: techinical efficiency change
    // techch: technological change
    // pech: pure techinical efficiency change
    // sech: scale efficiency change
    matrix `prodidxr_t' = J(`dmuCount', 1, `tsval_t')
    matrix `prodidxr_t' = `prodidxr_t', J(`dmuCount', 1, `tsval_t1')
    matrix `prodidxr_t' = `prodidxr_t', J(`dmuCount', 5, 0)
    forvalues dmui = 1/`dmuCount' {
        scalar `tfpch' = sqrt((`crsr_ct'[`dmui',1] ///
                        / `crsr_t'[`dmui',1]) ///
                        * (`crsr_t1'[`dmui',1] ///
                        / `crsr_ct1'[`dmui',1]))
        scalar `effch' = `crsr_t1'[`dmui',1]/`crsr_t'[`dmui',1]
        scalar `techch' = sqrt((`crsr_ct'[`dmui',1] ///
                        / `crsr_t1'[`dmui',1]) ///
                        * (`crsr_t'[`dmui',1] ///
                        / `crsr_ct1'[`dmui',1]))
        scalar `pech' = `vrsr_t1'[`dmui',1]/`vrsr_t'[`dmui',1]
        scalar `sech' = `effch'/`pech'
        matrix `prodidxr_t'[`dmui', 3] = ///
            (`tfpch', `effch', `techch', `pech', `sech')
    }
    matrix rownames `prodidxr_t' = `rnames'
    if (`t' == 1) matrix colnames ///
        `prodidxr_t' = from thru tfpch effch techch pech sech

    matrix `prodidxrslt' = nullmat(`prodidxrslt') \ `prodidxr_t'

    matrix `crossrslt' = nullmat(`crossrslt') \ ///
        (`prodidxr_t'[1...,1..2], `crsr_ct'[1...,1], `crsr_ct1'[1...,1])

        */
}
/*
    // -----------------------------------------------------------------------
    // REPORT
    // -----------------------------------------------------------------------
    di _n(2) as txt "Cross CRS-DEA Result:"
    matrix colnames `crossrslt' = from thru t t1
    matrix rownames `crossrslt' = `: rowfullnames `prodidxrslt''
    matrix list `crossrslt', noblank nohalf noheader f(%9.6g)

    di _n "Malmquist efficiency `ort'PUT Oriented DEA Results:"
    // matrix list `effrslt', noblank nohalf noheader f(%9.6g)
    qui {
                drop _all
                svmat `effrslt', names(col)
                // generate dmu
                gen str dmu = ""
                // order dmu, after(`tsn') // options not allowed. why?
                order dmu
                order `tsn'
                local matrownames: rownames(`effrslt')
                forvalues i = 1/`: word count `matrownames'' {
                        replace dmu = `"`: word `i' of `matrownames''"' in `i'
```

231

```
                        }
        format CRS_eff VRS_eff %9.6g
}
list
return matrix effrslt = `effrslt'

di _n "Malmquist productivity index `ort'PUT Oriented DEA Results:"
// matrix list `prodidxrslt', noblank nohalf noheader f(%9.6g)
restore, preserve
qui {
                drop _all
                svmat `prodidxrslt', names(col)
                // generate dmu
                gen str dmu = ""
                order dmu
                local matrownames: rownames(`prodidxrslt')
                forvalues i = 1/`: word count `matrownames'" {
                        replace dmu = `"`: word `i' of `matrownames'"' in `i'
                }
                // generate period
                gen str period = ""
                order period
                replace period = string(from) + "~" + string(thru)
        drop from thru
                format tfpch effch techch pech sech %9.6g
}
list
return matrix prodidxrslt = `prodidxrslt'
*/
    savedata, saving(`saving') `replace'
    restore, preserve
end

*******************************************************************************
* result data save
*******************************************************************************
program define savedata, rclass
    syntax [varlist] [if] [in] [, saving(string) replace]

    if (`"`saving'"'!="") {
        // if save file exist and don't replace, make the backup file.
        if (`"`replace'"' != "") {
            local dotpos = strpos(`"`saving'"',".")
            if (`dotpos' > 0) {
                mata: _file_exists(`"`saving'"')
            }
            else {
                mata: _file_exists(`"`saving'".dta")
            }
            if r(fileexists) {
                local curdt = subinstr(`"`c(current_date)'"'," "," ","",.) + /*
                    */ subinstr(`"`c(current_time)'"', ":", "", .)
                if (`dotpos' > 0) {
                    #del ;
                    local savefn = substr(`"`saving'"', 1, `dotpos' - 1) +
                        "_bak_`curdt'" +
                        substr(`"`saving'"',`dotpos', .);
                    #del cr
                    qui copy `"`saving'"' `"`savefn'"', replace
```

```
        }
        else {
            local savefn = "`saving'_bak_`curdt'" + ".dta"
            qui copy "`saving'.dta" "`savefn'", replace
        }
      }
    }
    capture save `saving', replace
  }
end


*****************************************************************************
* DEA Main - Data Envelopment Analysis Main
*****************************************************************************
program define deamain, rclass
  args dmuIn dmuOut frameMat rts ort stage tol1 tol2 trace

  tempname efficientVec deamainrslt

  // unused option. so, should be removed.
  local minsubscript = ""

  // stage step 1.
  if ("`trace'" == "trace") {
    di _n(2) as txt "RTS(`rts') ORT(`ort') 1st stage."
  }
  mata: _dealp("`frameMat'", "`dmuIn'", "`dmuOut'", "`rts'", "`ort'", ///
    1, `tol1', `tol2', "`minsubscript'", "`efficientVec'", "`trace'")
  matrix `deamainrslt' = r(dealprslt)

  // stage step 2.
  if ("`stage'" == "2") {
    if ("`trace'" == "trace") {
      di _n(2) as txt "RTS(`rts') ORT(`ort') 2nd stage."
    }
    matrix `efficientVec' = `deamainrslt'[1...,1]

    mata: _dealp("`frameMat'", "`dmuIn'", "`dmuOut'", "`rts'", "`ort'", ///
      2, `tol1', `tol2', "`minsubscript'", "`efficientVec'", "`trace'")
    matrix `deamainrslt' = r(dealprslt)
  }

  // // if output oriented, get theta from eta
  // if ("`ort'" == "OUT") {
  //    tempname eta
  //    forvalues i = 1/`=rowsof(`deamainrslt')' {
  //       scalar `eta' = el(`deamainrslt', `i', 1)
  //       matrix `deamainrslt'[`i',1] = 1/`eta'
  //       matrix `deamainrslt'[`i',2] = `deamainrslt'[`i',2...]/`eta'
  //    }
  // }

  // adjust negative value
  forvalues i = 1/`=rowsof(`deamainrslt')' {
    forvalues j = 1/`=colsof(`deamainrslt')' {
      if (`deamainrslt'[`i',`j'] < 0) {
        matrix `deamainrslt'[`i',`j'] = 0
      }
    }
  }

  return matrix deamainrslt = `deamainrslt'
```

```
            end


************************************************************************
* Data Import and Conversion
************************************************************************

        // Make DMU Matrix ------------------------------------------------
        program define mkDmuMat
            #del ;
            syntax varlist(numeric) [if] [in], DMUmat(name)
            [
                SPREfix(string)
            ];
            #del cr

            qui ds
            // variable not found error
            if ("`varlist'" == "") {
                di as err "variable not found"
                exit 111
            }

            // make matrix
            mkmat `varlist' `if' `in', matrix(`dmumat') rownames(dmu)
            matrix roweq `dmumat' = "dmu"
            matrix coleq `dmumat' = `=lower("`sprefix'")' + "slack"'
            matrix `dmumat' = `dmumat'
        end
```

B2.9 tfdea.ado

** Byungki Jung contributed as a Ph.D. student in KNDU, Rep. of Korea
** model follows Inman et al.(2006) and minimization algorithm of Inman et al.(2014)

```
capture program drop tfdea
program define tfdea, rclass
    #del ;
    syntax anything(name=inoutvars equalok) [if] [in] [using/]
    ,
    [
                    RTS(string) // return to scale; default : VRS
                    ORT(string)         // orientation; default : OUT
                    TF(string)          // current year; last year for computing rate of
chagne

                    DMU(varname)        // dmu variable name
                    MODEL(string)       // choose forecasting model; default =
specification
                    TK(varname)                   // DMU's first appearing year
    ];
    #del cr

    local varnames `inoutvars'
    gettoken word inoutvars : inoutvars, parse("=")
    while ~("`word'" == "=") {
            local invars `invars' `word'
            gettoken word inoutvars : inoutvars, parse("=")
    }
    local outvars `inoutvars'

    unab invars : `invars'
    unab outvars : `outvars'

    // setting of macro name and default options
    if ("`tk'" == "")  local tk = "year"    // first appearing year
                    // ?????? how to display error if there is no year?

    if ("`dmu'" == "") local dmu = "dmu"          // dmu name check

    // default returns to scale setting
    if ("`rts'" == "") local rts = "VRS"    // default rts = VRS
    else if ("`rts'" == "vrs" | "`rts'" == "BCC") local rts = "VRS"
    else if ("`rts'" == "crs" | "`rts'" == "CCR") local rts = "CRS"

    // default orientation setting
    if ("`ort'" == "") local ort = "OUT" // default ort = OUT
    else if ("`ort'" == "in" | "`ort'" == "IN" | "`ort'" == "INPUT") local ort = "IN"
    else if ("`ort'" == "out" | "`ort'" == "OUT" | "`ort'" == "OUTPUT") local ort =
"OUT"

                    // default forecasting model setting
        if ("`tf'" != "") local model = "SPECIFICATION"         // default mod =
specification
            else local model = "NOFORECAST"

    // end of syntax and macro setting
```

235

```
**************************************************************************
* _roc : compute a rate of change(ROC)
**************************************************************************
preserve
    // declare temparary variable and matrix name
    tempname dataset tktemp tkindex fdataset ftkindex dearslt alltheta tkeff
    tempname tkineff thetafinal rsltroc thetainitial roc specrslt elaprslt theta
    tempname I sumlambda refmat

    ** step 1. make dataset matrix for computing ROC and forecasting
    set more off
    sort `tk' `dmu'
    if ("`tf'" != "") local tf = real("`tf'")
    else local tf = `tk'[`c(N)]
    local time = real("`time'")
    local foretime = `tf' + `time'

        // matrix for compute rate of change(ROC) and it's tk index
        mkmat `tk' `invars' `outvars' if (`tk' <= `tf'), matrix(`dataset') rown(dmu)
        mkmat `tk' if(`tk' <= `tf'), matrix(`tktemp') rown(dmu)
                matrix colnames `tktemp' = tk
                local n1 = rowsof(`tktemp')          // number of observation for
computing ROC

        forvalues i = 1/`n1' {      // make matrix `tkindex' for iterating DEA
            if `tktemp'[`i',1] != `tktemp'[`i'+1,1] {
                    matrix `tkindex' = nullmat(`tkindex') \ `tktemp'[`i',1]
            }
        }      // end of forvalues
        local n2 = rowsof(`tkindex')          // number of iteration when
compute ROC

    ** step 2. compute efficiency (DEA) for each year that DMU appeared
        local i = 1
        local tki = `tkindex'[`i',1]
        matrix `alltheta' = J(`n1',`n2',.)      // efficiency matrix of each iteration
        while (`tki' <= `tf'){
                display "DEA iteration", `i', "of", `n2'
                quietly clear
                quietly svmat `dataset', names(col)
                quietly keep if (`tk' <= `tki')
                quietly dea `invars' = `outvars', rts(`rts') ort(`ort') stage(2)
                    matrix `dearslt' = r(dearslt)
                    local j = rowsof(`dearslt')
                    matrix `theta' = `dearslt'[.,"theta"]
                    matrix `refmat' = `dearslt'[.,"ref:"]
                    forvalues row = 1/`j' {
                        if (`theta'[`row',1] < 1) {
                                matrix `alltheta'[`row',`i'] = 1 /
`theta'[`row',1]
                        }
                        else if(`theta'[`row',1] == .){
                                matrix `alltheta'[`row',`i'] = 0
                        }
                        else {
                                matrix      `alltheta'[`row',`i']      =
`theta'[`row',1]
                        }
                    }
                local i = `i'+1
```

```
                 local tki = `tkindex'[`i',1]
}                // end of while

// efficiency score (theta) of current time (`tf')
matrix `thetafinal' = `alltheta'[1...,`n2']
                 matrix colnames `thetafinal' = theta_tf

// choose DMU's initial (`tk') efficiency when appeared
matrix `thetainitial' = J(`n1',1,.)
                 matrix colnames `thetainitial' = theta_tk
forvalues i = 1/`n1'{
                 forvalues j = 1/`n2' {
                          if (`alltheta'[`i',`j'] == 1) {
                                   matrix `thetainitial'[`i',1] = `alltheta'[`i',`j']
                          }
                          else if (`alltheta'[`i',`j'] == . & `alltheta'[`i',`j'+1] != .) {
                                   matrix `thetainitial'[`i',1] = `alltheta'[`i',`j'+1]
                          }
                 }
}                // end of forvalues

// choose DMU's `tkineff', last year remain SOA
restore, preserve
  quietly clear
  quietly svmat `thetainitial', names(col)
  quietly svmat `thetafinal', names(col)
  quietly gen tk_ineff = .
  quietly forvalues i = 1/`n1' {
                 replace tk_ineff = `tktemp'[`i',1] in `i' if theta_tk==1 & theta_tf != 1
  }
  mkmat tk_ineff, matrix(`tkineff')
                 matrix colnames `tkineff' = tk_ineff

restore, preserve

  // compute effective time of DMU k
  matrix `I' = J(`n1',1,1)
  matrix `tkeff' = `refmat' * `tktemp'
  matrix `sumlambda' = `refmat' * `I'
  forvalues i = 1/`n1' {
                 matrix `tkeff'[`i',1] = `tkeff'[`i',1] / `sumlambda'[`i',1]
  }
                 matrix colnames `tkeff' = tk_eff

** step 3. computing ROC
  matrix `roc' = J(`n1',1,.)
                 matrix colnames `roc' = ROC
  forvalues i = 1/`n1' {
                 if (`tkineff'[`i',1] != .) {
                          matrix `roc'[`i',1] = ///
                                   (`thetafinal'[`i',1])^(1/(`tkeff'[`i',1]-`tktemp'[`i',1]))
                 }
                 else {
                          matrix `roc'[`i',1] = .
                 }
  }

*!! need to update about weighted average method of Lim et al.(2014)
  // compute annual ROC by average
  local mroc = 0
  local numroc = 0
  forvalues i = 1/`n1' {
```

```
                        if `roc'[`i',1] != . {
                                local mroc = `mroc'+`roc'[`i',1]
                                local numroc = `numroc'+1
                        }
                }
                local mroc = `mroc' / `numroc'

                // result matrix of computing ROC
                matrix `rsltroc' = `tktemp', `thetainitial', `thetafinal', `tkeff', `roc'

        restore, preserve
        ** step 4. forecast technology by MODEL
                // Model : Specification
                if ("`model'" == "SPECIFICATION"){
                        _spec, invars(`invars') outvars(`outvars') dataset(`dataset') ///
                                        rts(`rts')  ort(`ort')  tk(`tk')  tf(`tf')  mroc(`mroc')
dmu(`dmu')

                        matrix `specrslt' = r(specrslt)
                }
                matrix `alltheta' = `tktemp', `alltheta'
        restore

        ** step 5. display results
                display as text "{hline `c(linesize)'}"
                display as result ""
                display as result "DEA Options: RTS(`rts') ORT(`ort')"
                display as result ""
                display as result "Rate of Change (ROC) calculation Results: "
                matrix list `rsltroc', noblank nohalf noheader f(%9.6g)
                display as result ""
                display as result "Annual Rate of Change (AROC) is: " `mroc' "(`numroc' DMU
chosen)"

                // Model : SPECIFICATION
                if ("`model'" == "SPECIFICATION")  {
                        display as result ""
                        display as result "TFDEA Forecasting Results: "
                        matrix list `specrslt', noblank nohalf noheader f(%9.6g)
                }

                // Model : Noforecast
                else if ("`model'" == "NOFORECAST"){
                        display "end"
                }

                // return
                return scalar mean_roc = `mroc'
                return scalar num_roc_dmu = `numroc'
                return matrix rocrslt = `rsltroc'
                return matrix theta_all = `alltheta'
                if ("`model'" == "SPECIFICATION") {
                        return matrix forecasting = `specrslt'
                }
                return matrix lambda = `refmat'

        end
```

```
*********************************************************************
* _SPEC : technology forecasting
*********************************************************************
program define _spec, rclass
    syntax, invars(varlist) outvars(varlist) dataset(name) ///
                        rts(string) ort(string) tk(string) tf(string) mroc(string) ///
                        dmu(string)

    preserve

    tempname ftkindex fdataset ndataset deasurslt supertheta superteff tfeff
    tempname tksuptemp tfexp rsltspec SEI selambda sumselambda

    local tf = real("`tf'")
    local mroc = real("`mroc'")

    sort `tk' `dmu'

    // matrix for compute technology forecasting and it's tk index
    mkmat `tk' `invars' `outvars' if (`tk' > `tf'), matrix(`fdataset') rown(dmu)
    mkmat `tk' if(`tk' > `tf'), matrix(`ftkindex') rown(dmu)
                local n3 = rowsof(`ftkindex')          //     number     of     observationfor
forecasting

    matrix `supertheta' = J(`n3',1,.)
                matrix colnames `supertheta' = SE_tf
    matrix `tfeff' = J(`n3',1,.)
                matrix colnames `tfeff' = tf_eff


    // super efficiency computation
    forvalues i = 1/`n3' {
                display "DEA_SUPEREFF iteration", `i', "of", `n3'
                quietly clear
                matrix `ndataset' = nullmat(`ndataset') \ `dataset' \ `fdataset'[`i',1...]
                                quietly svmat `ndataset', names(col)
                                quietly gen dmu = _n
                                local n4 = c(N)

                quietly dea_supereff `invars' `outvars', rts(`rts') ort(`ort') stage(2)
                                matrix `deasurslt' = r(dearslt)
                                matrix `supertheta'[`i',1] = `deasurslt'[`n4',"theta"]
                                matrix `selambda' = `deasurslt'[1...,"ref:"]
                                matrix `SEI' = J(`n4',1,1)
                                matrix `sumselambda' = `selambda'*`SEI'

                                ** compute effective time(`tfeff') in current frontier
                                matrix `superteff' = `deasurslt'[.,"ref:"] * `ndataset'[., "`tk'"]
                                matrix `tfeff'[`i',1] = `superteff'[`n4',1]/`sumselambda'[`i',1]
                                matrix drop `ndataset'
    }

    // calculate expected time for each DMU
    matrix `tfexp' = J(`n3',1,.)
                matrix colnames `tfexp' = tf_exp
    forvalues i = 1/`n3' {
                matrix `tfexp'[`i',1] = `tfeff'[`i',1] + ln(1/`supertheta'[`i',1])/ln(`mroc')
    }

    matrix `rsltspec' = nullmat(`rsltspec'), `ftkindex', `supertheta', ///
                                                `tfeff', `tfexp'

    restore

    return matrix specrslt = `rsltspec'

end
```

B2.10 dea_additive.ado

```
! version 1.0.0  26SEP2011
capture program drop dea_additive
program define dea_additive, rclass
    version 10.0

/** Terms Description:
* -------------------------------------------------------------------------
* RTS: Return To Scale
* CRS: Constant Return to Scale
* VRS: Variant Return to Scale
* -------------------------------------------------------------------------
*/

// syntax checking and validation----------------------------------------
// rts - return to scale
// input varlist = output varlist
// example:
//    additive Employee Area = Sales Profits, rts(CRS)
//    additive Employee Area = Sales Profits, sav
// -------------------------------------------------------------------------
    // returns 1 if the first nonblank character of local macro `0' is a comma,
    // or if `0' is empty.
    if replay() {
        dis as err "ivars and ovars required."
        exit 198
    }

    // get and check invarnames
    gettoken word 0 : 0, parse("=,")
    while ~("`word'" == ":" | "`word'" == "=") {
        if "`word'" == "," | "`word'" == "" {
            error 198
        }
        local invarnames `invarnames' `word'
        gettoken word 0 : 0, parse("=,")
    }
    unab invarnames : `invarnames'

    #del ;
    syntax varlist(min=1) [if] [in] [using/]
    [,
        RTS(string)      // ignore case sensitive,[{CRS|CCR} | {BCC|VRS}]
        TOL1(real 1e-14)  // entering or leaving value tolerance
        TOL2(real 1e-8)   // B inverse tolerance: 2.22e-12
        TRACE            // Whether or not to do the log
        SAVing(string)   // log file name
        REPLACE          // Whether or not to replace the log file
    ];
    #del cr

    local num_invar : word count `invarnames'
    local i 1
    while (`i'<=`num_invar') {
        local invarn : word `i' of `invarnames'
        local junk : subinstr local invarnames "`invarn'" "", ///
```

240

```
        word all count(local j)
        if `j' > 1 {
            di as error ///
                "cannot specify the same input variable more than once"
            error 498
        }
        local i = `i' + 1
    }

    // default model - CRS(Constant Return to Scale)
    if ("`rts'" == "") local rts = "CRS"
    else {
        local rts = upper("`rts'")
        if ("`rts'" == "CCR") local rts = "CRS"
        else if ("`rts'" == "BCC") local rts = "VRS"
        else if (~("`rts'" == "CRS" | "`rts'" == "VRS")) {
            di as err "option rts allow for case-insensitive " _c
            di as err "CRS (eq CCR) or VRS (eq BCC) or nothing."
            exit 198
        }
    }

    if ("`using'" != "") use "`using'", clear
    if (~(`c(N)' > 0 & `c(k)' > 0)) {
        dis as err "dataset required!"
        exit 198
    }

// end of syntax checking and validation -------------------------------------

    set more off
    capture log close dea_additivelog

    // to remove log header information, use "quietly" and "hline"
    di as text "{hline `c(linesize)'}"
    quietly log using "dea_additive.log", replace text name(dea_additivelog)
    preserve

    if ("`if'" != "" | "`in'" != "") {
        qui keep `in' `if'  // filtering : keep in range [if exp]
    }

    _dea_additive, ivars(`invarnames') ovars(`varlist') rts(`rts') ///
                tol1(`tol1') tol2(`tol2') `trace' saving(`saving') `replace'
    return add

    restore, preserve
    quietly log close dea_additivelog
    di as text "{hline `c(linesize)'}"
end

********************************************************************************
* DEA Additive - Data Envelopment Analysis Additive Model
********************************************************************************
program define _dea_additive, rclass
    #del ;
    syntax , IVARS(string) OVARS(string) RTS(string)
    [
        TOL1(real 1e-14) TOL2(real 1e-8)
```

```
                    TRACE SAVing(string) REPLACE
];
#del cr

preserve

// ----------------------------------------------------------------------

tempname dmuIn dmuOut frameMat deamainrslt dearslt vrsfrontier crslambda
mkDmuMat `ivars', dmumat(`dmuIn') sprefix("i")
mkDmuMat `ovars', dmumat(`dmuOut') sprefix("o")
local dmuCount = colsof(`dmuIn')
local minrank = 1

mata: _l_mkframemat("`frameMat'", "`dmuIn'", "`dmuOut'", "`rts'")
mata: _l_dealp ("`frameMat'", "`dmuIn'", "`dmuOut'", "`rts'", ///
           `tol1', `tol2', "`trace'")
matrix `deamainrslt' = r(dealprslt)

mata: _l_slacksum("`deamainrslt'", `=rowsof(`dmuIn')', `=rowsof(`dmuOut')')
matrix `deamainrslt'[1,1] = r(slacksum)
matrix `dearslt' = J(`dmuCount', 1, .), `deamainrslt' // rank column

// TODO if you need rank, substitution above a line.
// ----------------------------------------------------------------------
// mata: _dmurank("`deamainrslt'", ///
//       `=rowsof(`dmuIn')', `=rowsof(`dmuOut')', `minrank', `tol2')
// matrix `dearslt' = r(rank), `deamainrslt'
// ----------------------------------------------------------------------

// use mata function '_setup_dearslt_names' because the maximum string
// variable length needs to be kept under the 244 for all the time
mata: _setup_dearslt_names("`dearslt'", "`dmuIn'", "`dmuOut'")

// ----------------------------------------------------------------------
// REPORT
// ----------------------------------------------------------------------
di as result ""
di as input "options: RTS(`rts')"
di as result "`rts' DEA-Additive Efficiency Results:"
matrix list `dearslt', noblank nohalf noheader f(%9.6g)

if ("`saving'" != "") {
    // if the saving file exists and replace option not specified,
    // make the backup file.
    if ("`replace'" == "") {
        local dotpos = strpos("`saving'",".")
        if (`dotpos' > 0) {
            mata: _file_exists("`saving'")
        }
        else {
            mata: _file_exists("`saving'.dta")
        }
        if r(fileexists) {
            local curdt = subinstr("`c(current_date)'", " ", "", .) + /*
                */ subinstr("`c(current_time)'", ":", "", .)
            if (`dotpos' > 0) {
                #del ;
                local savefn = substr("`saving'", 1, `dotpos' - 1) +
```

```
                              "_bak_`curdt'" +
                              substr("`saving'",`dotpos', .);
                    #del cr
                    qui copy "`saving'" "`savefn'", replace
                }
                else {
                    local savefn = "`saving'_bak_`curdt'" + ".dta"
                    qui copy "`saving'.dta" "`savefn'", replace
                }
            }
        }

    restore, preserve
                svmat `dearslt', names(eqcol)
                capture {
                                renpfix _
                                renpfix ref ref_
                                renpfix islack is_
                                renpfix oslack os_
                }
                capture save `saving', replace
    }
    return matrix dearslt = `dearslt'
    restore, preserve
end


******************************************************************************
* Data Import and Conversion
******************************************************************************


// Make DMU Matrix ---------------------------------------------------
program define mkDmuMat
    #del ;
    syntax varlist(numeric) [if] [in], DMUmat(name)
    [
        SPREfix(string)
    ];
    #del cr

    qui ds
    // variable not found error
    if ("`varlist'" == "") {
        di as err "variable not found"
        exit 111
    }

    // make matrix
    mkmat `varlist' `if' `in', matrix(`dmumat') rownames(dmu)
    matrix roweq `dmumat' = "dmu"
    matrix coleq `dmumat' = `=lower("`sprefix'") + "slack'"
    matrix `dmumat' = `dmumat'
end

// Start of the MATA Definition Area -------------------------------------
version 10
mata:
mata set matastrict on

/**
```

```
* make frame matrix and set matrix value at the param frameMat
* rts - return to scale, ort - orientation
*/
function _l_mkframemat(
                string scalar frameMat,
                string scalar dmuIn,
                string scalar dmuOut,
                string scalar rts )
{
    real matrix F, DI, DO
    real scalar dmus, slackins, slackouts
    real scalar frows, fcols

    DI = st_matrix(dmuIn)
    DO = st_matrix(dmuOut)
    if (cols(DI) != cols(DO)) {
        _error(3200, "in and out count of dmu is not match!")
    }

    dmus = cols(DI) // or cols(DO), because cols(DI) == cols(DO)
    slackins = rows(DI); slackouts = rows(DO)
    if (rts == "CRS") {
        // target coefficient\slackins\slackouts
        frows = 1 + slackins + slackouts
                    // target coefficient,theta,dmus,slackins,slackouts,rhs
        fcols = 1 + 1 + dmus + slackins + slackouts + 1
    }
    else if (rts == "VRS") {
                    // target coefficient\slackins\slackouts\sum of lamda
        frows = 1 + slackins + slackouts + 1
                    // target coefficient,theta,dmus,slackins,slackouts,rhs
        fcols = 1 + 1 + dmus + slackins + slackouts + 1
    }
    else {
        _error(3498, "invalid rts optoin.")
    }

    // make frame matrix for CRS(CCR)
    F = J(frows, fcols, 0)
    F[1, 1] = 1
    replacesubmat(F, 2, 3, DI)
    replacesubmat(F, 2 + slackins, 3, DO)
    replacesubmat(F, 2, 3 + dmus, I(slackins))
    replacesubmat(F, 2 + slackins, 3 + dmus + slackins, -I(slackouts))

    // adjustment
    if (rts == "VRS") {
        replacesubmat(F, frows, 3, J(1, dmus, 1))
        F[frows,fcols] = 1
    }

    // return result
    st_matrix(frameMat, F)
}

/**
* DEA Loop - Data Envelopment Analysis Loop for DMUs
*/
function _l_dealp (
```

```
            string scalar frameMat,
            string scalar dmuIn,
            string scalar dmuOut,
            string scalar rts,
            real scalar tol1,
            real scalar tol2,
            string scalar trace )
{
    real matrix F, DI, DO, M, VARS, LPRSLT, DEALPRSLT, ARTIF
    real scalar dmus, slackins, slackouts, slacks, artificials, artificialrow
    real scalar frows, fcols, i, dmui
    real colvector effvec, slackidx
    string scalar tracename

    struct BoundCond matrix boundF, boundM
    struct LpParamStruct scalar param

    F  = st_matrix(frameMat)
    DI = st_matrix(dmuIn)
    DO = st_matrix(dmuOut)
    if (cols(DI) != cols(DO)) {
        _error(3200, "in and out count of dmu is not match!")
    }
    if (!(rts == "CRS" || rts == "VRS")) {
            _error(3498, "rts must be one of CRS, VRS")
    }

    // basic value setting for artificial variabels
    frows = rows(F); fcols = cols(F)
    dmus = cols(DI) // or cols(DO), because cols(DI) == cols(DO)
    slackins = rows(DI); slackouts = rows(DO)

    tracename = rts

    // -------------------------------------------------------------------------
    // define number of slacks by rts
    slacks = slackins + slackouts

    // define number of artificials by rts, ort, stage
    if (rts == "CRS") {
            artificials = slackouts; artificialrow = 2+slackins;
    }
    else if (rts == "VRS") {
            artificials = slackouts+1; artificialrow = 2+slackins
    }
    if (artificials > 0) {
            ARTIF = J(1, artificials, 1) \ J(frows-1, artificials, 0)
            replacesubmat(ARTIF, artificialrow, 1, I(artificials))
            F = F[,1..fcols-1], ARTIF, F[,fcols]
            frows = rows(F); fcols = cols(F) // revise frows, fcols
    }
    // -------------------------------------------------------------------------
    boundF = J(1, fcols, BoundCond());
    // set the boundary for the efficiency variable(theta, eta):
    // -INFINITE <= efficiency <= INFINITE
    boundF[1,2].val = 0; boundF[1,2].lower = 0; boundF[1,2].upper = .

    // set boundary for the weight variable(lamda, mu):
    // 0 <= weight <= INFINITE
```

245

```
            for (i=3; i<dmus+3; i++) {
                    boundF[1,i].val = 0; boundF[1,i].lower = 0; boundF[1,i].upper = .
            }

            // set boundary for the non-structural variable(slack, artificial).
            // 0 <= slacks and atrificials <= INFINITE
            for (i=dmus+3; i<fcols; i++) {
                    boundF[1,i].val = 0; boundF[1,i].lower = 0; boundF[1,i].upper = .
            }
            // liststruct(boundF); // for debug

            // set the lp's parameters
            param.rts          = rts
            param.isin         = 0 // max
            param.stagestep    = 2 // 2 step
            param.dmus         = dmus
            param.slacks       = slacks
            param.artificials  = artificials
            param.tol1         = tol1
            param.tol2         = tol2
            param.isminsubscript = 0 // false
            param.trace        = trace
            // liststruct(param); // for debug
            // -------------------------------------------------------------------
            DEALPRSLT = J(0, 1+ dmus + slacks, 0)
            for (dmui=1; dmui<=dmus; dmui++) {
                    M = F; boundM = boundF
                    replacesubmat(M, 2, fcols, DI[,dmui])
                    replacesubmat(M, 2+slackins, fcols, DO[,dmui])

                    // execute LP
                    VARS  = lp_phase1(M, boundM, dmui, tracename, param)
                    if (VARS[1,1] == .) {
                            LPRSLT = J(1, cols(DEALPRSLT), .)
                    }
                    else {
                            LPRSLT = lp_phase2(M, boundM, VARS, dmui, tracename,
param);
                    }
                    DEALPRSLT = DEALPRSLT \ LPRSLT
            }

            st_matrix("r(dealprslt)", DEALPRSLT)
    }

    function _l_slacksum( string scalar deamat,
                    real scalar dmuincount,
                    real scalar dmuoutcount )
    {
       real matrix M
       real rowvector slcaksum

       M = st_matrix(deamat)
       slcaksum = rowsum(M[|1,cols(M) - (dmuincount + dmuoutcount - 1)\.,.|])
       st_matrix("r(slacksum)", slcaksum)
    }
    end
// End of the MATA Definition Area --------------------------------------------
```

B2.11 dea_allocative.ado

```
*! version 1.0.0  26SEP2011
capture program drop dea_allocative
program define dea_allocative, rclass
    version 10.0

/** Terms Description:
 * ------------------------------------------------------------------------
 * RTS: Return To Scale
 * CRS: Constant Return to Scale
 * VRS: Variant Return to Scale
 * ------------------------------------------------------------------------
 */

    // syntax checking and validation----------------------------------------
    // input varlist = output varlist
    // example:
    //    dea_allocative Employee Area = Sales Profits, model(c) values(1 2)
    //    dea_allocative Employee Area = Sales Profits, model(r) values(2 2)
    // ------------------------------------------------------------------------
    // returns 1 if the first nonblank character of local macro `0' is a comma,
    // or if `0' is empty.
    if replay() {
        dis as err "ivars and ovars required."
        exit 198
    }

    // get and check invarnames
    gettoken word 0 : 0, parse("=,")
    while ~("`word'" == ":" | "`word'" == "=") {
        if "`word'" == "," | "`word'" == "" {
            error 198
        }
        local invarnames `invarnames' `word'
        gettoken word 0 : 0, parse("=,")
    }
    unab invarnames : `invarnames'

    #del ;
    syntax varlist(min=1) [if] [in] [using/],
            MODel(string)                   //  ignore   case    sensitive
{COST|REVENUE|PROFIT}
    [
            VALues(numlist >0)    //
            UNITVars(varlist numeric) // unit variables for unit values
            RTS(string)           //              ignore          case
sensitive,[{CRS|CCR}|{BCC|VRS}]
            TOL1(real 1e-14)  // entering or leaving value tolerance
            TOL2(real 1e-8)     // B inverse tolerance: 2.22e-12
            TRACE         // Whether or not to do the log
                DETAIL                              // Detail Result Report
            SAVing(string)    // log file name
            REPLACE        // Whether or not to replace the log file
    ];
    #del cr
```

```
local num_invar : word count `invarnames'
local i 1
while (`i'<=`num_invar') {
   local invarn : word `i' of `invarnames'
   local junk : subinstr local invarnames "`invarn'" "", ///
      word all count(local j)
   if `j' > 1 {
      di as error ///
         "cannot specify the same input variable more than once"
      error 498
   }
   local i = `i' + 1
}

// default model - CRS(Constant Return to Scale)
if ("`rts'" == "") local rts = "CRS"
else {
   local rts = upper("`rts'")
   if ("`rts'" == "CCR") local rts = "CRS"
   else if ("`rts'" == "BCC") local rts = "VRS"
   else if (~("`rts'" == "CRS" | "`rts'" == "VRS")) {
      di as err "option rts allow for case-insensitive " _c
      di as err "CRS (eq CCR) or VRS (eq BCC) or nothing."
      exit 198
   }
}

if ("`using'" != "") use "`using'", clear
if (~(`c(N)' > 0 & `c(k)' > 0)) {
   dis as err "dataset required!"
   exit 198
}

// make value matrix, check invarnames count and values count as model
tempname vmat
local sizeof_values : list sizeof values
local sizeof_unitvars : list sizeof unitvars
if (`sizeof_values' > 0 & `sizeof_unitvars' > 0) {
      dis as err "values and unitvars cannot be used at the same time."
   exit 198
}

if (`sizeof_values' > 0) {
      foreach value of numlist `values' {
            matrix `vmat' = (nullmat(`vmat'), `value')
      }
}
else if (`sizeof_unitvars' > 0){
      mkmat `unitvars', mat(`vmat')
}
else {
      dis as err "values and unitvars should be used at least."
   exit 198
}

local model = upper("`model'")
if ("`model'" == "C") local model = "COST";
else if ("`model'" == "R") local model = "REVENUE";
else if ("`model'" == "P") local model = "PROFIT";
```

```
      if ("`model'" == "COST") {
            if (colsof(`vmat') != `num_invar') {
                  di as error "the number of input variable the same with " _c
                  di as error "the number of values in unitvars."
                  error 498
            }
      }
      else if("`model'" == "REVENUE") {
            local num_outvar : list sizeof varlist
            if (colsof(`vmat') != `num_outvar') {
                  di as error "the number of output variable should be " _c
                  di as error "the same with the number of values in unitvars."
                  error 498
            }
      }
      else if("`model'" == "PROFIT") {
            local num_outvar : list sizeof varlist
            if (colsof(`vmat') != (`num_invar' + `num_outvar')) {
                  di as error "cannot different the sum of " _c
                  di as error "number of in/output variable and number of
values."
                  error 498
            }
      }
      else {
            di as err "option model allow for case-insensitive " _c
            di as err "{C|COST or R|REVENUE or P|PROFIT}"
            exit 198
      }

   // end of syntax checking and validation --------------------------------------

      set more off
      capture log close dea_allocative
      log using "dea_allocative.log", replace text name(dea_allocative)
      preserve

      if ("`if'" != "" | "`in'" != "") {
            qui keep `in' `if'  // filtering : keep in range [if exp]
      }

      if ("`model'" == "COST") {
                  dea_cost, ivars(`invarnames') ovars(`varlist') rts(`rts') ///
                  model(`model') unitcost(`vmat') tol1(`tol1') tol2(`tol2') ///
                  `trace' `detail' saving(`saving') `replace'
      }
      else if("`model'" == "REVENUE") {
                  dea_revenue, ivars(`invarnames') ovars(`varlist') rts(`rts') ///
                  model(`model') unitprice(`vmat') tol1(`tol1') tol2(`tol2') ///
                  `trace' `detail' saving(`saving') `replace'
      }
      else {  // if("`model'" == "PROFIT")
                  dea_profit, ivars(`invarnames') ovars(`varlist') rts(`rts') ///
                  model(`model') unitvalue(`vmat') tol1(`tol1') tol2(`tol2') ///
                  `trace' `detail' saving(`saving') `replace'
      }

      return add
```

```
    restore, preserve
    log close dea_allocative
end

********************************************************************************
* DEA Cost - Data Envelopment Analysis Cost Model
********************************************************************************
program define dea_cost, rclass
    #del ;
    syntax , IVARS(string) OVARS(string) RTS(string)
                        MODel(string) UNITCost(name)
    [
        TOL1(real 1e-14) TOL2(real 1e-8)
                TRACE DETAIL SAVing(string) REPLACE
    ];
    #del cr

    preserve

    // ------------------------------------------------------------------

    tempname dmuIn dmuOut frameMat
    tempname dearslt minIn theta
    mkDmuMat `ivars', dmumat(`dmuIn') sprefix("i")
    mkDmuMat `ovars', dmumat(`dmuOut') sprefix("o")
    local dmuCount = colsof(`dmuIn')
    local minrank = 1
    local detailYn = ("`detail'" != "") | ("`trace'" != "")

    // 1. Get Min Input
    mata: _l_mkframemat("`model'", "`frameMat'", "`dmuIn'", "`dmuOut'", "`rts'")
    mata: _l_dealp ("`model'", "`frameMat'", "`dmuIn'", "`dmuOut'", "`rts'", ///
            "`unitcost'", `tol1', `tol2', "`trace'")

if (`detailYn') {
    di as result "Min Cost DEA Result:"
    matrix `dearslt' = J(`dmuCount', 1, .), r(dealprslt) // rank column
    mata: _setup_dearslt_names("`dearslt'", "`dmuIn'", "`dmuOut'")
    matrix list `dearslt', noblank nohalf noheader f(%9.6g)
}

    matrix `dearslt' = r(dealprslt)
    local i = (2 + `dmuCount')
    matrix `minIn' = `dearslt'[1...,`i'..(`i' + rowsof(`dmuIn') - 1)]

    // 2. Get Theta
    local ort = "IN"
    local stage = 1
    local minsubscript = 0 // false
    mata: _mkframemat("`frameMat'", "`dmuIn'", "`dmuOut'", ///
                    "`rts'", "`ort'")
    deamain `dmuIn' `dmuOut' `frameMat' `rts' `ort' `stage' ///
                    `tol1' `tol2' `minsubscript' `trace'
    matrix `dearslt' = r(deamainrslt)
    matrix `theta' = `dearslt'[1...,1]

    // 3. Calculate Cost
    mata: _l_calc_cost("`unitcost'", "`dmuIn'", "`minIn'", "`theta'", `detailYn')
    matrix `dearslt' = r(mat)
```

Appendix B2.11 dea_allocative.ado

```
// -------------------------------------------------------------------------
// REPORT
// -------------------------------------------------------------------------
di as result ""
di as input "options: RTS(`rts')"
di as result "`rts' DEA-Cost Efficiency Results:"
matrix list `dearslt', noblank nohalf noheader f(%9.6g)

if ("`saving'" != "") {
        restore, preserve
    save_result `dearslt' `saving' `replace'
}
return matrix dearslt = `dearslt'

    restore, preserve
end

********************************************************************************
* DEA Revenue - Data Envelopment Analysis Revenue Model
********************************************************************************
program define dea_revenue, rclass
    #del ;
    syntax , IVARS(string) OVARS(string) RTS(string)
                    MODel(string) UNITPrice(name)
    [
        TOL1(real 1e-14) TOL2(real 1e-8)
                    TRACE DETAIL SAVing(string) REPLACE
    ];
    #del cr

    preserve

    // -------------------------------------------------------------------------

    tempname dmuIn dmuOut frameMat
    tempname dearslt maxOut eta
    mkDmuMat `ivars', dmumat(`dmuIn') sprefix("i")
    mkDmuMat `ovars', dmumat(`dmuOut') sprefix("o")
    local dmuCount = colsof(`dmuIn')
    local minrank = 1
    local detailYn = ("`detail'" != "") | ("`trace'" != "")

    // 1. Get Max Output
    mata: _l_mkframemat("`model'", "`frameMat'", "`dmuIn'", "`dmuOut'", "`rts'")
    mata: _l_dealp ("`model'", "`frameMat'", "`dmuIn'", "`dmuOut'", "`rts'", ///
                    "`unitprice'", `tol1', `tol2', "`trace'")

if (`detailYn') {
        di as result "Max Price DEA Result:"
        matrix `dearslt' = J(`dmuCount', 1, .), r(dealprslt) // rank column
        mata: _setup_dearslt_names("`dearslt'", "`dmuIn'", "`dmuOut'")
        matrix list `dearslt', noblank nohalf noheader f(%9.6g)
}

        matrix `dearslt' = r(dealprslt)
        local i = (2 + `dmuCount')
        matrix `maxOut' = `dearslt'[1..., `i'..(`i' + rowsof(`dmuOut') - 1)]
```

251

```
// 2. Get Eta
local ort = "OUT"
local stage = 1
local minsubscript = 0 // false
mata: _mkframemat("`frameMat'", "`dmuIn'", "`dmuOut'", ///
                  "`rts'", "`ort'")
deamain `dmuIn' `dmuOut' `frameMat' `rts' `ort' `stage' ///
                  `tol1' `tol2' `minsubscript' `trace'
matrix `dearslt' = r(deamainrslt)
matrix `eta' = `dearslt'[1...,1]


// 3. Calculate Cost
mata: _l_calc_revenue("`unitprice'", "`dmuOut'", "`maxOut'", "`eta'", `detailYn')
matrix `dearslt' = r(mat)


// ----------------------------------------------------------------------
// REPORT
// ----------------------------------------------------------------------
di as result ""
di as input "options: RTS(`rts')"
di as result "`rts' DEA-Revenue Efficiency Results:"
matrix list `dearslt', noblank nohalf noheader f(%9.6g)

if ("`saving'" != "") {
        restore, preserve
    save_result `dearslt' `saving' `replace'
}
return matrix dearslt = `dearslt'

    restore, preserve
end

**************************************************************************
* DEA Profit - Data Envelopment Analysis Profit Model
**************************************************************************
program define dea_profit, rclass
  #del ;
  syntax , IVARS(string) OVARS(string) RTS(string)
                        MODel(string) UNITValue(name)
  [
     TOL1(real 1e-14) TOL2(real 1e-8)
                TRACE DETAIL SAVing(string) REPLACE
  ];
  #del cr

  preserve

  // ----------------------------------------------------------------------

  tempname dmuIn dmuOut frameMat
  tempname dearslt
  mkDmuMat `ivars', dmumat(`dmuIn') sprefix("i")
  mkDmuMat `ovars', dmumat(`dmuOut') sprefix("o")
  local dmuCount = colsof(`dmuIn')
  local minrank = 1
  local detailYn = ("`detail'" != "") | ("`trace'" != "")

  // 1. Get Max Profit
```

```
    mata: _l_mkframemat("`model'", "`frameMat'", "`dmuIn'", "`dmuOut'", "`rts'")
    mata: _l_dealp ("`model'", "`frameMat'", "`dmuIn'", "`dmuOut'", "`rts'", ///
            "`unitvalue'", `tol1', `tol2', "`trace'")

if (`detailYn') {
    di as result "Max Profit DEA Result:"
    matrix `dearslt' = J(`dmuCount', 1, .), r(dealprslt) // rank column
    mata: _setup_dearslt_names("`dearslt'", "`dmuIn'", "`dmuOut'")
    matrix list `dearslt', noblank nohalf noheader f(%9.6g)
}

    matrix `dearslt' = r(dealprslt)


    // 2. Calculate Profit
    mata: _l_calc_profit("`unitvalue'", "`dmuIn'", "`dmuOut'", ///
                    "`dearslt'", `detailYn')
    matrix `dearslt' = r(mat)


    // -------------------------------------------------------------------
    // REPORT
    // -------------------------------------------------------------------
    di as result ""
    di as input "options: RTS(`rts')"
    di as result "`rts' DEA-Profit Efficiency Results:"
    matrix list `dearslt', noblank nohalf noheader f(%9.6g)

    if ("`saving'" != "") {
            restore, preserve
        save_result `dearslt' `saving' `replace'
    }
    return matrix dearslt = `dearslt'

    restore, preserve
end

********************************************************************************
* Save Result
********************************************************************************
program define save_result, rclass
    args dearslt saving replace

    // if the saving file exists and replace option not specified,
    // make the backup file.
    if ("`replace'" == "") {
            local dotpos = strpos("`saving'",".")
            if (`dotpos' > 0) {
                    mata: _file_exists("`saving'")
            }
            else {
                    mata: _file_exists("`saving'.dta")
            }
            if r(fileexists) {
                    local curdt = subinstr("`c(current_date)'", " ", "", .) + /*
                            */ subinstr("`c(current_time)'", ":", "", .)
                    if (`dotpos' > 0) {
                            #del ;
                            local savefn = substr("`saving'", 1, `dotpos' - 1) +
"_bak_`curdt'" +
```

```
substr("`saving'",`dotpos', .);
                                        #del cr
                                        qui copy "`saving'" "`savefn'", replace
                            }
                            else {
                                        local savefn = "`saving'_bak_`curdt'" + ".dta"
                                        qui copy "`saving'.dta" "`savefn'", replace
                            }
                    }
            }

        svmat `dearslt', names(eqcol)
        capture {
                    renpfix _
                    renpfix CUR cur_
                    renpfix TECH tech_
                    renpfix MIN min_
        }
        capture save `saving', replace
    end

    *******************************************************************************
    * DEA Main - Data Envelopment Analysis Main
    *******************************************************************************
    program define deamain, rclass
        args dmuIn dmuOut frameMat rts ort stage tol1 tol2 minsubscript trace

        tempname efficientVec deamainrslt

        // stage step 1.
        if ("`trace'" == "trace") {
            di _n(2) as txt "RTS(`rts') ORT(`ort') 1st stage."
        }
        mata: _dealp("`frameMat'", "`dmuIn'", "`dmuOut'", "`rts'", "`ort'", ///
            1, `tol1', `tol2', "`minsubscript'", "`efficientVec'", "`trace'")
        matrix `deamainrslt' = r(dealprslt)

        // stage step 2.
        if ("`stage'" == "2") {
            if ("`trace'" == "trace") {
                di _n(2) as txt "RTS(`rts') ORT(`ort') 2nd stage."
            }
            matrix `efficientVec' = `deamainrslt'[1...,1]

            mata: _dealp("`frameMat'", "`dmuIn'", "`dmuOut'", "`rts'", "`ort'", ///
                2, `tol1', `tol2', "`minsubscript'", "`efficientVec'", "`trace'")
            matrix `deamainrslt' = r(dealprslt)
        }

        return matrix deamainrslt = `deamainrslt'
    end

    *******************************************************************************
    * Data Import and Conversion
    *******************************************************************************

    // Make DMU Matrix ---------------------------------------------------------
    program define mkDmuMat
```

```
#del ;
syntax varlist(numeric) [if] [in], DMUmat(name)
[
    SPREfix(string)
];
#del cr

qui ds
// variable not found error
if ("`varlist'" == "") {
    di as err "variable not found"
    exit 111
}

// make matrix
mkmat `varlist' `if' `in', matrix(`dmumat') rownames(dmu)
matrix roweq `dmumat' = "dmu"
matrix coleq `dmumat' = `=lower("`sprefix'")' + "slack"'
matrix `dmumat' = `dmumat'
end

// Start of the MATA Definition Area -----------------------------------------
version 10
mata:
mata set matastrict on

// ---------------------------------------------------------------------------
// Internal mata and stata combination.
// ---------------------------------------------------------------------------

/**
 * calculate min cost
 */
function _l_calc_cost(
                string scalar unitCost,
                string scalar dmuIn,
                string scalar minIn,
                string scalar theta,
                real scalar detail )
{
    real matrix UC, DI, MI, TT // input
    real matrix TI, CC, TC, MC // cost calculate result
    real matrix CCR, TCR, MCR  // sum of cost calculate result
    real matrix OE, AE, TE, FR // cost efficiency final result

    string matrix DMU_CS  // dmu column stripes
    string matrix FR_CS      // ce final result matrix column stripes
    string matrix FR_RS      // ce final result matrix row stripes
    string matrix CS                  // temp column stripes

    // input
    UC = st_matrix(unitCost)
    DI = st_matrix(dmuIn)'
    MI = st_matrix(minIn)
    TT = st_matrix(theta)

    // cost calculate result
    TI = TT:*DI // Thechnical Input
    CC = UC:*DI // Current Cost
```

255

```
TC = UC:*TI // Technical Cost
MC = UC:*MI // Min Cost

// sum of cost calculate result
CCR = rowsum(CC)
TCR = rowsum(TC)
MCR = rowsum(MC)

// cost efficiency result
OE = (MCR:/CCR) // Overall Efficiency
AE = (MCR:/TCR) // Allocative Efficiency
TE = (TCR:/CCR) // Technical Efficiency

// final result
FR = (DI, CCR, TT, TI, TCR, MI, MCR, OE, AE, TE)

if (detail) {
        printf("\n{res}Input:\n");
    printf("\n{res}Unit Cost:\n"); UC
    printf("\n{res}DMU In:\n"); DI
        printf("\n{res}Min In:\n"); MI
        printf("\n{res}Theta:\n"); TT

        printf("\n{res}Temp Result:\n");
    printf("\n{res}Current Cost:\n"); CC
        printf("\n{res}Technical Cost:\n"); TC
        printf("\n{res}Min Cost:\n"); MC

        printf("\n{res}Final Result:\n"); FR
}

// return result
st_matrix("r(mat)", FR)

// ------------------------------------------------------------------------

DMU_CS = st_matrixrowstripe(dmuIn)
FR_RS = st_matrixcolstripe(dmuIn)

CS = DMU_CS\("","cost")
replacesubmat(CS, 1, 1, J(rows(CS), 1, "CUR"))
FR_CS = CS;

CS = ("","theta")\DMU_CS\("", "cost")
replacesubmat(CS, 1, 1, J(rows(CS), 1, "TECH"))
FR_CS = FR_CS\CS

CS = DMU_CS\("", "cost")
replacesubmat(CS, 1, 1, J(rows(CS), 1, "MIN"))
FR_CS = FR_CS\CS

FR_CS = FR_CS\("","OE")\("","AE")\("","TE")

// name the row and column of dea result matrix
st_matrixrowstripe("r(mat)", FR_RS)
st_matrixcolstripe("r(mat)", FR_CS)
}

/**
```

```
* calculate max revenue
*/
function _l_calc_revenue(
            string scalar unitPrice,
            string scalar dmuOut,
            string scalar maxOut,
            string scalar eta,
            real scalar detail )
{
  real matrix UP, DO, MO, ET // input
  real matrix TO, CP, TP, MP // revenue calculate result
  real matrix CPR, TPR, MPR  // sum of revenue calculate result
  real matrix OE, AE, TE, FR // revenue efficiency final result

  string matrix DMU_CS   // dmu column stripes
  string matrix FR_CS     // ce final result matrix column stripes
  string matrix FR_RS     // ce final result matrix row stripes
  string matrix CS              // temp column stripes

  // input
  UP = st_matrix(unitPrice)
  DO = st_matrix(dmuOut)'
  MO = st_matrix(maxOut)
  ET = st_matrix(eta)

  // cost calculate result
  TO = ET:*DO // Thechnical Output
  CP = UP:*DO // Current Price
  TP = UP:*TO // Technical Price
  MP = UP:*MO // Max Price

  // sum of cost calculate result
  CPR = rowsum(CP)
  TPR = rowsum(TP)
  MPR = rowsum(MP)

  // cost efficiency result
  OE = (CPR:/MPR) // Overall Efficiency
  AE = (TPR:/MPR) // Allocative Efficiency
  TE = (CPR:/TPR) // Technical Efficiency

  // final result
  FR = (DO, CPR, ET, TO, TPR, MO, MPR, OE, AE, TE)

  if (detail) {
          printf("\n{res}Output:\n");
    printf("\n{res}Unit Price:\n"); UP
    printf("\n{res}DMU Out:\n"); DO
          printf("\n{res}Max Out:\n"); MO
          printf("\n{res}Eta:\n"); ET

          printf("\n{res}Temp Result:\n");
    printf("\n{res}Current Price:\n"); CP
          printf("\n{res}Technical Price:\n"); TP
          printf("\n{res}Max Price:\n"); MP

          printf("\n{res}Final Result:\n"); FR
  }
```

257

```
// return result
st_matrix("r(mat)", FR)

// ---------------------------------------------------------------------

DMU_CS = st_matrixrowstripe(dmuOut)
FR_RS = st_matrixcolstripe(dmuOut)

CS = DMU_CS\("","price")
replacesubmat(CS, 1, 1, J(rows(CS), 1, "CUR"))
FR_CS = CS;

CS = ("","eta")\DMU_CS\("", "price")
replacesubmat(CS, 1, 1, J(rows(CS), 1, "TECH"))
FR_CS = FR_CS\CS

CS = DMU_CS\("", "price")
replacesubmat(CS, 1, 1, J(rows(CS), 1, "MAX"))
FR_CS = FR_CS\CS

FR_CS = FR_CS\("","OE")\("","AE")\("","TE")

// name the row and column of dea result matrix
st_matrixrowstripe("r(mat)", FR_RS)
st_matrixcolstripe("r(mat)", FR_CS)

}

/**
 * calculate max profit
 */
function _l_calc_profit(
                string scalar unitValue,
                string scalar dmuIn,
                string scalar dmuOut,
                string scalar dearslt,
                real scalar detail )
{

        real matrix UV, DI, DO, DR      // input: Unit Value, DMU In/Out, DEA Result
        real matrix UC, UP, CP          // Unit Cost, Unit Price, Current Profit
        real matrix MI, MC              // Min In, Min Cost
        real matrix MO, MR, MP          // Max Out, Max Revenue, Max
Profit
        real matrix CPR, MCR, MRR       // Current Profit Result, Min Cost Result,

        // Max Revenue Result
        real matrix OE, FR              // result: Overall Efficiency, Final
Result

        string matrix FR_CS     // ce final result matrix column stripes
        string matrix FR_RS     // ce final result matrix row stripes
        string matrix CS        // temp column stripes

        real scalar dmus, invars, outvars, vars

        // input
        UV = st_matrix(unitValue)
        DI = st_matrix(dmuIn)
```

```
DO = st_matrix(dmuOut)
DR = st_matrix(dearslt)

dmus    = cols(DI)
invars  = rows(DI)
outvars = rows(DO)
vars    = invars + outvars
if (vars != cols(UV)) {
        _error(3200, sprintf("%s%s",
                "size of in/out of dmu and size of unit values ",
                "are not match!" ))
}

UC = UV[,1..invars]
UP = UV[,1+invars..vars]
CP = (UV' :* (-DI\DO))'

DR = DR[,2..1+dmus]
DR = ((DI\DO)*(DR'))'  // restore

MI = DR[,1..invars]
MO = DR[,1+invars..vars]

// profit calculate result
MC = UC :* MI
MR = UP :* MO

// sum of profit calculate result
CPR = rowsum(CP)
MCR = rowsum(MC)
MRR = rowsum(MR)

// profit efficiency result
MP = MRR :- MCR
OE = CPR :/ MP

// final result
FR = (MO, MRR, MI, MCR, MP, CPR, OE)

// Logging
if (detail) {
        "Output:"
        "Unit Value:"; UV
        "Unit Cost:"; UC
        "Unit Profit:"; UP
        "Current Profit:"; CP

        "DMU In:"; DI
   "DMU Out:"; DO
        "DEA Result:"; DR
        "Min In:"; MI
        "Max Out:"; MO

        "Temp Result:";
   "Min Cost:"; MC
        "Max Revenue:"; MR

        "Final Result:"; FR
}
```

```
// return result
st_matrix("r(mat)", FR)

// ------------------------------------------------------------------------

FR_RS = st_matrixcolstripe(dmuIn)

CS = st_matrixrowstripe(dmuOut)
replacesubmat(CS, 1, 1, J(rows(CS), 1, "MAX_H"))
FR_CS = CS\("MAX","revenue");

CS = st_matrixrowstripe(dmuIn)
replacesubmat(CS, 1, 1, J(rows(CS), 1, "MIN_H"))
FR_CS = FR_CS\CS\("MIN","cost");

FR_CS = FR_CS\("MAX", "profit")\("CUR","profit")\("", "OE")

// name the row and column of dea result matrix
st_matrixrowstripe("r(mat)", FR_RS)
st_matrixcolstripe("r(mat)", FR_CS)
}

/**
* make frame matrix and set matrix value at the param frameMat
* rts - return to scale, ort - orientation
*/
function _l_mkframemat(
                string scalar model,
                string scalar frameMat,
                string scalar dmuIn,
                string scalar dmuOut,
                string scalar rts )
{
  real matrix F, DI, DO
  real scalar dmus, variables, slackins, slackouts
  real scalar frows, fcols

  DI = st_matrix(dmuIn)
  DO = st_matrix(dmuOut)
  if (cols(DI) != cols(DO)) {
    _error(3200, "in and out count of dmu is not match!")
  }

  dmus = cols(DI) // or cols(DO), because cols(DI) == cols(DO)
  slackins = rows(DI); slackouts = rows(DO)

  if (model == "COST") variables = slackins
  else if (model == "REVENUE") variables = slackouts
  else variables = 0 // if (model == "PROFIT")

  if (rts == "CRS") {
    // target coefficient\slackins\slackouts
    frows = 1 + slackins + slackouts
                // target coefficient,theta,dmus,slackins,slackouts,rhs
    fcols = 1 + 1 + dmus + variables + slackins + slackouts + 1
  }
  else if (rts == "VRS") {
                // target coefficient\slackins\slackouts\sum of lamda
```

```
        frows = 1 + slackins + slackouts + 1
                // target coefficient,theta,dmus,variables,slackins,slackouts,rhs
        fcols = 1 + 1 + dmus + variables + slackins + slackouts + 1
    }
    else {
        _error(3498, "invalid rts optoin.")
    }

    // make frame matrix for CRS(CCR)
    F = J(frows, fcols, 0)
    F[1, 1] = 1
    replacesubmat(F, 2, 3, DI)
    replacesubmat(F, 2+slackins, 3, DO)
    if (model == "COST") {
                replacesubmat(F, 2, 3+dmus, -I(variables))
                replacesubmat(F, 2, 3+dmus+variables, I(slackins))
                replacesubmat(F, 2+slackins, 3+dmus+variables+slackins, -I(slackouts))
    }
    else if (model == "REVENUE") {
                replacesubmat(F, 2+slackins, 3+dmus, -I(variables))
                replacesubmat(F, 2, 3+dmus+variables, I(slackins))
                replacesubmat(F, 2+slackins, 3+dmus+variables+slackins, -I(slackouts))
    }
    else { // if (model == "PROFIT")
                replacesubmat(F, 2, 3+dmus, I(slackins))
                replacesubmat(F, 2+slackins, 3+dmus+slackins, -I(slackouts))
    }

    // adjustment
    if (rts == "VRS") {
        replacesubmat(F, frows, 3, J(1, dmus, 1))
        F[frows,fcols] = 1
    }

    // return result
    st_matrix(frameMat, F)
}

// ------------------------------------------------------------------------
// Internal mata only.
// ------------------------------------------------------------------------

/**
 * DEA Loop - Data Envelopment Analysis Loop for DMUs
 */
function _l_dealp (
                string scalar model,
                string scalar frameMat,
                string scalar dmuIn,
                string scalar dmuOut,
                string scalar rts,
                string scalar valueMat,
                real scalar tol1,
                real scalar tol2,
                string scalar trace )
{
    real matrix F, DI, DO, M, VARS, LPRSLT, DEALPRSLT, ARTIF, VM, RVM
    real scalar dmus, slackins, slackouts, slacks, artificials, artificialrow
    real scalar frows, fcols, i, dmui, variables, minYn, vari
```

```
real colvector effvec, slackidx
string scalar tracename

struct BoundCond matrix boundF, boundM
struct LpParamStruct scalar param

F  = st_matrix(frameMat)
DI = st_matrix(dmuIn)
DO = st_matrix(dmuOut)
if (cols(DI) != cols(DO)) {
    _error(3200, "in and out count of dmu is not match!")
}
if (!(rts == "CRS" || rts == "VRS")) {
        _error(3498, "rts must be one of CRS, VRS")
}
VM = st_matrix(valueMat)

// basic value setting for artificial variabels
frows = rows(F); fcols = cols(F)
dmus = cols(DI) // or cols(DO), because cols(DI) == cols(DO)
if (rows(VM) != dmus) {
        VM = J(dmus, 1, VM);
}

slackins = rows(DI); slackouts = rows(DO)
if (model == "COST") {
        minYn = 1 // minimized
        variables = slackins
}
else if (model == "REVENUE") {
        minYn = 0 // maximized
        variables = slackouts
}
else { // if (model == "PROFIT")
        minYn = 0 // maximized
        variables = 0
}

tracename = rts

// -----------------------------------------------------------------------
// define number of slacks by rts
slacks = variables + slackins + slackouts

// define number of artificials by rts, ort, stage
if (rts == "CRS") {
        artificials = slackouts; artificialrow = 2+slackins;
}
else if (rts == "VRS") {
        artificials = slackouts+1; artificialrow = 2+slackins;
}
if (artificials > 0) {
        ARTIF = J(1, artificials, 1) \ J(frows-1, artificials, 0)
        replacesubmat(ARTIF, artificialrow, 1, I(artificials))
        F = F[,1..fcols-1], ARTIF, F[,fcols]
        frows = rows(F); fcols = cols(F) // revise frows, fcols
}
// -----------------------------------------------------------------------
boundF = J(1, fcols, BoundCond());
```

```
// set the boundary for the efficiency variable(theta, eta):
// -INFINITE <= efficiency <= INFINITE
boundF[1,2].val = 0; boundF[1,2].lower = 0; boundF[1,2].upper = .

// set boundary for the weight variable(lamda, mu):
// 0 <= weight <= INFINITE
for (i=3; i<dmus+3; i++) {
        boundF[1,i].val = 0; boundF[1,i].lower = 0; boundF[1,i].upper = .
}

// set boundary for the non-structural variable(slack, artificial).
// 0 <= slacks and atrificials <= INFINITE
for (i=dmus+3; i<fcols; i++) {
        boundF[1,i].val = 0; boundF[1,i].lower = 0; boundF[1,i].upper = .
}
// liststruct(boundF); // for debug

// set the lp's parameters
param.rts          = rts
param.isin         = minYn // min
param.stagestep    = 1 // 1 step
param.dmus         = dmus
param.slacks       = slacks
param.artificials  = artificials
param.tol1         = tol1
param.tol2         = tol2
param.isminsubscript = 0 // false
param.trace        = trace
// liststruct(param); // for debug
// -------------------------------------------------------------------
DEALPRSLT = J(0, 1+ dmus + slacks, 0)
for (dmui=1; dmui<=dmus; dmui++) {
        M = F; boundM = boundF

        if (model == "COST") {
                replacesubmat(M, 2+slackins, fcols, DO[,dmui])
        }
        else if (model == "REVENUE") {
                replacesubmat(M, 2, fcols, DI[,dmui])
        }
        else { // if (model == "PROFIT")
                replacesubmat(M, 2, fcols, DI[,dmui])
                replacesubmat(M, 2+slackins, fcols, DO[,dmui])
        }

        // execute LP
        VARS  = lp_phase1(M, boundM, dmui, tracename, param)
        if (VARS[1,1] == .) {
                LPRSLT = J(1, cols(DEALPRSLT), .)
        }
        else {
                if (model != "PROFIT") {
                        vari = dmus + 2 // variable start index
                        for (i = 1; i <= variables; i++) {
                                M[1,] = M[1,] + ((VARS :== vari++)
* VM[dmui,i])
                        }
                LPRSLT  =  l_lp_phase2(M,  boundM,  VARS,
dmui, tracename, param);
```

```
                                        }
                                        else { // if (model != "PROFIT")
                                            vari = 2 // dmu start index
                                            RVM        =         -VM[dmui,1..slackins],
VM[dmui,1+slackins::cols(VM)]
                                            RVM        =         colsum(RVM'        :*
F[2..1+slackins+slackouts,3..2+dmus])
                                            for (i = 1; i <= dmus; i++) {
                                                M[1,] = M[1,] + ((VARS :== vari++)
* RVM[1,i])
                                            }
                                            LPRSLT  =  l_lp_phase2(M,  boundM,  VARS,
dmui, tracename, param);
                                        }
                                    }
                                    DEALPRSLT = DEALPRSLT \ LPRSLT
                }

         st_matrix("r(dealprslt)", DEALPRSLT)
    }

    real matrix function l_lp_phase2 (
                        real matrix M,
                        struct BoundCond matrix boundM,
                        real matrix VARS,
                        real scalar dmui,
                        string scalar aTracename,
                        struct LpParamStruct scalar param )
    {
        real matrix orgVARS, LPRSLT
        real scalar j, phase
        real vector slackidx
        string scalar tracename, msg
        struct LpResultStruct scalar lpresult

        orgVARS = VARS

        tracename = aTracename + "-PII"
        if (param.trace == "trace") {
            displayas("txt")
            printf("\n---------[PHASE II]---------")
            printf("\n[DMUi=%g]%s: initialize matrix.\n",
                dmui, tracename); M
            printf("\n[DMUi=%g]%s: VARS.\n", dmui, tracename); VARS
        }

        phase = 2
        lpresult = lp(M, boundM, VARS, dmui, phase, tracename, param)

        // ------------------------------------------------------------
        // phase 2 final.
        // ------------------------------------------------------------
        if(lpresult.rc) {
                LPRSLT = J(1, 1+param.dmus+param.slacks, .)
        }
        else {
                // lpresult = theta(1) + dmus + slacks
                LPRSLT = J(1, 1+param.dmus+param.slacks, 0)
                for (j=1; j<=rows(lpresult.XB) ; j++) {
```

```
                              if (VARS[1,j+1] > 0) LPRSLT[1, VARS[1,j+1]] =lpresult.XB[j,
1]
                      }
       }

       if (param.trace == "trace") {
           msg = sprintf("[DMUi=%g]%s-FINAL", dmui, tracename);
           printf("\n%s: original VARS.\n", msg); orgVARS
           printf("\n%s: VARS.\n", msg); VARS
           printf("\n%s: XB.\n", msg); lpresult.XB
           printf("\n%s: LPRSLT.\n", msg); LPRSLT
       }

       return(LPRSLT)
   }

   end
// End of the MATA Definition Area ---------------------------------------------
```

B2.12 dea_ci.ado

```
*! version 1.0.0  03MAY2014
capture program drop dea_ci
program define dea_ci, rclass
    version 11.0

    // syntax checking and validation---------------------------------------

    // ---------------------------------------------------------------------
    // returns 1 if the first nonblank character of local macro `0' is a comma,
    // or if `0' is empty.
    if replay() {
        dis as err "ivars = ovars required."
        exit 198
    }

    // quick check
    #del ;
    syntax anything(name=inoutvars equalok) [if] [in] [using/]
    ,
    envars(varlist)      // environment variable list
    [
        Level(integer 95)    // set confidence level; default is level(95)
        SEParator(integer 5) // draw separator line after every # variables;
        reps1(integer 100)   // perform # bootstrap replications; default is 100
        reps2(integer 2000)  // perform # replications; default is 2000
        noLAPtime            // Timer

        dmu(varname)      // indicate dmu variable name.
        rts(string)       // ignore case sensitive,[{CRS|CCR} | {BCC|VRS}|DRS|IRS]
        ort(string)       // ignore case sensitive,[{IN|INPUT} | {OUT|OUTPUT}]
        stage(integer 1) // dea stage 1 or 2
        trace             // Whether or not to do the log
        *                 // other dea options(varname is options)
    ];
    #del cr

    // get invars and outvars
    local varnames `inoutvars'
    gettoken word inoutvars : inoutvars, parse("=")
    while ~("`word'" == "=") {
        local invars `invars' `word'
        gettoken word inoutvars : inoutvars, parse("=")
    }
    local outvars `inoutvars'

    unab invars : `invars'
    unab outvars : `outvars'

    // dmu variable name(default "dmu") check.
    if ("`dmu'" == "") {
        local dmu = "dmu"
    }

    // default model - CRS(Constant Return to Scale)
    if ("`rts'" == "") {
```

```
    local rts = "CRS"
}

// default orientation - Input Oriented
if ("`ort'" == "") local ort = "IN"
else {
    local ort = upper("`ort'")
    if ("`ort'" == "I" | "`ort'" == "IN" | "`ort'" == "INPUT") {
        local ort = "IN"
    }
    else if ("`ort'" == "O" | "`ort'" == "OUT" | "`ort'" == "OUTPUT") {
        local ort = "OUT"
    }
    else {
        di as err "option ort allows for case-insensitive " _c
        di as err "(i|in|input|o|out|output) or nothing."
        exit 198
    }
}
if ("`trace'" == "trace") {
    di as txt "invars:[`invars']"
    di as txt "outvars:[`outvars']"
    di as txt "envars:[`envars']"
    di as txt "reps1:[`reps1']"
    di as txt "laptime:[`laptime']"

    di as txt "rts:[`rts']"
    di as txt "ort:[`ort']"
    di as txt "options:[`options']"
}

    if ("`using'" != "") use "`using'", clear
    if (~(`c(N)' > 0 & `c(k)' > 0)) {
        dis as err "dataset required!"
        exit 198
    }

// end of syntax checking and validation --------------------------------------

// REP1 : loop count of stage1
// REP2 : loop count of stage2
    set more off
    capture log close dea_ci_log

    // to remove log header information, use "quietly" and "hline"
    di as text "{hline `c(linesize)'}"
    quietly log using "dea_ci.log", replace text name(dea_ci_log)
    preserve

    if ("`if'" != "" | "`in'" != "") {
        qui keep `in' `if'  // filtering : keep in range [if exp]
    }

    // if variable `dmu' not found, generate variable.
    capture qui novarabbrev ds `dmu'
    if (c(rc) != 0) { // maybe c(rc) is r(111)
        qui gen str `dmu' = "`dmu'" + string(_n)
    }
```

```
    local org_matsize = c(matsize)
    local new_matsize = `reps2' * (wordcount("`envars'") + 1)
    if (`new_matsize' > `org_matsize') {
        qui set matsize `new_matsize'
    }


if ("`laptime'" != "nolaptime") {
    timer clear 1
    timer clear 2
}
    _main, invars(`invars') outvars(`outvars') envars(`envars') ///
        level(`level') reps1(`reps1') reps2(`reps2') `laptime' ///
        dmu(`dmu') rts(`rts') ort(`ort') stage(`stage') ///
        `trace' `options'

    tempname thrslt deacirslt
    matrix `thrslt' = r(thrslt)
    matrix `deacirslt' = r(deacirslt)
    _report, thrslt(`thrslt') deacirslt(`deacirslt') ///
        level(`level') separator(`separator') ///
        rts(`rts') ort(`ort')

if ("`laptime'" != "nolaptime") {
    di _n(2) as txt "laptime: 1 is dea, 2 is truncated regression"
    timer list
    timer clear 1
    timer clear 2
}
    return add
    if (`new_matsize' > `org_matsize') {
        qui set matsize `org_matsize'
    }
    set more on

    restore, preserve
    quietly log close dea_ci_log
    di as text "{hline `c(linesize)'}"

end

********************************************************************************
* MAIN -
********************************************************************************
program define _main, rclass

    syntax, invars(varlist) outvars(varlist) envars(varlist) ///
        level(integer) reps1(integer) reps2(integer) ///
        dmu(varname) rts(string) ort(string) stage(integer) ///
        [trace laptime *]

    // declare the tempname
    tempname dearslt thrslt cirslt
    tempname TM EM B2M HHSM T // B2M: Beta2 Metrix

    capture drop theta_h theta_hs theta_hh

if ("`laptime'" != "nolaptime") {
    timer on 1
```

```
}

    // -----------------------------------------------------------------------
    // STAGE1
    // -----------------------------------------------------------------------
    // step1: calculate the theta_h with dea
    qui dea `invars' = `outvars', rts(`rts') ort(`ort') stage(`stage') `options'
    matrix `dearslt' = r(dearslt)
    matrix `TM' = `dearslt'[1...,"theta"]
    mata: _roundmat("`TM'", 1e-14) // round off
    matrix colnames `TM' = theta_h
    svmat `TM', names(col)
    if ("`ort'" == "IN") {
        qui replace theta_h = 1 / theta_h
    }
    gen float theta_hs = 0
    gen float theta_hh = 0

if ("`trace'" == "trace") {
    di _n(2) as txt "[theta_h values as dea result.]:"
    list
}

    // step2: truncated regression theta_h on environment variables
    qui truncreg theta_h `envars', ll(1) noconstant level(`level')
    scalar sigma_h = e(sigma)
    matrix `EM' = e(b)

    // FIXME:
    /*
    if (e(p) > 0.1) {
        di as err "The model is not statistically significant with " _c
        di as err "the specified p-value."
        exit 198
    }
    */

if ("`trace'" == "trace") {
    di _n(2) as txt "[ereturn list as truncreg result.]:"
    ereturn list sigma
    di _n(2) as txt "[matrix list e(b) as truncreg result.]:"
    matrix list e(b)
}

    // generate the revising in-out variables.
    foreach invar of varlist `invars' {
        local varname = "_`invar'_s"
        local r_invars = "`r_invars' `varname'"
        gen `varname' = `invar'
    }
    foreach outvar of varlist `outvars' {
        local varname = "_`outvar'_s"
        local r_outvars = "`r_outvars' `varname'"
        gen `varname' = `outvar'
    }

    forvalues i = 1/`="`reps1'" {
        capture drop _epsilon _theta_s _theta_hsi
```

```
// step3: 1st bootstrap stage, L1 times : computing dea
// step3.1: calculate the epsilon1 using sigma_h in step 2.
gen float _epsilon = sigma_h * invnormal(normal(1/sigma_h)) ///
                + (1 - normal(1/sigma_h)) * uniform())

// step3.2: calculate theta_s: _theta_s = ZiB + ei
gen float _theta_s = _epsilon
foreach envar of varlist `envars' {
    matrix `T' = `EM'[1,"eq1:`envar'"]
    qui replace _theta_s = _theta_s + `envar' * `T'[1,1] // beta_h
}
```

```
if ("`trace'" == "trace") {
    di _n(2) as txt "[`i'][_theta_s = ZiB + ei]:"
    list
}
```

```
// step3.3: reset the dataset using theta_h in step1:and theta_s
if ("`ort'" == "IN") {
    foreach invar of varlist `invars' {
        qui replace _`invar'_s = `invar' * (_theta_s / theta_h)
    }
}
else { // if ("`ort'" == "OUT") {
    foreach outvar of varlist `outvars' {
        qui replace _`outvar'_s = `outvar' * (theta_h / _theta_s)
    }
}
```

```
if ("`trace'" == "trace") {
    di _n(2) as txt "[`i'][reset the dataset using theta_h]:"
    list
}
```

```
// step3.4: compute dea with changed dataset in step 3.3:
qui dea `r_invars' = `r_outvars', ///
        rts(`rts') ort(`ort') stage(`stage') `options'
        matrix `dearslt' = r(dearslt)
        matrix `TM' = `dearslt'[1...,"theta"]
        mata: _roundmat("`TM'", 1e-14) // round off
        matrix colnames `TM' = "_theta_hsi"
svmat `TM', names(col)

// Loop-i times
if ("`ort'" == "IN") {
    qui gen _theta_hs_`i' = (1 / _theta_hsi)
}
else {
    qui gen _theta_hs_`i' = _theta_hsi
}
```

```
if ("`trace'" == "trace") {
    di _n(2) as txt "[`i'][result of calculate the theta_hs]:"
    list, ab(16)
}
```

```
} // end of forvalues
capture drop _epsilon _theta_s _theta_hsi `r_invars' `r_outvars'
```

```
qui {
   // step3.5: calculate mean and variance of theta_hs
   egen _theta_hs = rowmean(_theta_hs_1-_theta_hs_`reps1')
   egen _sigma_b = rowsd(_theta_hs_1-_theta_hs_`reps1')
   replace theta_hs = _theta_hs
   replace _sigma_b = _sigma_b ^ 2
   gen bias = theta_hs - theta_h

      // step4: compute bias-corrected efficiency estimates
      replace theta_hh = theta_h
      replace theta_hh = theta_h - bias if (_sigma_b < (bias^2)/3)
      order bias, before(theta_hh)
}
novarabbrev {
   capture drop _theta_hs_* _theta_hs _sigma_b
}

   mkmat theta_h theta_hs bias theta_hh, matrix(`thrslt') rownames(`dmu')
   matrix roweq `thrslt' = "dmu"
   return matrix thrslt = `thrslt'

if ("`trace'" == "trace") {
   di _n(2) as txt "[result of stage1]:"
   list `dmu' theta_h theta_hs bias theta_hh, ab(16)
}

if ("`laptime'" != "nolaptime") {
   timer off 1
   timer on 2
}
   // ------------------------------------------------------------------
   // STAGE2
   // ------------------------------------------------------------------
   // step5:
   qui truncreg theta_hh `envars', ll(1) noconstant
   scalar sigma_hh = e(sigma)
   matrix `B2M' = e(b)
   matrix `B2M' = `B2M'[1,"eq1:"]

if ("`trace'" == "trace") {
   di _n(2) as txt "[step5]:[results of truncreg for sigma_hh and beta_hh]:"
   scalar list sigma_hh
   matrix rownames `B2M' = "beta_hh ="
   matrix list `B2M', noblank nohalf noheader f(%9.6g)
}

   // step6: calculate the beta_hs and sigma_hs
   forvalues i = 1/`=`reps2" {
      capture drop _epsilon2 _theta_ss

      // step6.1: calculate the epsilon2
      gen float _epsilon2 = sigma_hh * invnormal(normal(1/sigma_hh) ///
                   + (1 - normal(1/sigma_hh)) * uniform())

      // step6.2: calculate theta_s: _theta_ss = Zi*Bi_hh + ei
      gen float _theta_ss = _epsilon2
      foreach envar of varlist `envars' {
         scalar beta_hh = `B2M'[1,colnumb(`B2M',"eq1:`envar'")]
```

271

```
        qui replace _theta_ss = _theta_ss + `envar' * beta_hh
    }

if ("`trace'" == "trace") {
    di _n(2) as txt "STAGE2[STEP6.2][`i'][_theta_ss = Zi*Bi_hh + ei]:"
    list, ab(16)
}

    // step6.3: calculate the beta_hhs and sigma_hhs.
    qui truncreg _theta_ss `envars', ll(1) noconstant
    matrix `HHSM' = nullmat(`HHSM') \ e(b)

if ("`trace'" == "trace") {
    di _n(2) as txt "STAGE2[STEP6.3][`i'][beta_hhs and sigma_hhs]:"
    matrix list `HHSM', noblank nohalf noheader f(%9.6g)
}

    } // end of foreach
    capture drop _epsilon2 _theta_ss


    // step7: calculate the CI(confidence intervals) of beta and sigma
    preserve
    qui drop _all
    local rslt_names = "`envars' sigma_hh"
    matrix colnames `HHSM' = `rslt_names'
    qui svmat `HHSM', names(col)
    foreach var of varlist `rslt_names' {
        qui ci `var'
        matrix `cirslt' = nullmat(`cirslt') \ (r(N),r(mean),r(se),r(lb),r(ub))
    }
    matrix colnames `cirslt' = obs mean se lb ub
    matrix rownames `cirslt' = `rslt_names'
    restore, preserve

if ("`trace'" == "trace") {
    di _n(2) as txt "STAGE2[STEP7][results of ci]:"
    matrix list `cirslt', noblank nohalf noheader f(%9.6g)
}

if ("`laptime'" != "nolaptime") {
    timer off 2
}

    // return
    return matrix deacirslt = `cirslt'

end

********************************************************************************
* REPORT -
********************************************************************************
program define _report, rclass
    syntax, thrslt(name) deacirslt(name) level(integer) separator(integer) ///
        rts(string) ort(string)

    // --------------------------------------------------------------------
    // REPORT
    // --------------------------------------------------------------------
```

```
    di as result ""
    di as result "`rts'-`ort'PUT Oriented DEA Efficiency Results:"
    matrix list `thrslt', noblank nohalf noheader f(%9.6g)

    local tl1 "    Obs"
    local ttl "   Coef."

    #delimit ;
    di _n(2) in smcl in gr
    "Truncated regression on Efficiency estimate:" _n(2)
  `"    Variable {c |}   `tl1'    `ttl'    Std. Err.    `spaces'[`=strsubdp("`level'")'% Conf.
Interval]"'
    _n "{hline 13}{c +}{hline 63}" ;
    #delimit cr

    local nlines 0
    // forvalues i = 1/`=rowsof(`deacirslt')' {
    foreach rowname in `:rownames `deacirslt'" {
        local i = rownumb(`deacirslt', "`rowname'")
        local ccol 16
        local efmt %10.0f
        if (mod(`nlines++',`separator')==0) {
            if `nlines'!=1 {
                di in smcl as txt ///
                "{hline 13}{c +}{hline 63}"
            }
        }
        local ofmt "%9.8g"
        di in smcl in gr ///
            %12s abbrev("`rowname'",12) " {c |}" _col(`ccol') ///
            in yel `efmt' `deacirslt'[`i',colnumb(`deacirslt', "obs")] ///
            _col(29) `ofmt' `deacirslt'[`i',colnumb(`deacirslt', "mean")] ///
            _col(41) `ofmt' `deacirslt'[`i',colnumb(`deacirslt', "se")] ///
            _col(57) `ofmt' `deacirslt'[`i',colnumb(`deacirslt', "lb")] ///
            _col(69) `ofmt' `deacirslt'[`i',colnumb(`deacirslt', "ub")] ///
            in gr "`mark'"
    }

    return matrix thrslt = `thrslt'
    return matrix deacirslt = `deacirslt'
end

// Start of the MATA Definition Area -----------------------------------------
version 10
mata:
mata set matastrict on

// if function name start with '_', call at the stata.

/**
 * used to look for special values:
 * @param mat - matrix name
 * @param cmp - compare type(ge, gt, eq, lt, le: default is eq)
 * @param value - comparing value.
 */
function _all (string scalar mat, string scalar cmp, real scalar value)
{
    real matrix M;
    real scalar bool;
```

```
        M = st_matrix(mat)

        if (cmp == "ge") {
            bool = all (M :>= value);
        }
        else if (cmp == "gt") {
            bool = all (M :> value);
        }
        else if (cmp == "lt") {
            bool = all (M :< value);
        }
        else if (cmp == "le") {
            bool = all (M :<= value);
        }
        else { // if (cmp == "eq") {
            bool = all (M :== value);
        }
        st_numscalar("r(bool)", bool)
    }

    /**
     * used to look for special values:
     * @param mat - matrix name
     * @param cmp - compare type(ge, gt, eq, lt, le: default is eq)
     * @param value - comparing value.
     */
    function _any (string scalar mat, string scalar cmp, real scalar value)
    {
        real matrix M;
        real scalar bool;

        M = st_matrix(mat)

        if (cmp == "ge") {
            bool = any (M :>= value);
        }
        else if (cmp == "gt") {
            bool = any (M :> value);
        }
        else if (cmp == "lt") {
            bool = any (M :< value);
        }
        else if (cmp == "le") {
            bool = any (M :<= value);
        }
        else { // if (cmp == "eq") {
            bool = any (M :== value);
        }
        st_numscalar("r(bool)", bool)
    }

    end
    // End of the MATA Definition Area -------------------------------------------
```

274

INDEX

275

RTS, *see* returns to scale

SBM, *see* Slack Based Model

scale efficiency change, 73

SECH, *see* scale efficiency change

SEM, *see* Super Efficiency Model

Slack Based Model, 28, 30

sourceforge, 2

Stata Conference, iv

Stata Journal, 2

Statistical Inference, 80

Super Efficiency Model, 50, 52

TE, *see* Technical Efficiency

TECHCH, *see* technical change

technical change, 72

Technical Efficiency, 35, 42, 46

Technology Forecasting using DEA, 64, 65, 68

tfdea, 66

TFDEA, *see* Technology Forecasting using DEA

tfdea.ado, 235

user-written command, 2, 111

variable returns to scale, 5. 23

VRS, *see* variable returns to scale

ABOUT THE AUTHOR

Dr. Choonjoo Lee is Professor of Defense Science Department and the former Dean of Graduate School of Defense Management at the Korea National Defense University. Dr. Lee received his Ph.D. degree in Technology Management, Economics and Policy Program from the Seoul National University, his M.S. degree in Nuclear Engineering from University of California at Berkeley, his Master of Public Policy degree from KDI School of Public Policy and Management, and his B.S. degree in Physics from Korea Military Academy. His research topics include Defense R&D policy, AI enabled Critical Infrastructure Protection, Defense Analytics, and S&T and National Security. He has served in senior policy positions within the government institutions. These include a member of expert committee at National Science and Technology Council and special advisor to the Army Chief of Staff and government agencies.

Made in the USA
Columbia, SC
30 April 2025